"The early fathers and mothers of the Church have provided us with a well of wisdom that was fed by their openness to God, so much so that their words flowing from that relationship have almost the quality of scripture about them. Charles has lowered his bucket and raised up a gift, brimming full of the grace of God. It is such a treasure to have so much of the original texts accompanied by very brief reflections that invite us to do our own work of opening ourselves to the truth and wisdom of God."

—**BISHOP GODFREY FRYAR**
Provincial Minister, Franciscan Third Order Asia-Pacific

"This collection of daily readings from our spiritual forebears is not meant for us to indulge in nostalgia; when read meditatively, they speak to our modern condition and challenge us to resist conforming to this world and experience real spiritual transformation. The editors are to be commended for their wide-ranging and judicious selections."

—**SIMON CHAN**
Earnest Lau Professor of Systematic Theology, Trinity Theological College, Singapore

"A wonderful meditational reader culled from carefully selected primary sources representing the ecumenical voices of the past—our very own past we can no longer afford to ignore. Ringma and Alexander have done a great service by reconnecting us all back to our common heritage."

—**WIL HERNANDEZ**
Executive Director, CenterQuest (CQCenterQuest.org)

"For the many who believe in a post-Christian world, this rich resource of spiritual reflection drawn from that very tradition, shows what a huge loss it would be to accept that fate."

—**RACHAEL KOHN**
Presenter of The Spirit of Things, ABC National Radio, Australia

"*Of Martyrs, Monks and Mystics* is a remarkable collection of primary sources offering a contemporary insider view of what is being described. The result is a sparkling array of freshness from many lesser-known lives such as Gertrude the Great, Macarius of Egypt and the Dutch poet Hadewijch conversing with us alongside Julian of Norwich, John Cassian and Clare of Assisi. I found the breadth, depth and consistency of insight in this anthology of ancient wisdom through storytelling and sayings; prayers and poems to be a real gift as such wisdom is timeless. Indeed, it struck me again and again that this is a book that not only needs to be read slowly and prayerfully but also applied and lived as present-day wisdom. The good news is that the editors/compilers clearly have unique gifts of both mind and heart to assist us to do so."

—**TREVOR MILLER**
Abbot of Northumbria Community

Of Martyrs, Monks, and Mystics

Of Martyrs, Monks, and Mystics

A YEARLY MEDITATIONAL READER OF
ANCIENT SPIRITUAL WISDOM

*

EDITED BY
Charles Ringma
& Irene Alexander

CASCADE *Books* • Eugene, Oregon

OF MARTYRS, MONKS, AND MYSTICS
A Yearly Meditational Reader of Ancient Spiritual Wisdom

Copyright © 2015 Wipf and Stock Publishers. All rights reserved. Except for brief quotations in critical publications or reviews, no part of this book may be reproduced in any manner without prior written permission from the publisher. Write: Permissions, Wipf and Stock Publishers, 199 W. 8th Ave., Suite 3, Eugene, OR 97401.

Cascade Books
An Imprint of Wipf and Stock Publishers
199 W. 8th Ave., Suite 3
Eugene, OR 97401

www.wipfandstock.com

ISBN 13: 978-1-4982-0928-1

Cataloging-in-Publication data:

Of martyrs, monks, and mystics : a yearly meditational reader of ancient spiritual wisdom / edited by Charles Ringma and Irene Alexander.

xvi + 422 p. ; 23 cm. —Includes bibliographical references.

ISBN 13: 978-1-4982-0928-1

1. Devotional calendars. 2. Spiritual life—Christianity. I. Title.

BV4811 O35 2015

Manufactured in the U.S.A.

For
Naasicaa and Annasophia,
Patrick-Charles, Lachlan and Bronte,
Phoenix and Harmina,
Chelo and Elias.
Beloved grandchildren. Bearers of a new tomorrow.

and for
Irene Alexander
Teresa Jordan
Karen Hollenbeck-Wuest
Three remarkable women. They helped birth this anthology.

Contents

Preface ix
Introduction xiii

January 1
February 35
March 65
April 99
May 131
June 165
July 197
August 231
September 265
October 297
November 331
December 363

A Brief History of Authors and Writings Cited 397
Bibliography 403
Topical Index 411
Author Index 414
Scripture Index 416

Preface

There are some strange and yet exciting winds blowing in contemporary culture. While on the one hand we seem to be solidly locked into the ongoing scientific and technological shaping of our world, the powerful role of economic considerations in the way in which life is determined, and the ongoing consumer madness of our lifestyles, there are also surprising counter-winds.

These winds whisper of ecological care, more sustainable lifestyles, down-scaling, simplicity, humanizing our institutions, rebuilding the common good, creating community and the quest for justice.

In the midst of all of this, and beyond it, there are other voices as well. These voices speak of a recovery of spirit, the need for the re-enchantment of the modern world, focus on the growth of wisdom rather than mere rationality, the need for a new social imagination and the need for a re-engagement with meditative and contemplative practices.

Within this frame, it is interesting to note the growing fascination with monasticism, centering prayer, spiritual formation, spiritual direction and the practice of the spiritual disciplines. Along with this growing interest, we can also note the contemporary intrigue with the Desert Fathers and Mothers, Benedictine spirituality, Celtic spirituality, St. Francis and the medieval Christian mystics.

This helps to account for the popularity of Thomas Moore's *The Re-Enchantment of Everyday Life* (1996), Kathleen Norris's *The Cloister Walk* (1996), and the writings of Thomas Merton and Henri Nouwen. It also helps us understand the interest in the two contemporary films about monastic communities, *Of Gods and Men* and *Into Great Silence*, and the fact that many people, instead of taking normal holidays in resorts, are now taking time out to spend a week or a weekend in a monastic community.

Along with all of this, there is a growing sense in many of the contemporary churches that we have ended up with a shallow and programmatic consumer Christianity, which is too beholden to our contemporary consumer culture. Hence, Christians feel that they are in a "desert," and they are longing to bathe again in refreshing streams. The words of the Canadian songwriter Leonard Cohen are appropriate here when he notes that the "blizzard of the world has . . . overturned the order of the soul." Or to put that in words more directly related to the Christian church, in our rightful quest to be a relevant and serving church in the world, we have failed to sustain our intimacy with God—and for many, the wells of inner life have run dry.

This meditational reader with reflections drawn from primary sources of the early church fathers, the early church martyrs, voices from the Desert hermits, the long Monastic tradition, the Celtic saints, and the medieval mystics is meant to be a rich resource of fourteen centuries of Christian living, praying, reflection, serving, and suffering. These are wells from which we can drink and be refreshed. This long history of pre-Reformation Christianity ought to be part of the heritage of every contemporary Christian and every seeker for the ancient wisdom.

Some words of grateful thanks are very much in order. Alethea Hubley, the librarian of Trinity Theological College, Brisbane, Australia, has been more than generous in giving me access to the library and allowing me regularly to break return of books' deadlines. Teresa Jordan has greatly enhanced this meditational reader with her evocative images for each month. Karen Hollenbeck-Wuest has not only fine-edited this book, but also brought the older English of many of the translations of the primary sources into contemporary English. Pieter Kwant, my literary agent, once again deserves thanks for seeing this book into print. And Irene Alexander has completed a remarkable feat by finding many of the primary sources for this anthology. And finally, I am grateful for my early exposure to the church fathers during my seminary days at the Reformed Theological College, Geelong, Australia; my much later introduction to the writings of Merton and Nouwen; my time at Regent College with its rich tradition of emphases on spiritual theology; and my later in life exposure to Franciscan spirituality and the major themes of the Celtic Christian tradition. What is in the pages of this book has not been a mere scholarly concern but a hunger for inspiration and renewal.

Charles R. Ringma,
Brisbane, Australia, 2014

Introduction

Leonard Cohen in one of his songs celebrates that "there is a crack in everything; that's how the light gets in." There are many ways in which one can interpret these pregnant lines. But one way is to suggest that no matter how rigid a system may become, or how moribund a tradition, or how stultifying an institution, sooner or later, cracks will appear.

The reason cracks appear is because over time, such situations become unsustainable. The human being longs for a roomy space, fresh air, a better future, freedom, creativity, and the ability "to fly." And when the unsustainable present begins to crack, new possibilities begin to swim in view. Sometimes the new is wholly new. But more often the "new" is a recovery of what we, in the present, have neglected or lost. Thus the "new," "the light," may be a re-appropriation of the old.

My hope is that in this meditational reader of ancient spiritual wisdom, something of "the light" of earlier saints will shine upon us. This does not mean that we denigrate the present and only laud the past. Rather, we wish to recognize the weaknesses of present-day Christianity and look to earlier periods of church history for contemporary inspiration. Moreover, voices from the past are often quite different, and in their light, we might be challenged and, over time, transformed.

So let's explore some of the ways in which the ancient wisdom can bring light to our contemporary spirituality.

What is so refreshing about this ancient wisdom is that the people in this anthology had a love of God and the things of God's kingdom and reign not for self-gain or the blessings of heaven, but for God's own sake and glory. This was not a love of God in order to gain personal benefits. This was no utilitarian spirituality, but a love of God that had God's honor in view. From this we can learn much. So much of contemporary Christianity is all about us and our blessings. We almost seem to have God at our beck and call. Instead of acknowledging God's lordship and thus living a life of obedience, we have created a fair-weather Christianity that knows little of the cost of discipleship.

Furthermore, what is life-giving about the spirituality of our forebears is that they were not caught in the contemporary bind in which we find ourselves with our sacred/secular polarities. This was not a Sunday piety and a Monday-to-Saturday secularism. Instead, they had a sacramental view of life. All of life was sacred. All of life was impregnated with God's Spirit. God as creator affirmed life and the world. God as redeemer brought healing to where our lives and our world bore the marks of sin and brokenness. Moreover, in the incarnation God makes the earthly a vehicle for the heavenly. Thus everywhere in the ordinary, the sacred presence of God can be discerned and embraced. This thinking found its culmination in the Eucharist where in bread and wine the Risen Christ through the Spirit comes to enliven and to nurture us.

One of the things that strikes us is that our ancient forebears were not escapists. While there were some unhealthy dualistic tendencies and while the monastic tradition did remove people from mainstream society, the overall thrust of this ancient wisdom was that in the quest for growth in the love of God the love of neighbor could come to fuller expression. This was equally true of the men and the women who were part of monastic communities. These communities in their long history not only shaped their members in piety but also in agriculture, the arts, learning, hospitality and service. The early hospices and schools and services to the poor were the fruits of these communities. As such, rather than being world-denying, this long tradition was world-formative.

From this heritage we can learn much. A Christianity that only prepares people for heaven, is not a full-orbed Christianity. In fact, it is warped. True Christianity knows the call of service to the neighbor and the shaping of the world to more fully reflect God's reign of peace and justice. This vision of a world-formative Christianity calls us away from our narrow self-preoccupations. It invites us to become a richer and fuller self, a self marked by self-transcendence through entering into the life and purposes of God.

It is not possible to read this ancient wisdom without being struck by the theme of union with God. Our forebears not only believed in God as the source of salvation, but believed that the whole of their lives should be linked and bound to this God. Thus they sought to become like God through radical identification. Through a Christo-mysticism and a Spirit-revitalization they sought to become partakers of the divine nature. For our forebears the longing was for an ever greater conformity to Christ. Their hope was for Christ to take form and shape in the very fabric of their lives. For some, like St. Francis, this included being gifted with the stigmata.

One of the further themes that captures one's imagination in reading from this vast Christian tradition is that these followers of Jesus were so

INTRODUCTION

committed to their faith that they were willing to give their lives. While the long history of Christianity has always had its martyrs, including in our present day (think only of Oscar Romero), the early centuries were written in martyr's blood. We need only think of Polycarp, St. Justin Martyr, or Origen, who in the AD 250 persecution of Decius, was imprisoned and subjected to long torture. He died soon after.

This highlights a further kind of baptism. By faith, we are baptized into Christ. By water, we are baptized into the faith community. For empowerment we are baptized in the Spirit. But there is also a "red" baptism, a martyr's death—the surrender of one's life for the sake of the gospel. And while most of us may not be called to such a surrender, we are called to a life of relinquishment for the sake of the Kingdom of God. This poses a challenge to our contemporary sensibilities, where our Christianity is one of convenience. Jesus is the great add-on to our life's priorities, acting as an insurance policy to get us to heaven while we live here in whichever way we like. A "red" baptism, or its approximate equivalent, changes all of that. In this God is no longer the great Father Christmas, but the God who calls us to obedience, suffering, and relinquishment. This then ushers us into one of the key Pauline themes of living the paschal mystery: that death leads us to life, both the "old" life dying in us and the new life of Christ increasingly growing in us. This paschal spirituality may well lead to the call to radical renunciation and discipleship.

While our forebears ever wrestled with the knowability of God, they knew how to bow before mystery. They celebrated God's otherness. They knew the limitations of human reasoning. They embraced both the revelation of God and the mystery of God, including the mystery of the incarnation. As a consequence, they were willing to follow this God even in the desert and in the dark places of human suffering.

We know little of this. We want a God we can manage and even control. We want a God who is there, not a God who hides in mystery. We want a God who makes things light, not a God who invites us into darkness. Thus our forbears can point us to a whole new way of living the Christian life beyond the predictable spiritual consumerism of our time.

It really does not matter to what theme we attend, this ancient wisdom has an inspiration and challenge for us. Whether it is community, contemplation, conversion or communion, or incarnation, impartation or indwelling, or revelation, renewal, redemption or regeneration, our ancient forebears can point the way.

In these pages then, may you find comfort, hope and direction. May the seed of the martyrs, the monks and the mystics find fertile ground in you. And may a harvest of goodness and justice be its abiding fruit.

January

PSALM 27:8–9   JANUARY 1

The Seeking Heart

At the heart of being human lies an endless longing. We long for generativity, creativity, and fulfillment. At the heart of Christian spiritually lies the longing for the vision of God and for the joy of communion.

St. Anselm knew much about this longing. He prays,

> Behold, O Lord, my heart is before you. I strive, but I cannot do what I want to do. Therefore do what my heart cannot do. Bring me into the secret chamber of your love.
>
> I ask, I seek, I knock. You who made me to ask, make me also to receive. You who made me to seek, grant me also to find. You who taught me to knock, open to my knocking.
>
> To whom will you give, if you deny the one that asks? Who will find, if the one who seeks is disappointed? What do you give to those who do not pray, if you deny your love to those who do pray?
>
> You have given me my desire; from you may I have also the fulfillment of desire. Cleave to the Lord, my soul, cleave to the Lord earnestly! O good Lord, do not cast me away!
>
> I faint with hunger for your love. Cherish me, and let me be satisfied with your loving-kindness, enriched by your favour, fulfilled by your love.
>
> May your love take me and possess me, because you are with the Father and the Holy Spirit, the one and only God, blessed for ever, world without end.

Anselm of Canterbury:
Meditation Concerning the Redemption of Mankind, 7

Reflection

The longing for God is the deepest longing of humanity made in the image and likeness of God.

PSALM 43:3   JANUARY 2

The Light of Your Word

The Word of God is a mirror and a lamp. In it we can see ourselves and our need for healing and wholeness. And in its pages we gain direction for how we can live with purpose and joy.

St. Augustine sought to live his life in the light of God's liberating word. He writes,

> At your bidding the moments fly by. Grant me then a space for my meditations on the hidden things of your law. Do not close the door against those who knock. For you did not will that the hidden secrets of so many pages would be written in vain. Nor are forests without their stags that retire within them, ranging and walking, feeding, lying down and ruminating.
>
> Perfect me, O Lord, and reveal the secrets of your law to me. Behold, your voice is my joy. Your voice exceeds the abundance of all pleasure. Give me what I love, for I do love your law. And this love, too, you have given.
>
> Do not abandon your gifts, nor despise those who thirst for you. Let me confess to you everything that I find in your books and let me hear the voice of your praise. Let me drink from you and meditate on the wonderful things of your law—from the very beginning, when you made heaven and the earth, unto the everlasting reign of your Kingdom.
>
> *The Confessions of Saint Augustine*, 12.2

Reflection

The Word of God has been given to be read and to read us. In being read, we need to enter into a solitude of the heart and into a purpose of will in order to live and proclaim what the Lord would say to us.

2 THESSALONIANS 2:13–16   JANUARY 3

The Blessed Trinity

In the love and unity of the Father, the Son, and the Holy Spirit, we find the sustenance and inspiration for a life of mutuality, cooperation, and joy. Living in the grace of the Trinity, we are called to live like the Trinity.

Hildegard of Bingen reflected much on the beauty of the Trinity. She writes,

> Therefore you see "a bright light," which represents the Father. And "in the light is the figure of a man the color of sapphire," which designates the Son, who was born of the Father before time began and then within time became incarnate in the world through humankind.
>
> And the "all blazing with a gentle glowing fire" represents the Holy Spirit, by whom the only Son of God was conceived in the flesh, without any flaw, and born of the Virgin and poured out as true light into the world.
>
> "And that bright light bathes the whole of the glowing fire, and the glowing fire bathes the bright light; and the bright light and the glowing fire pour over all humankind, so that the three are one light in one power and one strength."

Hildegard of Bingen: Scivias, 161

Prayer

Lord, thank you that you have invited me and all your people
into the beauty of your life of love, mutuality and care.
You are my true home. In the shelter of your care, may I make a safe place
for others.
Amen.

PSALM 89:5-8　　　　　　　　　　　　　　　　JANUARY 4

Seeing the Beauty of God

God is not only to be believed. God is also to be sought. And God is to be thought about and reflected upon. This is an invitation to the practices of solitude and meditation.

John Cassian was one of the important early voices in articulating something of the contemplative life. He writes,

> The contemplation of God can be understood in a variety of ways. For we not only discover God by admiring his incomprehensible nature.... But we also see God through the greatness of creation, and as we consider his justice, and the aid of his daily providence.
>
> We also contemplate God when we reflect on what he has done through his saints in every generation. And we can sense his presence when we admire the power with which he governs, corrects, directs, and rules all things.... His presence is known when we consider the sand of the sea and the number of the waves measured by him and known to him.
>
> In wonder, we consider how the drops of rain, the hours and the days of the ages and all things past and future are present to his knowledge. And overwhelmed with gratitude, we reflect on his ineffable mercy and the free grace through which he has called us and receives us.
>
> *The Conferences of John Cassian*, 1.15

Reflection

In meditation we may reflect on the Word of God
and the acts of God in creation and redemption.
We may also reflect on our own inner being.
This is the path to wonder, gratitude and joy.

PHILIPPIANS 4:8–9   JANUARY 5

The Power of Virtue

The movement of grace within us is not a desperate uprooting, but a gentle transformation. Problems are overcome, not avoided. And goodness blossoms even in the difficult places.

St. Francis was a mystic and visionary. He was also an evangelist. But above all, he was a person of prayer with keen psychological insight. His reflection on the beauty of virtue challenges us:

> Where there is charity and wisdom,
> there is neither fear nor ignorance.
> Where there is patience and humility,
> there is neither anger nor disturbance.
> Where there is poverty with joy,
> there is neither covetousness nor avarice.
> Where there is inner peace and meditation,
> there is neither anxiousness nor dissipation.
> Where there is fear of the Lord to guard the house,
> there the enemy cannot gain entry.
> Where there is mercy and discernment,
> there is neither excess nor hardness of heart.

Francis and Clare: The Complete Works, 35

Prayer

Lord, may goodness flourish in all the places of my woundedness and in the broken places of our world. Amen.

True Love

A love that springs from within and seeks the well-being of others is a love that is true. But this love will be sorely tested in the ebb and flow of life. Self-giving love is not without its measure of suffering.

The German Christian mystic, Meister Eckhart, writes about the nature of true love within the gospel tradition:

> All God's commandments come from his love and from the goodness of his nature. If they did not spring from love, they could not be his. She who lives lovingly lives by what is good in her nature and within the love of God—a love that asks no questions. If I have a friend and love him so that he may benefit me and do what I wish, then I do not love my friend at all but rather myself.
>
> I am to love my friend for his own sake, for the goodness and virtue of him, for all that he himself is and then I shall truly love him, in the only real sense of that word.
>
> This is how it is with the person who lives in God's love, who does not seek her own welfare, either in God or herself or any other, who loves God only for his goodness, for the sake of the goodness of his nature and all that he himself is. That is true love.
>
> *Meister Eckhart: A Modern Translation*, 188

Reflection

We know something about the love of family and reciprocity. We need to grow in the love of service, surrender and relinquishment.

JOHN 4:13–14 — JANUARY 7

The Longing God

The God of the biblical story is not an unfeeling divine robot. God is a God who suffers with us and on our behalf. God is the God who yearns for and watches over humanity and the created order to bring it to fullness.

The Christian mystic, Julian of Norwich, through revelation and visions, understood something of the longing heart of God. She writes,

> Since Christ is our Head, he must be both glorious and impassible. But since he is also the Body in which all his members are joined, he is not yet fully either of these.
>
> Therefore, the same desire and thirst that he had upon the cross—and this desire, longing, and thirst was with him from the very first, I fancy—he has still, and shall continue to have until the last soul to be saved has entered into its blessedness.
>
> For just as there is in God the quality of sympathy and pity, so too in him is there that thirst and longing. And in virtue of this longing which is in Christ, we in turn long for him too. No soul comes to heaven without it. This quality of longing and thirst springs from God's eternal goodness, just as pity does.
>
> Though, to my mind, longing and pity are quite distinct, it is the same goodness that gives point to the spiritual thirst; a thirst which persists in Christ as long as we are in need and which draws us up into his blessedness. All of this was seen in the revelation of his compassion.
>
> *Revelations of Divine Love*, 108–9

Thought

May the longing heart of God become our very heartbeat.

MATTHEW 18:21–22   JANUARY 8

The Grace of Forgiveness

In a broken world mending is a key task. And what so easily gets broken are our relationships. To heal relationships is a hope for a better world. And forgiveness lies at the heart of healing and reconciliation.

There is much spiritual wisdom in the sayings of the Desert Fathers and Mothers. They knew a lot about the power of forgiveness. Here is one of their accounts:

> It happened that a brother in the community of the Abbot Elias fell into sin. The brothers expelled him from the monastery, and he fled to St. Antony, who dwelled on the inner mountain. The saint kept him there some time and then sent him back to the monastery. When the brothers saw him, they immediately drove him away again.
>
> Once more, he fled to St. Antony and said, "My father, they will not receive me." Then the saint was grieved, and he sent a message to the brothers: "A certain vessel was wrecked at sea, and all her cargo was lost. Yet with great labour, the sailors brought the ship to land. Do you now wish to sink the ship that has been rescued by pushing it back into the sea?" The brothers meditated upon this message, and when they understood it, they were greatly ashamed. At once, they received again the brother who had sinned.

The Wisdom of the Desert, 45–46

Reflection

To forgive is a grace that both the one giving forgiveness
and the one receiving forgiveness need to receive.
There may be blockages in this flow of goodness.
Where are those blockages? Can they be removed?

ROMANS 12:9–13   JANUARY 9

A Community of Goodness

The church, marked by the cross of Christ and sculpted by the life-giving Spirit, is called to be a community of love, forgiveness and care. It can only live up to this call in a spirit of servanthood and humility.

St. Cyprian, one of the early church fathers, in his treatise on *The Unity of the Catholic Church*, paints a picture for us of what the community of faith should be like. He writes of the Holy Spirit,

> The dove is a purely simple and joyful living creature. It is not venomously bitter; it does not bite savagely; its claws do not slash with violence. It loves human company, and it enjoys the experience of a single home. When doves give birth, they bring forth their offspring together. When they travel in flight, they flock together. They spend their lives in sociable mutuality, marking peace with a kiss of the beak and being in one mind about all things.
>
> As a church, we are called to demonstrate this pure simplicity and divine affection with one another. Our love for one another should imitate the doves in kindness and gentleness. There is no room in the Christian's heart for the wildness of wolves or the savagery of dogs, the deadly poison of snakes or the bloody cruelty of wild beasts.
>
> Bitterness cannot grow together and be joined with sweetness. Nor can darkness mingle with light, nor storms with fine weather, nor war with peace, nor barrenness with fruitfulness, nor drought with springing wells, nor a storm with a calm.
>
> *On the Church: Select Treatises by Saint Cyprian*, 160–61

Prayer

Lord, heal us as your people. May your goodness and grace triumph in our midst and banish from our lives all fear, jealousy, and unforgiveness. May the gentle Spirit rule in us! Amen.

ISAIAH 49:13   JANUARY 10

God the Comforter

There are people who see God in very severe terms. An austere life must mean that there is an austere God. But God does not fit our descriptions and expectations. God is above all, merciful, and is the great comforter.

St. Anselm, archbishop of Canterbury, while a great theologian, was also a writer of exquisite spirituality. Enter into this gentle prayer:

> Jesus, as a mother you gather your people to you,
> you are gentle with us as a mother with her children.
> Often you weep over our sins and our pride,
> tenderly you draw us from hatred and judgement.
> You comfort us in sorrow and bind up our wounds,
> in sickness you nurse us and with pure milk you feed us.
> Jesus, by your dying, we are born to new life,
> by your anguish and labour we come forth in joy.
> Despair turns to hope through your sweet goodness,
> through your gentleness, we find comfort in fear…
> Lord Jesus, in your mercy heal us,
> in your love and tenderness, remake us.
> In your compassion, bring grace and forgiveness,
> for the beauty of heaven, may your love prepare us.

Celebrating Common Prayer: A Version of the Daily Office SSF, 232

Reflection

I am safe with you, Lord Jesus. May I live in your presence.
May I act out of your love.

DEUTERONOMY 15:7–8   JANUARY 11

Generosity

To be generous is sharing oneself and not only one's abilities and resources. This expresses a way of life that lies at the very heart of who God is. Thus it is a godly act to be generous.

The fourth-century church father, St. Basil, has this to say about a life of generosity:

> Listen, you rich men and women to the kind of advice I am giving to the poor because of your inhumanity. Far better endure under dire straits than undergo the troubles that are bred of usury! But if you rich were obedient to the Lord, what need of these words? What is the advice of the Master? Lend to those from whom you do not hope to receive.
>
> And what kind of loan is this, it is asked, from which all idea of the expectation of repayment is withdrawn? . . . When you mean to supply the need of a poor man or woman for the Lord's sake, the transaction is at once a gift and a loan. Because there is no expectation of reimbursement, it is a gift. Yet because of the munificence of the Master, who repays on the recipient's behalf, it is a loan.
>
> Do you not wish the Master of the universe to be responsible for your repayment? If any wealthy man or woman in the town promises you repayment on behalf of others, do you not accept his or her suretyship? But you do not accept God, who more than repays on behalf of the poor.
>
> Give the money lying useless, without weighting it with increase, and both shall be benefited.
>
> *Nicene and Post-Nicene Fathers*, vol. 8, xlviii

Thought

At the heart of the gospel lies the vision of generosity that blesses both the receiver and giver.

GALATIANS 6:2   JANUARY 12

Being Gentle with Others

We should neither be hard on ourselves or on others. Instead, we need to be gentle with ourselves and with those who cause us distress or difficulty. In this way, we reflect something of God's great kindness towards us.

The well-known ancient writer on Christian spirituality, Thomas à Kempis, had this to say about being gentle with others and carrying their burdens:

> Whatever we are unable to reform in ourselves or in others, we must clearly put up with until God chooses to change it. View this as being, perhaps, the better state, for by undergoing this test it teaches us patience without which all our actions carry little merit. And while enduring these misfortunes, pray God to grant you his support that you may quietly bear them.
>
> If anyone, after having been corrected once or twice, still does not conform, do not take issue with him, but commit the matter to God so that God's will may be done and that he may be honoured in all his servants. After all, God alone knows how to draw good out of evil.
>
> Be patient in bearing the imperfections of others, no matter what they be, just as others have to put up with your faults. If you cannot remake yourself in the way you would like why, then, do you expect another to fashion herself according to the pattern you set for her?
>
> We want others to be perfect, but we do nothing to amend our own faults.

The Imitation of Christ in Four Books, 20

Prayer

Lord, give me grace to be more forgiving and generous with others and more demanding of myself to live in your truth. Amen.

PSALM 27:4 — JANUARY 13

With Seeing Eyes

We need to become more reflective. We need to slow down to see and hear. But for this to take place, we need a new heart and a whole new way of being, if we wish to see with new eyes.

The great Franciscan theologian, Bonaventure, had this to say about St. Francis and his ability to see with new eyes:

> He beheld in beauty Him who is the most beautiful,
> and, through the images of Himself imprinted on creation,
> he everywhere sought to reach the Beloved,
> making of all things a ladder by which he might ascend
> to embrace Him who is altogether lovely.
>
> For by the impulse of his unprecedented devotion
> he tasted that fountain of goodness that streams forth,
> as in rivulets, in every created thing,
> and he perceived a heavenly harmony in the concord
> of the virtues and actions granted unto them by God,
> and sweetly exhorted them to praise the Lord,
> even as the Prophet David had done.
>
> *The Little Flowers and the Life of St. Francis,* 358

Reflection

To gaze on Christ in faith and love is to become more like him.

Behold: Jesus!

We are invited to see Jesus as the savior of the world, the creator God, the lord of history, the head of the church and the lover of my soul.

The English medieval mystic and Augustinian Canon, Walter Hilton, puts Jesus center stage in the confession of our faith. He writes,

> Jesus is endless might, wisdom and goodness, righteousness, truth, holiness and mercy. What Jesus is in himself no soul can see or hear, but by the effects of his working, he may be seen by the light of grace—like this:
>
> His might is seen by making all his creatures of nothing; his wisdom in orderly disposing of them; his goodness in saving them; his mercy in forgiveness of sins; his holiness in gifts of grace; his righteousness in severely punishing sin; his gentleness in the true rewarding of good works.
>
> And all this is expressed in holy writ, and this a soul sees there. . . . And be well assured that such gracious knowings in holy writ—or in other writings, which are made by the assistance of God's grace—are nothing else but sweet letters, sent and made betwixt a loving soul and Jesus the beloved. Or else, that I may speak more truly, betwixt Jesus the true lover and the souls beloved of him.
>
> *The Scale (or Ladder) of Perfection,* 2.3.13

Reflection

Jesus is at the very heart of the Christian story.
He is savior and Lord.
He is also friend and companion of the journey of faith and life.

1 Corinthians 11:23–26 — January 15

The Eucharist

Christ has shown us his life and left us his words. He has also given us his Spirit and the feast of Holy Communion by which he comes to us ever anew, and we are nourished by his provision.

The second-century document known as the *Didache* contains this thoughtful eucharistic prayer:

> We give you thanks, Holy Father, for your holy name, which you have caused to dwell in our hearts, and for the knowledge and faith and immortality that you have made known to us through Jesus your servant.
> To you be the glory forever.
> You, almighty Master, created all things for your name's sake, and gave food and drink to humans to enjoy, so that they might give you thanks; but to us you have graciously given spiritual food and drink, and eternal life through your servant . . .
> Remember your church, Lord, to deliver it from all evil and to make it perfect in your love; and from the four winds gather the church that has been sanctified into your kingdom, which you have prepared for it.
> For yours is the power and glory forever . . .
> If anyone is holy, let him or her come;
> if anyone is not, let him or her repent.
> Maranatha! Amen.
>
> *Didache*, ch. 10

Reflection

Holy Communion is the gift of Christ for the community of faith expressing our need of him and of each other.

COLOSSIANS 1:17   JANUARY 16

Christ the Center

> *Jesus, the carpenter's son from the rogue province of Galilee, is, so the church confesses, the Son of God and the one in whom, after the resurrection, all things hold together.*

The fourteenth-century Christian mystic St. Catherine of Siena, in *The Dialogue*, wrote down this vision of the exalted Christ. She speaks from the perspective of God:

> I sent my Son in order that he should be lifted on high on the wood of the cross. For on the cross, He drew everything to himself and revealed my ineffable love for you, for the human heart is always attracted by love. Greater love I could not show you than to lay down my life for you. My Son was treated in this way by love, so that the ignorant would not be able to resist being drawn to me.
>
> In very truth, my Son said that when he was lifted on high, he would draw all things to himself. This is to be understood in two ways. First, when the human heart is drawn by the affection of love, it is drawn with all the powers of the soul: the memory, the intellect, and the will. Now, when these three powers are harmoniously joined together in my name, everything else you do, whether in deed or thought, will be pleasing, and joined together by the effect of love, because love is lifted on high, following the sorrowful crucified one. If the heart and the powers of the soul are drawn to him, all the actions are also drawn to him.
>
> Second, everything has been created for your use, to serve your needs. But you who have the gift of reason were made not for yourselves but for me, in order to serve me with all your heart and all your affection.
>
> *Dialogue of St. Catherine of Siena*, 4.3.10

Reflection

Christ is more than Lord of my heart. He is Lord of the universe.

ISAIAH 57:15　　　　　　　　　　　　　　JANUARY 17

Humility

In the modern world of self-assertion, humility is not our favorite word. In Christian spirituality, however, humility has nothing to do with groveling, but everything to do with an attentive openness to God.

The unknown fourteenth-century English author of *The Cloud of Unknowing* had this to say about a spirit of humility:

> In itself, humility is nothing else but our true understanding and awareness of ourselves as we really are. It is certain that if we could see and be conscious of ourselves as we really are, we would be truly humble. There are two causes for this meekness.
>
> One is the degradation, misery and weakness into which we have fallen by sin. As long as we live in this life, we will never be completely free from the effects of sin, no matter how holy we become.
>
> The other is the superabundant love and goodness of God himself, before which all nature trembles, the learned are fools, and all the saints and angels are blinded. Were it not for the wisdom of the godhead, which sustains everything by grace in accordance with its capacity, I cannot think what might happen.
>
> *The Cloud of Unknowing,* 148

Reflection

Humility is to know who God is and who we are in relation to this God. This knowing leads to worship, gratitude and obedience.

Psalm 18:35–36   January 18

God Our Protector

When we trust God as our protector, we express our faith and prayer in the ebb and flow of life. This is not a magic formula against life's difficulties, but a desire to be and to live in God's sheltering presence.

St. Patrick's *Breastplate* is a prayer that seeks not only God's protection, but also God's presence. Here is a part of that prayer:

> I bind to myself today:
> God's power to guide me,
> God's might to uphold me,
> God's wisdom to teach me,
> God's eye to watch over me,
> God's ear to hear me,
> God's word to give me speech,
> God's hand to protect me,
> God's way to lie before me,
> God's shield to shelter me,
> God's host to secure me:
> against the snares of demons, against the seductions of temptations,
> against the lusts of nature, against everyone who seeks to harm me.

The Confessions of St. Patrick, 99

Reflection

We need to be upheld and protected far more than we realize.

2 CORINTHIANS 13:5   JANUARY 19

Self-Examination

> *In the journey of faith one needs to be careful not to become overly introspective. One can't always be taking one's religious pulse. On the other hand, we do need to face our failings and compulsions.*

We can learn much from this serious personal reflection of the great church father of Western Christianity, St. Augustine. He writes,

> Behold, O Truth, it is in you that I see that I should not be moved at my own praises for my own sake, but for the sake of my neighbor's good. And whether this is actually my way, I truly do not know. On this score I know less of myself than you do.
>
> I beg you now, O my God, to reveal myself to me also, that I may confess to my brothers, who are to pray for me in those matters where I find myself weak.
>
> Let me once again examine myself the more diligently. If, in my own praise, I am moved with concern for my neighbor, why am I less moved if some other man or woman is unjustly dispraised than when it happens to me? Why am I more irritated at that reproach which is cast on me than at one which is, with equal injustice, cast upon another in my presence?
>
> Am I ignorant of this also? Or is it still true that I am deceiving myself, and do not keep the truth before you in my heart and tongue? Put such madness far from me, O Lord, lest my mouth be to me "the oil of sinners, to anoint my head."
>
> *The Confessions of St. Augustine,* 208–9

Prayer

Lord, may the light of your truth and love and mercy shine in my heart, healing all that is broken and not pleasing to you. Amen.

PSALM 63:1   JANUARY 20

The Seeking Heart

The heart of Christian spirituality is both finding and ongoing seeking. It is homecoming and journeying. It is drinking and being thirsty.

The great thirteenth-century Dutch medieval mystic and poet Hadewijch speaks about the seeking nature of love. She writes,

> She who wishes to taste veritable Love,
> Whether by random quest or sure attainment,
> Must keep to neither path nor way.
> She must wander in search of victory over Love,
> Both on the mountains and in the valleys,
> Devoid of consolation, in pain, in trouble;
> Beyond all the ways men and women can think of,
> That strong steed of Love bears her.
> For reason cannot understand
> How Love, by Love, sees to the depths of the Beloved,
> Perceiving how Love lives freely in all things.
> Yes, when the soul has come to this liberty,
> The liberty that Love can give, It fears neither death nor life.
> The soul wants the whole of Love and wants nothing else.

Hadewijch: The Complete Works, 89

Thought

Let love be our stay, our guide, and our way.

1 CORINTHIANS 2:2-5   JANUARY 21

The Blessed Trinity

The confession of the Trinity is no mere intellectual exercise. It is a great grace to be invited into the blessed life of the Trinity and to reflect that blessing in the way we live as family, church and community.

The Christian mystic Julian of Norwich speaks about the way in which the Father, the Son, and the Spirit are a blessing to the person of faith. She writes,

> Thus in our Father, God almighty, we have our being. In our merciful Mother we have reformation and renewal, and our separate parts are integrated into the perfect person. In yielding to the gracious impulse of the Holy Spirit we are made perfect.
>
> Our essence is in our Father, God almighty, and in our Mother, God all-wise, and in our Lord the Holy Spirit, God all-good. Our essential nature is entire in each Person of the Trinity, who is one God.
>
> Our sensual nature is in the Second Person alone, Jesus Christ. In him is the Father too, and the Holy Spirit. In him and by him have we been taken out of hell with a strong arm; and out of the earth's wretchedness have been wonderfully raised to heaven, and united, most blessedly, to him who is our true being.
>
> And we have developed in spiritual wealth and character through all Christ's virtues, and by the gracious Holy Spirit.
>
> *Revelations of Divine Love*, 166–67

Reflection

The Father, Son and Holy Spirit, one God,
live and work in love and harmony to bring into being a new people and a new creation.
We are invited to join in with this happy task.

MATTHEW 10:42   JANUARY 22

Practical Service

> *While we are thankful for those who have visions and have prophetic powers, we are also grateful for those who care and cook meals. The Spirit gives many gifts, there are many different ministries, and there are many ways in which to be a blessing to others.*

One of the sayings of the Desert Fathers has to do with the blessedness of practical service. Here is the story:

> A certain Apollonius, who had been a merchant and renounced the world, came to live on Mount Nitria: and since he could learn no art, hindered as he was by weight of years, nor could practice the abstinence laid down in Holy Writ, he laid down a rule of continence for himself.
>
> For out of his own purse and labor he bought every kind of remedy and food-stuffs in Alexandria, and provided the brothers that were ailing with whatever they needed.
>
> You might see him from early morning till the ninth hour traversing up and down through all the monasteries, whether of men or women, in and out of door after door where there were any sick, carrying with him raisins and pomegranates, and eggs, and fine wheaten flour, especially for the ailing.
>
> To such a life for which alone he was adapted, did this servant of Christ devote his old age.
>
> *The Desert Fathers,* 171

Prayer

Lord, help me to understand my true identity and to know my gifts. And bless me, then, to serve others well in the power of your grace and in the joy of who I am. Amen.

2 CORINTHIANS 4:7 JANUARY 23

Mere Vessels

We have been created to embody and manifest the glory of God. But such glory is in unsafe hands when it is given to us. We, therefore, need to become the wounded carriers of God's presence and blessing.

Hildegard of Bingen, in her letter to Elisabeth of Schonau, a fellow visionary, touches on the topic of our vulnerability. She writes,

> Hear, O anxious daughter, for the ambitious suggestions of the ancient serpent often weary those whom God has inspired. For when that same serpent sees an elegant gem, he roars, saying, "What is this?" And he burns their minds with many miseries, tempting them to fly over the clouds, as if they were gods, just as he did.
>
> Now hear again. Whoever desires to accomplish the works of God, let them always consider that they are earthen vessels, for they are mere human beings. And let them always reflect on what they are and what they will be and to leave heavenly things to the one who is of heaven. For they are exiles, not knowing heavenly things, but only reciting the mysteries of God, just as a trumpet only makes a sound, but does not cause it. Someone must blow into it in order to make a sound.
>
> But let the mild, gentle, poor and needy put on the breastplate of faith. Let them become like simple children, whose trumpet sounds come from the horn of the Lamb.
>
> *Epistolae: Medieval Women's Latin Letters*, 125

Reflection

We so easily take what God gives and make out that is comes from us.
We thus displace God's glory.
But as we grow in humility we can more readily give the gifts of God their rightful place.

JAMES 1:12–16   JANUARY 24

Temptation

Temptation comes to all of us. It is the move to make us less than what we could be. And it grieves the heart of God.

The great church father St. Jerome did not only display his learning. He also wrote about his struggles and temptations:

> How often, when I was living in the desert, in the vast solitude which gives to hermits a savage dwelling place, parched by a burning sun, did I fancy myself among the pleasures of Rome! I used to sit alone because I was filled with bitterness. Sackcloth disfigured my unshapely limbs and my skin from long neglect had become as black as an Ethiopian's.
>
> Tears and groans were every day my portion; and if drowsiness chanced to overcome my struggles against it, my bare bones, which hardly held together, were bruised against the ground. Of my food and drink I say nothing: for, even in sickness, the solitaries have nothing but cold water, and to eat one's food cooked is looked upon as self-indulgence.
>
> Now, although in my fear of hell I had consigned myself to this prison, where I had no companions but scorpions and wild beasts, I often found myself [in my imagination] amid bevies of girls. My face was pale with fasting, but though my limbs were chilled, yet my mind was burning with desire, and the fires of lust kept bubbling up before me when my flesh was as good as dead.
>
> Helpless, I cast myself at the feet of Jesus, I watered them with my tears, I wiped them with my hair: and then I subdued my rebellious body with weeks of abstinence. I do not blush to avow my abject misery; rather I lament that I am not now what I once was.
>
> *Jerome, Letter XXII: To Eustochium, 7*

Prayer

Lord, I too have my besetting sins and temptations.
I cannot overcome them.
Grant me your grace and forgiveness and move me into the wholeness of your love. Amen.

PSALM 18:1-2   JANUARY 25

God Our Shield

Living in the grace of Christ, the power of the Spirit, and the goodness of God's care, we can be safe even when the storms are raging.

In the famous *Breastplate* prayer, St. Patrick celebrates the protective love of God in Christ—and, we may add, through the power of the Spirit.

> I invoke today all these virtues
> Against every hostile merciless power
> Which may attack my body and my soul,
> Against the incantations of false prophets,
> Against the black laws of heathenism,
> Against the false laws of heresy,
> Against the deceits of idolatry
> Against spells of…smiths and druids,
> Against every knowledge that is harmful to body and soul.
> Christ protect me today
> Against every poison, against burning,
> Against drowning, against death-wound,
> That I may receive abundant reward.
> Christ with me, Christ before me, Christ behind me,
> Christ within me, Christ beneath me, Christ above me,
> Christ at my right, Christ at my left.
>
> *The Confessions of St. Patrick*, 100

Reflection

Christ, my shield, my fortress, my safe place. Secure in you, may I be bold in the world.

ROMANS 6:5–11   JANUARY 26

Christ in Our Place

What we did not do and now of ourselves cannot do, in living in obedience to God, Christ has done for us. He has shown us the way. And in joining with Christ we are now empowered to live his way.

The great church father of Western Christian orthodoxy, St. Athanasius, had this to say about the atoning work of Christ:

> The Word takes on a body capable of death, so that by partaking in the Word that is above all, it might be worthy to die instead of all. . . . Hence the Word did away with death for all who are like him by the offering of a substitute . . .
>
> For this reason was Christ born, appeared as man, and died and rose again . . . that, wherever men and women have been lured away, he may recall them, and reveal to them his own true Father; as he himself says, "I came to seek and to save that which was lost."

Documents of the Christian Church, 34–35

Thought

In whatever way we may understand the reason for the incarnation
and Christ's death on the cross,
it is foundational that Christ needed to save us,
reconcile us to the Father and make us whole.

MARK 1:16–20   JANUARY 27

Servants of Christ

We are called to believe in Christ. We are called to become like him. But we are also called to become his followers and servants.

Bonaventure had this to say about St. Francis as he sought to be a servant of Christ:

> True piety, which according to the Apostle
> is helpful for all things,
> had so filled Francis's heart and penetrated its depths
> that it seemed to have appropriated the man of God
> completely into its dominion.
>
> This is what drew him up to God through devotion,
> transformed him into Christ through compassion,
> attracted him to his neighbour through condescension
> and symbolically showed a return
> to the state of original innocence
> through universal reconciliation with each and every thing.

The Life of St. Francis, 79

Reflection

To be the servant of Christ is first an act of worship and then an act of service.
And this service seeks the healing and renewal of all things.

ACTS 18:26–27   JANUARY 28

God's Preparatory Way

God works in strange ways to gain our attention. But God's way is always gracious. God prepares us to receive what God seeks to give.

Hugh of Saint Victor, a twelfth-century theologian and mystic, identified some of the ways in which God does his preparatory work. He writes,

> Accordingly, since a time of repentance had been granted, humans were set in this world in a place of repentance, so that they might correct evil things and recover good things. The purpose of this was that, when humankind comes at last to judgment, they might receive, not the penalty for sin, but the glory prepared for them as a reward of righteousness.
>
> It remains then, that while there is time, men and women should seek advice and ask for help for their correction and liberation. But as they are found to be sufficient of themselves for neither, it is necessary that God, who by his grace delays judgment, should by the same grace meanwhile supply advice for the escape, and after the advice, bestow help.
>
> So, then, it is fitting that God should, for the time being, lay aside the role of judge, and first take on the role of an adviser and afterward that of helper. God must act in such a way, as at first to leave humankind entirely to themselves, so that they may experience their own ignorance and understand that they need advice—and thereafter may feel their weakness and recognize that they need help.
>
> *A Scholastic Miscellany: Anselm to Ockham*, 302

Prayer

Lord, grant that I may have the eyes to see and the ears to hear and the heart to comprehend your ways with me, so that I may enter into the way you are opening up for me. Amen.

ROMANS 5:6–8   JANUARY 29

God's Great Generosity

> *There is only one way to truly recognize God—and that is to enter into and embrace God's gracious love for each one of us.*

St. Anselm wants to take his readers beyond speculation into the very goodness of God. He writes,

> Ah, for what generous love and loving generosity
> compassion flows out to us!
> Ah, what feelings of love should we sinners have
> towards the unbounded goodness of God!
> For you save the righteous
> who are commended by their righteousness,
> and you set free those
> who by their unrighteousness are condemned;
> the one by the help of what they have deserved,
> the other in spite of what they have deserved.
> In those you look to find the good you gave them;
> in these you overlook the evil which you hate.
> Ah, boundless goodness, far beyond all understanding
> on me be your compassion which comes from such generosity!
> Let that which flows from you, flow into me.

The Prayers and Meditations of Saint Anselm with the Proslogion, 250–51

Thought

Receptivity is the gateway of the Christian life.

Luke 6:27–28 & 1 Timothy 2:1–2   January 30

Prayer for Enemies

At the heart of Christian spirituality is the art and passion of prayer. Prayer is expressing our friendship with God. But prayer is also for the benefit of others, including one's enemies.

The early Christian martyr Polycarp expresses a heart of forgiveness to those who would bring harm. He writes,

> But may the God and Father of our Lord Jesus Christ, and Jesus Christ himself, who is the Son of God and our everlasting high priest, build you up in faith and truth, and in all meekness, gentleness, patience, long-suffering, forbearance and purity.
>
> And may he give you a place among his saints, and us with you, and all that are under heaven who will yet believe in our Lord Jesus Christ, and in his Father, who raised him from the dead.
>
> Pray for all the saints.
>
> Pray also for kings and potentates and princes, and for those who persecute and hate you, and for the enemies of the cross, so that your fruit may be manifest to all, and that you may be perfect in him.
>
> *The Epistle of Polycarp to the Philippians*, ch. 12

Reflection

While we should never condone any form of evil,
whether personal or institutional,
we are called to forgive those who bring us harm.
In this, we are called to follow and embrace the way of Christ,
who extended forgiveness to those who crucified him.

JEREMIAH 29:11-12 JANUARY 31

Prayer

To the modern mind, prayer seems to be irrelevant. But at the heart of the biblical story and in the history of Christian spirituality, prayer is the heartbeat of the Christian life.

John Cassian, who was one of the leaders in shaping monasticism, gives us some important insights into the nature of prayer. He writes,

> Each moment, prayer changes according to the purity and state of the soul, based on what happens to us, or by our efforts in renewing ourselves. Therefore it is quite clear that we cannot always offer up uniform prayers.
>
> For we all pray one way when feeling lively and another way when oppressed by the weight of sadness or despair. We pray one way when we are invigorated by spiritual achievements and another way when we are cast down by the burden of attacks. We pray differently, depending on whether we are asking pardon for our sins or to obtain grace or virtue or for the destruction of some sin. We pray one way when we are pricked to the heart by thoughts of hell and the fear of future judgment and another way when we are aglow with hope and the desire of good things to come. We pray one way when we are taken up with affairs and dangers and another when we are at peace and security. We pray one way when we are enlightened by the revelation of heavenly mysteries and another when we are depressed by a sense of barrenness in virtues and dryness in feeling.
>
> *The Conferences of John Cassian,* 2.10.8

Reflection

While there are liturgical prayers that we pray, much of our praying is the language of the heart. As such, our prayers take on all the hues and textures of life.

February

ACTS 9:15–16 — FEBRUARY 1

A Missional Calling

We are called to faith. We are also called to outwork our faith. We are called to faith in Christ. We are also called to serve Christ in the world.

St. Patrick was a visionary and a missionary. He speaks of his calling to this ministry in *Patrick on the Great Works of God*. He writes,

> But after I reached Ireland, I pastured the flocks each day, and I prayed many times a day. More and more, the love of God and my fear of him grew, and my faith increased, and my spirit was moved, so that in a day I prayed up to a hundred payers, and just as many at night.
>
> I used to stay out in the forests and on the mountain, and I would wake up before daylight to pray in the snow, in icy coldness, in rain, and I never felt ill nor spiritually lazy because, as I now see, the Spirit was burning in me at that time.
>
> And it was there, of course, that one night in my sleep I heard a voice saying to me: "You do well to fast: soon you will depart for your home country."
>
> And again, a very short time later, there was a voice prophesying: "Behold, your ship is ready."
>
> *The Confessions of St. Patrick*, 16–17

Thought

A missional calling usually grows within us.
And it is the gift of prayer that gives shape to this calling.

PSALM 90:1–2   FEBRUARY 2

God our Dwelling Place

> *The heart of Christian spirituality does not center on the belief that God occasionally visits us, or that it is good to pray from time to time, but that God becomes our dwelling place and our home forever.*

The medieval mystic Gertrude the Great wrote much about God as the great lover and friend in whom we can find shelter. Hear her voice:

> You continued to act lovingly toward me and to continually draw my soul from vanity and to yourself. One day between the festival of the Resurrection and the Ascension, I went into our courtyard . . . and seated myself near the fountain. I began to consider the beauty of the place. It charmed me with its clear and flowing stream, the verdure of the trees which surrounded it, and the flight of the birds—especially the doves.
>
> Above all, I loved the sweet calm of this place. . . . And I asked myself what would make this place even better for me. I thought that the friendship of a wise and intimate companion, who would sweeten my solitude or render it useful to others, would do that.
>
> It was then that you, my Lord and my God, who are a torrent of inestimable pleasure, not only surprised me with the first impulse of this desire, but also willed to be the fulfillment of it. You inspired me with the thought that if I return your graces to you in continual gratitude, as a stream returns to its source; if I increase in the love of virtue, and put forth the flowers of good works like the trees; if I despise the things on earth and fly upward as freely as the birds, I can free my senses from the distraction of exterior things.
>
> Then my spirit would be empty of obstacles and my heart would be an agreeable dwelling for you.
>
> *Life and Revelations of Saint Gertrude*, 76

Reflection

The gift of nature's beauty can be an opening for God's presence.
Emptiness, as well as the gifts of our human condition,
can make a way for God.

PSALM 42:1-2 — FEBRUARY 3

Yearning for God's Presence

Our longing for God and our life of prayer is not simply to gain blessings from God. We long to love God for who God is and to worship God in his glory, goodness and grace.

The English mystic Richard Rolle, the Hermit of Hampole, speaks of this yearning heart in his classic, *The Mending of Life*. He writes,

> O sweet and delectable light that is my Maker unmade, enlighten the face and sharpness of my inner eye with clearness unmade, that my mind—utterly cleansed from uncleanness and made marvellous with gifts—may swiftly flee into the high mirth of love. Kindled with your savour, I may sit and rest, joying in you, Jesus.
>
> O Love everlasting, enflame my soul to love God, so that nothing may burn in me but his embraces. O good Jesus, who shall grant me to feel you, who now may neither be felt nor seen?
>
> Shed yourself into the entrails of my soul. Come into my heart and fill it with your clearest sweetness. Moisten my mind with the hot wine of your sweet love, so that forgetful of all ills and all scornful visions and imaginations, and having only you, I may be glad and joyful in Jesus, my God.
>
> From now on, sweetest Lord, do not go from me, but continually dwell with me in your sweetness; for your presence only is solace to me, and your absence only leaves me heavy.
>
> *The Mending of Life*, ch. 11

Prayer

Lord, turn my heart and mind towards you.
Impart your love and grace to me, and may the wings of your Spirit carry me close to you. Amen.

EPHESIANS 1:17–19   FEBRUARY 4

A Song of the Nurturing Jesus

Jesus, the obedient Son of the Father and the exalted Lord, is the great sustainer and nurturer. He is the life-giver. He loves and cares as a mother.

The English mystic Julian of Norwich speaks of Jesus as a mother. She writes,

> Jesus is our true mother, the protector of the love that knows no end.
> We have our being from Jesus,
> where the foundation of motherhood begins.
> God revealed that in all things,
> as truly as God is our father, so truly God is our mother.
> God is the power and goodness of fatherhood,
> God is the goodness and loving kindness of motherhood.
> God is the Trinity and God is the Unity,
> God is all our life: nature, mercy and grace.
> God is the one who makes us to love,
> and the endless fulfilling of all true desires;
> For where the soul is highest and noblest,
> there it is humble and lowly.
> God desired Christ to be our mother, our brother and our Saviour,
> for God knows us now and loved us before time began.

Celebrating Common Prayer: A Version of the Daily Office SSF, 234–35

Reflection

Our life and fruitfulness is through the nurture of God.

JEREMIAH 1:14–16   FEBRUARY 5

Calamity

Christians are not specially protected from difficulty, natural disasters and wars. St. Augustine saw the city of Hippo, where he was bishop, besieged by Vandals for fourteen months before the city fell. Augustine died a month later.

The bishop Possidius, who was there at the time of this great calamity, writes about Augustine,

> These days, therefore, that he lived through and endured . . . were the most bitter and mournful of his old age. For he saw cities overthrown in destruction, and the resident citizens, together with the buildings on their lands, partly annihilated by the enemy's slaughter, and others driven into flight and dispersed.
>
> He saw churches stripped of priests and ministers, and holy virgins and all the monastics scattered in every direction. Here he saw some succumb to torture, and others slain by the sword, while still others in captivity and losing their innocence and faith both of soul and body, received from their foes the harsh and evil treatment of slaves.
>
> He saw the hymns and praises of God perish from the churches; the church buildings in many places consumed by fire, the regular services which were due to God cease from their appointed places, the holy sacraments no longer desired . . .
>
> And it happened one time while we were seated with him at table and were conversing together that he said to us: "I would have you know that, in this time of our misfortune I ask this of God: either that he may be pleased to free this city which is surrounded by the foe, or if something else seems good in his sight, that he make his servants brave for enduring his will, or at least that he may take me from this world unto himself."

Possidius, Life of St. Augustine, ch. 28

Reflection

The city fell. Some did not have the strength to endure.
But God is merciful—and Augustine died.

GALATIANS 3:25-27   FEBRUARY 6

A Christo-mysticism

> *Faith is not simply believing something about Jesus, but believing in Jesus. In faith, we enter into a relationship with Jesus, which binds us together.*

The most famous of the Dutch medieval mystics, Jan van Ruysbroeck (John Ruusbroec), in *The Little Book of the Enlightenment*, has this to say about a Christo-mysticism or this in-Christ relationship:

> Christ prayed that he might be in us, and we in him. We find this in many places in the Gospel. This is a union that is without an intermediary, for God's love not only flows outward, but also draws inward toward unity. And all those who experience and perceive this become interior, enlightened men and women.
>
> Their higher powers are raised above all their practices to the bare essence of their being. Simplified above reason, these powers become full and overflowing. In this simplicity, the spirit finds itself united with God without an intermediary. And this union, together with the exercise which is proper to it, will endure eternally...
>
> Then Christ further prayed the highest prayer: that all his beloved might be made perfectly one, even as he is one with the Father—not in the way that he is one single divine substance with the Father, for that is impossible for us, but as one in the same unity where he is, without distinction, one enjoyment and one beatitude with the Father in essential love.

John Ruusbroec: The Spiritual Espousals and Other Works, 267

Prayer

Lord, grant that through the grace of Christ
and the power of the Holy Spirit,
I may more fully enter into your life and light.
Draw me into the mystery of the love of Father, Son and Holy Spirit.
Amen.

1 JOHN 4:1 — FEBRUARY 7

To Weigh Up

In many of the circumstances of life we have to make choices: "Is this the right thing to do? Or is that what we must do?" So we need to discern, to weigh things up and to evaluate.

John Cassian, in writing about a spirituality for monks, focuses on the importance of discernment. This is what he has to say:

> Finally, there is the test to be applied to a money-changer, a test which, as I have already stated, has to do with checking the weight. This is how it is practiced.
>
> If our thoughts suggest that something must be done, we must handle it with the utmost scrupulosity. It must be placed on the scales of our heart and weighed with the most exacting care.
>
> Is it filled with what is good for all? Is it heavy with the fear of God? Is it genuine in the feelings which underlie it?
>
> Is it lightweight because of human show or because of some thrust toward novelty? Has the burden of vainglory lessened its merit or diminished its luster?
>
> This prompt testing should be done as something public. That is, it is measured against the acts and witness of the apostles. If it looks to be whole, complete, and in conformity with these latter, then let us hold on to it. Or if it seems defective, dangerous, and not of equal weight with these, let us cautiously and carefully reject it.
>
> John Cassian, *Conferences*, 57

Reflection

In seeking to be discerning about what we say and do,
we must avoid being overly self-critical and overly rash.
Rather, we must trust the Spirit to guide us.

ISAIAH 66:13 — FEBRUARY 8

The God of All Consolation

We have somehow ended up with the God of demand and have neglected the God of consolation. Maybe this is because, in the spasms of late modernity, we have become hard on ourselves and others. There seems to be little common grace in our world.

St. Anselm is ever seeking the God of consolation in his prayers. He does so because he recognizes his need for comfort in the light of his own brokenness and the difficulties of life. He prays,

> Come now, Lord, appear to me and I will be consoled;
> show me your face and I will be saved;
> display your presence and I have obtained my desire;
> reveal your glory and my joy will be full.
> "My soul thirsts for you, my flesh longs after you."
> My soul thirsts for God, the fountain of life;
> "when shall I come to appear before the presence of God?"
>
> My consoler, for whom I wait, when will you come?
> O that I might see the joy that I desire;
> that I might be satisfied with the appearing of your glory for which I hunger;
> that I might be satisfied with the riches of your house for which I sigh;
> that I might drink of the torrent of your pleasures for which I thirst.

The Prayers and Meditations of Saint Anselm with the Proslogion, 98

Meditation

The Lord is my refuge and my delight.
May that delight fan the flame of heart and hand.

PHILIPPIANS 2:14–15   FEBRUARY 9

A Life of Faithfulness

> *The challenge of our time is not to proclaim more Christian words, but to become the embodied word of Christ in our world.*

The unknown author of *The Epistle of Barnabas,* an early post-apostolic writing, has this to say to Christians about living a life of faithfulness and integrity:

> Let us, therefore, give heed unto the last days. For the whole time of our faith will profit us nothing unless now, in the season of iniquity and among the stumbling-blocks that are coming, we resist the temptations of the evil one, as it is befitting for God's children to do. Let us flee from all vanity and hate perfectly the deeds of the evil way. Do not withdraw into your own houses and dwell alone, as though you were already justified, but come together and seek out together the common good.
>
> For the Scripture says, "Woe to those who are wise in their own opinion and learned in their own eyes." Let us be spiritual: let us become a perfect temple for God. As much as we are able, let us practice the fear of God and strive to keep his commandments, so that we may rejoice in his righteousness.
>
> The Lord will judge the world without partiality; all shall receive according to what they have done. If they are good, righteousness shall go before them, but if they are evil, the wages of wickedness will go before them.
>
> Let us be careful that we do not take rest and sleep in our sins just because we have already been justified, so that the ruler of wickedness does not gain mastery over us and thrust us from the kingdom of the Lord.
>
> *Epistle of Barnabas,* ch. 4

Prayer

Lord, by your grace and through the Spirit, may I live to your glory, to the well-being of your people and to the blessing of the neighbor. Keep me safe from harm's way. Amen.

MATTHEW 10:21–23　　　　　　　　　　FEBRUARY 10

Persecution

Christianity has always been—and may it always be—a martyr's religion. This martyrdom has to do with the witness of faith—not for imposing one's cause on someone else.

St. Cyprian of Carthage, in one of his many letters, speaks of the persecution that believers of his day were experiencing. He gives this encouragement:

> When you see our people scattered and driven to flight through fear of persecution, none of you, dearly beloved, has reason for feeling distressed at no longer finding your community assembled together and at no longer hearing your bishops preach.
>
> At such a time, it is just not possible for everyone to be gathered in one place; they need to be killed, even though they themselves may not kill.
>
> In those days, whenever our brothers or sisters happen to be parted from the flock temporarily, by force of circumstances, and find themselves separated from the flock in body, but not in spirit, let them not be dismayed at the terrors of their flight. As they look for refuge and concealment, let them not be alarmed at the loneliness of their desert region.
>
> No one is alone who has Christ as a companion in flight; no one is alone who, by preserving the temple of God, has God always near, wherever he or she may be.
>
> *The Letters of St. Cyprian of Carthage*, vol. 3, 62–63

Reflection

The idea that God is with us even when Christians are persecuted, rather than that God prevents these terrible events from happening, calls us to a deep reflection regarding God's way with us.

EPHESIANS 6:12–13   FEBRUARY 11

Deliverance

> *The salvation which Christ brings restores us to God, cleanses us from sin, makes us whole and delivers us from the power of the Evil One. Deliverance brings us into a place of freedom.*

St. Patrick, in his *Declaration of the Great Works of God*, speaks of an experience of deliverance from the power of Satan. He writes,

> The very same night, while I was sleeping, Satan attacked me violently, as I will remember so long as I am in this body.
>
> Something like a huge rock fell on top of me, and I lost all power over my limbs. Though I was ignorant in spiritual matters, it came to me that I should call upon Elijah. Meanwhile, I saw the sun rising in the sky, and while I was crying out, "Elijah, Elijah," with all my might, the brilliance of the sun fell upon me and immediately shook me free of all the weight.
>
> I believe that I was aided by Christ my Lord, and that his Spirit was crying out for me. In the day of my affliction, I hope that it will be just as it says in the gospel: "in that hour," the Lord declares, "it is not you who speaks, but the Spirit of your Father speaking in you."
>
> *The Confessions of St. Patrick*, 20

Prayer

Lord, grant that I may not be afraid of all the Evil One may throw at me. Give me the faith to call on your name and to resist the power of Satan. Amen.

MATTHEW 15:25–27 FEBRUARY 12

Even Crumbs Are Enough

We know God at the edges of God's ways. We have glimpses of God's love. We see flashes of God's glory. Even the crumbs of God's goodness can more than satisfy us.

Louis the Pious became king of the Franks after the great Charlemagne. Dhouda of Septimania, who was the wife of Bernard, the king's trusted counselor, was a woman of great spiritual faith and wisdom. In her *Manual for My Son*, she writes about trusting God:

> My son, we must both search for God since we live in the will of God. It is in God that we live and move and have our being. I seek the Lord in order to be strong, for of myself I am as unworthy and inconsequential as a shadow.
>
> It is absolutely necessary for me to ask the Lord's help unceasingly so that I might know and understand. Even a problematic puppy, who sits under the master's table with the others, can often succeed in catching and eating the crumbs that fall from the master's table. The One who could make the mouth of dumb animals speak with understanding is indeed most powerful.
>
> The Lord who prepares a table in the desert for faithful followers and gives them a measure of wheat to fulfill their needs, can also satisfy my desires as a handmaid of the Lord from that goodness. Within the holy church I am at least under the table, able to watch the small dogs (that is, the ministers of the holy altars) even if it is at a distance.
>
> But I can still collect crumbs of spiritual understanding from under that table. Such crumbs of beautiful, valuable, and clear insights are appropriate both for you and for me. I am sure of this, for our God does not abandon the poor in spirit.

Mystics, Visionaries, and Prophets, 81

Thought

The challenge facing the present-day community of faith is to make sure that no one feels they have a lesser place in the church.

MARK 3:13–15 — FEBRUARY 13

In the Footsteps of the Master

If we ask the question, how should we live and what should we do?—the answer is clear: live like Jesus and do what he did.

Bonaventure paints for us a picture of St. Francis as one who sought most of all to wander with joy in the footsteps of Jesus. He writes,

> As he went through diverse districts,
> he preached the gospel with fervour,
> and the Lord worked with him and
> confirmed his words with the signs that followed.
> For in the power of God's name,
> Francis, the herald of truth,
> cast out demons,
> healed the sick,
> and, what is more, by the might of his preaching,
> softened and made penitent hard hearts,
> restoring health to the body and the mind at the same time,
> as all his miracles do prove.
>
> *St Bonaventure: The Life of St. Francis of Assisi*, 91

Prayer

> Lord, grant by your grace that I may seek
> to minister Christ's love and goodness
> to those around me. Amen.

PSALM 139:11–12   FEBRUARY 14

Darkness

The places of darkness and desolation in our lives need not be the empty places, though they often seem to be. Instead, these empty places can be where we are de-centered and renewed.

The English Christian mystic Walter Hilton has this to say about the places of darkness in our lives:

> Then what is the thing that makes this darkness? Truly, nothing but a gracious desire to have the love of Jesus. For the desire and longing that the soul has for the love of God—to see him and have him—drives out of the heart all worldly vanities and fleshly affections. Gathered into itself, the soul busies itself with thinking about how it may come to the love of him.
> At that time, whether praying or meditating, the soul may freely and devotedly behold Jesus. And this brings the soul to this right *nothing*, which is not altogether dark nor truly nothing. For though it is dark, it is not altogether dark because Jesus, who is both love and light, is in this darkness, whether it be painful or restful.
> If the darkness is painful, then it is Jesus in the soul, toiling in desire and longing after light, but not yet resting in love, nor showering forth his light. Therefore this is called night and darkness, inasmuch as the soul is hid from the false light of the world and has not yet had a full feeling of true light, but is awaiting the blessed love of God which it desires.
>
> *The Scale (or Ladder) of Perfection*, 2.2.5

Reflection

The places of darkness in our spiritual journey
need not be the terminus points,
but can be places of transition.
But these are difficult places, for we are in-between,
and the light has not yet fully broken through.

LUKE 10:38–42   FEBRUARY 15

Martha and Mary

> *These two women have long been depicted in the Christian tradition as symbols of the active and contemplative life. But clearly we need to be both.*

One of the stories of the Desert Fathers highlights how work and prayer, service and contemplation need to be held together:

> A pilgrim friar came to visit the Abbot Silvanus, who lived upon Mount Sinai. Seeing the monks work with their hands, he said to them: "Why do you labour for the meat that perishes? Do you not know that it is written, 'Mary chose the good part'?"
>
> Then Abbot Silvanus said to Zacharias, one of his disciples: "Give this pilgrim a book to read and put him in an empty cell."
>
> Zacharias did so, and the pilgrim remained there until the evening, wondering why he was not called to dinner. Waiting and listening some time longer, still no one came for him, and not being able to bear it, he left the cell and went to the abbot and said: "Have not the monks dined?" And the abbot replied: "We have all dined." And the pilgrim said: "Why then did you not send for me?" And the abbot answered in mockery: "You are a spiritual man and have no need of bodily food; but we are bodily men, and seeing that we need food, we labour to earn it; but you, who have with Mary chosen the good part, you can read and pray all day, because you do not need food."
>
> These words brought the stranger to repentance, and he said: "I see, my brothers, that there is need of both Martha and Mary, for while Martha labours, Mary can, in consequence, worship at the feet of the Saviour; and the active and contemplative life are both required, and the one helps the other."
>
> *Legends of Saints and Martyrs*, 57–58

Reflection

There is never only one way to live the Christian life and to serve others. The spiritual and the practical are threads woven into one fabric and are necessary to live well, pray well, and serve well.

LUKE 1:38   FEBRUARY 16

A Song for Mary

Mary, the mother of Jesus, has always been highly regarded in the writings of the church. She is, above all, a great symbol of obedience in the face of mystery.

Hildegard of Bingen has written a wonderful poem about Mary the mother of Jesus:

> Hail Mary,
> Author of life
> by rebuilding salvation,
> you destroyed death
> and crushed the serpent under your heel.
> Eve raised herself before the serpent,
> stiff-necked and full of pride.
> But you crushed the serpent
> when you bore the Son of God,
> come down from Heaven.
>
> The Spirit of God breathed him forth.
> O sweet, loving mother, hail,
> You brought forth into the world your Son sent from Heaven.
>
> *The Letters of Hildegard of Bingen*, vol. 2, 161

Reflection

May I too, O guiding angel, say: Be it unto me as the Lord wills.

Ephesians 5:15-16　　　　　　　　February 17

Christians in Society

While some streams of Christian spirituality have suggested that Christians should radically withdraw from the world, the central emphasis of Christian spirituality has always been one of worldly engagement.

The unknown author of *The Letter to Diognetus* makes it clear that Christians are to live in the world along with their fellow citizens, but they are called to live differently:

> Christians are not distinguished from the rest of mankind by either country, speech, or customs. The fact is, they nowhere settle in cities of their own; they use no special language; they cultivate no eccentric mode of life...
>
> Yet they dwell in both Greek and non-Greek cities, as each one's lot was cast. And they conform to the customs of the country in dress, food, and mode of life generally.
>
> The whole tenor of their way of living stamps it as worthy of admiration, and as admittedly extraordinary. They reside in their respective countries, but only as pilgrims.
>
> They take part in everything as citizens, and put up with everything as foreigners. Every foreign land is their home, and every home, a foreign land.
>
> They marry like all others, and beget children; but they do not expose their offspring. Their board [possessions] they share with all, but not their bed. They find themselves in the flesh, but do not live according to the flesh.
>
> They spend their days on earth, but hold citizenship in heaven. They obey the established laws, but in their private lives they rise above all laws.
>
> *The Christian Way of Life*, 62–63

Reflection

We are called to be in the world, but not of the world,
and world-concerned, but heavenly minded.

MATTHEW 26:26–29 FEBRUARY 18

Eucharist

In holy communion we celebrate the blessings that flow to us from the passion of Christ. We are grateful for the community formed by Christ's death and resurrection, and we look forward to the life to come.

The early church father Justin Martyr, in his *First Apology*, speaks of the Eucharist and its meaning. He writes,

> We call this food the "Eucharist." None are allowed to partake of it except those who believe that our teachings are true and have been cleansed in the bath for the forgiveness of their sins and for their regeneration, and who live as Christ commanded.
>
> Not as common bread nor as common drink do we receive these. But just as through the word of God, Jesus Christ, our savior, became incarnate and took on flesh and blood for our salvation, so, we have been taught, the food over which thanks has been given by the prayer of his word, and which nourishes our flesh and blood by assimilation, is both the flesh and blood of that incarnate Jesus.
>
> The apostles, in their memoirs, which are called gospels, have handed down that they were commanded to do this: Jesus took bread, and, after giving thanks, said "Do this in remembrance of me; this is my body." In like manner, he also took the cup, gave thanks, and said "This is my blood."
>
> *The Eucharist*, 34

Prayer

Lord, may you nourish and renew me in this feast of your passion. Amen.

Prayer and Thanksgiving

To pray is a multi-faceted activity. Above all, it expresses our friendship with God, and this will always involve the happy task of thanksgiving.

The English mystic Julian of Norwich, in her reflections on prayer, talks about the centrality of thanksgiving. She writes,

> For the meek and endless thanks that we will be given, God wants us to pray continually. God accepts our good intentions and work, no matter how we feel. It pleases God that we work, both in our prayers and in our good living, by the help of his grace, turning all our faculties to him . . .
>
> With prayer belongs thanksgiving. Thanksgiving is a true inward knowing, with great reverence and love, the work that our good Lord is stirring us to do with all our might and enjoyment.
>
> Sometimes the abundance breaks out with a voice and says, "Good Lord, Grant mercy! Blessed may you be!" Sometimes, when our hearts are dry and unfeeling, or when the temptations of the enemy overpower us, reason and grace drive us to cry upon our Lord, recalling his blessed passion and great goodness. And then the virtue of our Lord's word comes to the soul and quickens the heart and leads it by his grace into its true purpose, enabling it to pray blissfully and truly to enjoy our Lord. Thanksgiving is blessed in his sight.
>
> *Revelations of Divine Love Shewed to a Devout Ankress*, 73

Meditation

Reflect on all that you have been given, and give thanks to God.

LUKE 22:39-44   FEBRUARY 20

Our Gethsemane

If our spiritual walk is to follow in the footsteps of Christ, then similar key events in Jesus' life will resonate with our own lives. Thus we, too, will have to face our Gethsemanes, where we will struggle in surrendering to God's mysterious will.

St. Augustine gives us an instance of one of his intense early struggles of faith:

> There was a garden belonging to our lodging, of which we had the use—as we did the whole house—for our host did not live there. The tempest in my heart hurried me to this garden, where no one might hinder the fiery struggle which I had engaged against myself, until it was resolved, O Lord, as you foresaw, though I did not. Only, for a while, I was mad for health, dying for life, knowing the misery that I was, but not knowing the good that I would soon become.
>
> Into this garden I fled, and Alypius after me, step by step—for I had no secret that he did not share, and how could he forsake me in so great distress? We sat as far from the house as possible, and I, raging with tempestuous indignation, groaned in spirit with myself, as I acknowledged how I had not entered into your will and covenant, O my God, even though all my bones had cried out that this was the way to follow, extolling it above all else.
>
> For the pathway into your will, we do not travel in ships, nor in four-horsed chariots, nor yet on foot. In order to set upon the road toward your will and attain our journey's end, all that is required of us is that we have the will to go. But our will must be strong and single-minded—not a half-wounded, staggering will that tumbles about, struggling with itself while one part rises and the other part falls.
>
> *Confessions of St. Augustine,* 214

Reflection

In the journey of faith,
these struggles of surrender not only
lie at the beginning point of our conversion,
but at various points along the way.
This may call us, not only to a surrender of the will, but of our whole being.

ROMANS 1:16–17   FEBRUARY 21

The Power of the Gospel

> *In every age and culture the gospel of Jesus Christ brings salvation and hope and new life. Its spread throughout the earth reflects the purpose of God that all might hear, all might believe and all might be saved.*

Gregory the Great in his *Epistle LXII* to Brunichild, Queen of the Franks, speaks of the gospel coming to the English:

> We render thanks to Almighty God, who, among all the other gifts of His loving-kindness that He bestowed upon your Excellency, has so filled you with a love of the Christian religion that whatever you know to pertain to the gain of souls, whatever to the propagation of the faith, you cease not to carry into effect with devout mind and pious zeal.
>
> As to the great favour and assistance wherewith your Excellency aided our most reverend brother and fellow-bishop Augustine on his progress to the nation of the Angli [English], fame had already not been silent; and afterwards certain monks, returning to us from him, gave us a particular account thereof.
>
> And indeed, let others to whom your benefactions are less known wonder at these evidences of your Christianity; for to us who know them by experience they are not subject to wonder, but of rejoicing, because through what you bestow upon others you delight yourself.
>
> Now of what sort and how great are the miracles which our Redeemer has wrought in the conversion of the above-written nation is already known to your Excellency. On which account you ought to have great joy, since the succours afforded by you claim to themselves the larger share therein, it having been through your aid, after God, that the word of preaching became widely known in those parts. For one who aids the good work of another makes it his own.
>
> *Nicene and Post-Nicene Fathers*, vol. 13, 73

Reflection

Let us all share in joy of the gospel coming to those who hear it gladly.

ACTS 1:8 — FEBRUARY 22

The Gift of the Spirit as Unifier

While some Christians emphasize the power imparted by the Spirit, and others focus on the gifts and fruits of the Spirit, our fundamental focus should be on how the Spirit draws us into fellowship with the Father and the Son and each other.

The church father Gregory of Nyssa, in his *Homilies on the Song of Songs*, speaks about the Spirit uniting us into a bond of peace with God and the community of faith. He writes,

> When perfect love has driven out fear, or fear has been transformed into love, then everything that has been saved will be a unity growing together through the one and only Fullness, and everyone will be, in one another, a unity in the perfect Dove, the Holy Spirit . . .
>
> In this way, encircled by the unity of the Holy Spirit as the bond of peace, all will be one body and one spirit. . . . But it would be better to quote the very words of the Gospel literally: "That they may all be one; even as you, Father, are in me and I am in you, that they also may be in us" (John 17:21).
>
> Now the bond of this unity is glory. And that this glory is the Holy Spirit, all who are familiar with Scripture will agree if they are attentive to the word of the Lord: "The glory which thou hast given me, I have given to them" (John 17:22). He has indeed really given them such glory when he said: "Receive the Holy Spirit" (John 20:22).
>
> *The Roots of Christian Mysticism*, 273

Prayer

Lord, pour out your life-giving Spirit on us anew in order to draw us more deeply into your life, to revive us and your church, and to empower us for your service. Amen.

1 TIMOTHY 2:3-6 — FEBRUARY 23

The Shape of Belief

Our faith draws us into a faith relationship with Christ, but it also calls us to believe key truths that constitute our faith. Faith, therefore, involves both our hearts and our minds.

The early church father Tertullian, in his *Prescription Against Heretics*, spells out the Rule of Faith, which contains the central beliefs held by the church at that time:

> To state here and now what we maintain—which is, of course, what we believe: that there is but one God, who is none other than the Creator of the world, who produced everything from nothing through his Word, sent forth before all things. This Word is called his Son, and in the name of God was seen in diverse ways by the patriarchs and matriarchs, was ever heard in the prophets and finally was brought down by the Spirit and Power of God the Father into the Virgin Mary, was made flesh in her womb, was born of her and lived as Jesus Christ. Thereafter, he proclaimed a new law and a new promise of the kingdom of heaven, worked miracles, was crucified, on the third day rose again, was caught up into heaven and sat down at the right hand of the Father. God then sent in the place of Jesus Christ the power of the Holy Spirit to guide believers. He will come with glory to take the saints up into the fruition of life eternal and the heavenly promises, and he will judge the wicked to everlasting fire, after the resurrection of both good and with the restoration of their flesh.
>
> *Early Latin Theology*, 39–40

Reflection

While Scripture and theology may seem increasingly less important to contemporary Christians, our beliefs can't be only personal and emotive. Our beliefs also have to be communal, intelligent, and defensible.

PSALM 147:1–3   FEBRUARY 24

Contemplation and Action

Just as the worship of God and our receiving of God's healing grace belong together, so too, our life of prayer and contemplation and witness and service weave one tapestry.

The German Christian mystic Meister Eckhart has some important things to say regarding the relationship between contemplation and action. He writes,

> In this life, no one can reach the point at which they are excused from outward works. Even if someone follows the contemplative life, he or she cannot altogether keep from flowing out and mingling in the life of action.
>
> Just as a penniless person may yet be generous in the will to give, and just as a person of wealth who gives nothing cannot be called generous, so no man or woman who has virtues may refrain from using them at the proper time and place.
>
> Hence those who lead the contemplative life and do not do outward works are quite mistaken and entirely on the wrong track. What I say is that someone who lives the contemplative life may—indeed, must—be absolutely free from outward works when engaged in the act of contemplation, but afterwards, his or her duty lies in outward service. For no one can live the contemplative life without a break, and an active life bridges the gap in the life of contemplation.
>
> *The Best of Meister Eckhart*, 137

Thought

Life cannot be pulled apart and put into neat little boxes.
Life is to be integrated.
Thus prayer and service belong together.
So do reflection and action.

EPHESIANS 3:14–17   FEBRUARY 25

Growing in Grace

None can say that they have arrived in the journey of faith, for the journey is ongoing. There is always more to know and more to understand. But above all, there is the call for deepening love and growth in a life of obedience.

Thomas à Kempis writes about a life of longing to be closer to God:

> Good Jesus, sweet and gentle, have mercy on me and grant me, who am but a poor beggar, that when I receive Holy Communion I may sometimes experience just a touch of that heartfelt love for you.
>
> Thus, my faith in you will find strengthening, my hope in your goodness will have its increase, and my love, set on fire by having tasted the heavenly manna, will never again grow faint.
>
> Your mercy is powerful enough to grant me this most desired grace, and compassionate enough to bestow this spirit of fervour on me at a time when it suits your divine pleasure.
>
> Though I do not burn with the same degree of longing as the very devout do, nevertheless, by your grace, I desire to have the same intense craving as they have. I pray and earnestly desire to be numbered among your devout lovers and to dwell in their holy company.

The Imitation of Christ in Four Books, 208

Prayer

Lord, there seems to be so much that is up and down
in my relationship with you.
Please hold me and help me to grow in love and commitment. Amen.

PSALM 51:10-12   FEBRUARY 26

A Prayer of the Heart

In Christian spirituality we are invited to pray the Jesus Prayer, or the Prayer of the Heart. Such a prayer is beyond pressing needs and issues. It is, instead, a prayer regarding a way of being in and with God, and the way of life that issues out of that.

St. Francis of Assisi in his writings left us this prayer:

> Almighty, eternal, just, and merciful God,
> grant us in our misery the grace
> to do for you what we know you want us to do,
> and always to desire what pleases you.
>
> So that inwardly purified, inwardly illumined,
> and kindled by the flame of the Holy Spirit,
> we may be able to follow
> the footsteps of your Son, our Lord Jesus Christ.
>
> And, by your grace alone,
> may we come to you, Most High,
> who lives and reigns in perfect Trinity and simple Unity,
> and are glorified God almighty
> forever and ever. Amen.

The Writings of Saint Francis of Assisi, 52

Meditation

In the shadow of your wings, O God, I wish to be nurtured
and in your footsteps, O Christ, I wish to follow.

HEBREWS 5:5–10   FEBRUARY 27

The Father, the Son, and the Holy Spirit

The work of creation doesn't just belong to God the Father, while the work of redemption was not the exclusive domain of the Son. All the activities of God are activities of all three in perfect unity.

The medieval Christian mystic Mechthild of Magdeburg, in her *Flowing Light of the Godhead*, has a vision of the cooperation of the members of the Trinity. She writes,

> Then the eternal Son spoke with great refinement: "Dear Father, my nature shall also bear fruit. Now that we want to begin to do wondrous things, let us make man and woman in our image. Even though I foresee great tragedy, I will still love them forever."
>
> The Father said: "Son, a powerful desire stirs in my breast as well, and I swell with love alone. Therefore, we will become fruitful so that we will be loved in return, and so that our glory will be recognized in some small way. I will make a bride for myself, who will greet me with her mouth and wound me with her beauty. Only then will love really begin."
>
> Then the Holy Spirit spoke to the Father: "Yes, dear Father, I will deliver the bride to your bed."
>
> And the Son spoke: "Father, you well know that I will yet die for love. Even still, may we make these creatures joyfully in great holiness."
>
> *The Flowing Light of the Godhead*, 114

Reflection

While God's eternal purposes in creation and redemption
are shrouded in mystery,
we do know that in the biblical story,
we see a wonderful cooperation between the persons of the Trinity.

2 SAMUEL 12:1-8   FEBRUARY 28

Our Secret Sins

There are wrongdoings that we are willing to admit. But there are also sins that are deeply hidden. These, too, will need to see the light.

The English medieval Christian mystic St. Aelred of Rievaulx, in his famous *Mirror of Love*, speaks of his secret inner life:

> I was bound by the knot of a certain friendship, delightful to me above all the delights of my life. The gracious bond of friendship pleased me, but always I was afraid of my offence, and I was sure that it would be broken off at some time in the future. I thought about the joy with which it had begun, and I awaited what would follow, and I could foresee the end.
>
> I realized that its beginning was reprehensible, the middle state offensive and the end would inevitably be damnation. The death I awaited terrified me, because I was certain that punishment would await my soul after death. And men said, looking at my circumstances, but not knowing what was going on within me, "Isn't he doing well! Isn't he though!"

Quoted in *Friendship and Community: The Monastic Experience*, 301-2

Meditation

Into your scarred hands, O Christ,
I place my wounded self.
And in the light of thy face,
I acknowledge my secret sins.
Have mercy upon me O God!

March

PSALM 27:9 — MARCH 1

The Hidden Face of God

> *The God of the biblical story is a God who reveals and hides himself. God's revelation can overwhelm us, but in God's hiddenness, God still accompanies us.*

The unknown author of *The Cloud of Unknowing* speaks to us about the God who is also absent and what such withdrawal may mean:

> For make no mistake about this; God may at times withdraw sweet emotions, joyful enthusiasm, and burning desires but he never withdraws his grace from those he has chosen, except in the case of deadly sin.
>
> Of this I am certain. All the rest, emotions, enthusiasm, and desires, are not in themselves grace, only the tokens of grace. And these he may often withdraw, sometimes to strengthen our patience, sometimes for other reasons, but always for our spiritual good, though we may never understand.
>
> Grace, we must remember, in itself, is so high, so pure, and so spiritual that our senses and emotions are actually incapable of experiencing it.
>
> The sensible fervour they experience are the tokens of grace, not grace itself. These our Lord will withdraw from time to time to deepen and mature our patience.
>
> *The Cloud of Unknowing and The Book of Privy Counseling*, 184–85

Reflection

We are always looking for the signs of God, whether that be in our own interiority, in the church, in nature, or in the world. Sometimes we have to walk and live in the light of a naked faith.

GALATIANS 5:6 MARCH 2

A Living Faith

Faith is not a parent hand-me-down. Nor is faith what one simply accepts. Faith is a living trust in the God who is revealed in Christ. By this faith, we orient the whole of our lives, our loves and our service.

St. Anselm of Canterbury, in his *Monologion*, speaks about this dynamic faith:

> Therefore, however great one's faith in supreme truth is, it will be useless and, as it were, dead, unless it lives and is nurtured by love. Faith accompanied by love is by no means idle, for if an opportunity arises, it exercises itself in an abundance of works. It could not do so without love. For that which loves supreme justice cannot scorn what is just, nor can it approve of what is unjust.
>
> Therefore, anything that creates has life, for if it did not have life, it could not create. Thus faith that is generative is alive, because it is animated by the life of love, without which it could not exist. And in the same way, idle faith is not alive, because it lacks the life of love—and if it had that life, it would not be idle.
>
> If someone who has lost sight is referred to as blind, then we should also refer to those, who ought to be able to see and yet cannot, as blind. In like manner, *faith without love* should be called *dead*—not because it has lost its life (which is love), but because it does not have the life that it ought always to have. We can recognize faith that works through love as alive, and idle faith that works through contempt, as dead. It may, therefore, be said that the faith that believes *in* what it ought to believe is alive, while the faith that merely believes what it ought to believe is dead.
>
> *Monologion*, ch. 77

Prayer

Lord, grant me a grace-filled and joy-filled faith
that longs to love and serve. Amen.

Ephesians 2:4–7 — March 3

Bound in the Spirit to Christ

The great human longing throughout the ages has been to find our home in God. In Christian spirituality this longing is realized in becoming united to Christ in the Spirit.

St. Catherine of Genoa, a married (and later celibate) laywoman, hospital chaplain, and mystic, in her book of visions, *Purgation and Purgatory*, speaks of this desire to become one with God:

> All this I saw as clearly as if I touched them,
> but I cannot find the words to express them.
> These things that I speak about work within me
> in secret and with great power.
> The prison in which I seem to be
> is the world, the body its bonds;
> and they weigh upon the lesser me within,
> which is impeded from making its way to its true end.
>
> To assist it in its weakness,
> God's grace has allowed the soul
> to participate in his life,
> to become one with him,
> in the sharing of his goodness.
>
> *Purgation and Purgatory; The Spiritual Dialogue*, 86

Meditation

United to Christ is the heartbeat of the Christian life.
This union is ever-growing. Its culmination is in the life to come.

1 SAMUEL 15:26 — MARCH 4

A Prophetic Challenge

While we may always wish to hear the word of affirmation, there are times when we need to hear the word of challenge. Though such a word may seem to undo us, it carries the seeds of hope and renewal.

St. Ambrose was a fearless bishop in early Christianity. In his *Letter 51* concerning a massacre at Thessalonica, he challenges the Emperor Theodosius regarding his complicity:

> I have not written this to confuse you, but rather to incite you to put this sin away from your kingdom. This you will do by humbling your soul before God. You are a man, and temptation has come upon you. You must conquer it. Sin can only be put away by tears and penitence. No angel, nor archangel can do it. Only the Lord himself, who alone can say, "I am with you," forgives those who have sinned. And he only forgives those who repent.
>
> I urge, I beg, I exhort, I warn. For it is a grief to me that you—who were an example of unusual piety, who were known for clemency, who would not suffer individual offenders to be put in peril—are not mourning that so many innocent people have perished. Though you have waged battle successfully, and in other matters you are worthy of praise, piety has always been the crown of your actions. The devil envied your most excellent possession. Conquer him now, while you still possess the means to conquer him. Do not add another sin to your sin by following a course of action that has injured so many.
>
> *Letters of St. Ambrose*, 450

Reflection

The challenge to others to do what is just
can only come from those who live justly,
with great humility, but also with courage
that is inspired by the Spirit.

Revelation 21:6–7 — March 5

God Is All in All

We celebrate who God is both in the small coracles of our own hearts, but also in the worship of the community of faith and in the vastness of the universe.

Julian of Norwich speaks of the greatness of God out of her visionary experience:

> In this he showed me a little thing, the size of a hazelnut, lying in the palm of my hand, round as a ball. I looked at it and thought, "What may this be?" And I heard the answer, "It is all that is made."
>
> I marveled that it could last, for it was so small that I thought it might suddenly disappear. And I was answered in my mind: "It lasts and ever shall last, because God loves it, and so everything has its being through the love of God."
>
> In this little thing I saw three parts. The first is that God made it; the second is that he loves it; the third is that God keeps it. God is in truth the maker, the lover, the keeper. For until I am substantially united to him, I may never have love, rest, nor real happiness. That is to say, until I am so joined to him that there is absolutely nothing between my God and me . . .
>
> Of all that is made, nothing can compare to the love of God, who is uncreated. Because we are not his in heart and in soul here, we are preoccupied with earthly business and continually seek after worldly things. We love and seek our rest in these trivial things that will give us no rest, rather than seeking to know God, who is all-mighty, all-wise, and all-good. For he is our true rest. God wants to be known, and it pleases him when we rest in him. Nothing less than him will never satisfy us.
>
> *A Shewing of God's Love*, 9–10

Prayer

Lord, bring my restless heart and restless ways
into the safe harbor of your love. Amen.

Beyond Riches

The heartbeat of Yahweh is for the poor. The heartbeat of our contemporary sensibilities is about much-having. We need to be converted to the ways of God.

The unknown author of *The Shepherd of Hermas*, a second-century Christian pastoral document, maps out something of a Christian attitude to riches:

> Take care, all you who serve the Lord, and have him in your heart as you do the works of God, remembering his commandments and the promises he made, and believing that he will bring them to pass if his commandments are observed. Instead of land, therefore, buy afflicted souls, as you are able, and visit widows and orphans, and do not overlook them. Spend your wealth and all your possessions, which you received from the Lord, upon lands and houses of this kind.
>
> For to this end, the Master made you rich, that you might perform these services for him. It is much better to purchase lands, possessions, and houses of this kind, which you will find in your own city when you come to reside in it. This is a noble and sacred expenditure, which will not bring you sorrow or fear, but joy. Do not make extravagant expenditures like those who do not know God. Rather, as servants of God, practise your own extravagance, in which you can rejoice; and do not profane, touch, nor covet what is another's, for it is evil to covet someone else's things. But do your own work, and you will be saved.
>
> *The Shepherd of Hermas*, 3.1

Prayer

Lord, touched by the generosity of your grace,
may I reflect that generosity to others,
and may I learn to live with a truly open heart and hand.

1 PETER 2:21 MARCH 7

Suffering with God

At the heart of the Christian message is the God who suffers for us. But a parallel theme is the calling to suffer with God, so that God's concerns are ours and God's pain becomes ours.

The fourteenth-century German Christian mystic Meister Eckhart has as one of his important themes our identification with God. Being in and with God involves our suffering with God. He writes,

> "God is with us in trouble" means that he himself suffers with us. Indeed, anyone who recognizes the truth knows that I am speaking truthfully. God suffers with men and women, indeed he suffers in his own way before and incomparably more than those who suffer for his sake.
>
> Now I say, if then God is willing to suffer, it is quite right that I should suffer, for if I think rightly, I will what God wills. I pray every day and God bids me pray: "Lord, your will be done." And yet, when God wills suffering, I will complain about the suffering. This is quite wrong. I also say confidently that God suffers so gladly with us and for our sakes, that, if we suffer for the sake of God alone, he will suffer without suffering.
>
> Suffering is so blissful for him that for him suffering is not suffering. And therefore, if we thought rightly, suffering would not be suffering for us, but it would be happiness and consolation.... If I should suffer with a person whom I loved, and who loved me, then I ought to just as gladly suffer with God, who suffers for me and suffers for my sake, through the love which he has for me.
>
> *Meister Eckhart: The Essential Sermons, Commentaries, Treatises, and Defense,* 233

Reflection

The suffering God invites us into his suffering heart
to see a new world born.
Thus we bear the birth pangs of God in prayer and service.

SONG OF SOLOMON 1:2–4　　　　　　　　　MARCH 8

Drink Deeply

When we come to faith in Christ, our longings are not yet satisfied. Instead, our longings deepen, sometimes to the point of agony. For we desire to be drawn ever more deeply into the love of the Beloved.

Bonaventure, the minister general of the Franciscan Order and professor at the University of Paris, speaks of the passion of Christ in poetic images that invoke the human longing for union and fulfillment. He writes in his *The Tree of Life*:

> Rise, therefore the beloved of Christ,
> be like the dove
> that makes its nest in the heights in the mouth of a cleft.
> There, like a sparrow that finds a home,
> do not cease to keep watch;
> there, like a turtledove,
> hide the offsprings of your chaste love;
> there, apply your mouth
> to draw water from the Saviour's fountains
> for this is the river
> arising from the midst of paradise
> which, divided into four branches
> and flowing into devout hearts,
> waters and makes fertile the whole earth.

The Soul's Journey into God; The Tree of Life; The Life of St. Francis, 155

Reflection

Be my home and shelter, O God.
Revitalize my faith and love.
Be my all in all.

JOHN 3:5-6　　　　　　　　　　　　　　　　　　MARCH 9

Begetting

The God who created the world, who himself is unbegotten, is the God who seeks to bring forth sons and daughters who reflect his image and who seek to live in the inspiration of his Son through the Spirit.

St. Anselm, using feminine language, speaks of Christ as the one who brings forth the new community of faith and love:

> And you, Jesus, are you not also a mother?
> Are you not the mother who, like a hen,
> gathers her chickens under her wings?
> Truly, Lord, you are a mother;
> for those who have been brought forth by others
> are in fact accepted by you . . .
> You brought them forth by your death.
> For if you had not been in labour,
> you could not have borne death;
> and if you had not died, you would not have given birth.
> For, longing to bear sons and daughters into life,
> you tasted of death, and by dying you begot them.
>
> Quoted in *English Spirituality*, 117

Prayer

Lord, may your life which begot me become the impulse for my fruitfulness. Amen.

ACTS 2:43-47 — MARCH 10

Practices of Early Christian Faith Communities

The DNA founded in Jesus and practiced in the communities of the New Testament continued to find creative expression in the post-apostolic era.

The early church father Justin, in his *Apology*, describes Christian worship in the second-century churches. He writes,

> Now we continually remind each other of these things. The wealthy among us help the needy, and we keep together always. For all that we are given, we bless the maker of all through his son Jesus Christ and through the Holy Spirit.
>
> And on the day which is called Sunday, all who live in the cities or the country gather together in one place, and the memoirs of the apostles or the writings of the prophets are read, as long as time permits. When the reader ceases, the president instructs and exhorts us to imitate these good examples.
>
> Then we all rise together and pray, and, when our prayers are ended, bread and wine and water are brought, and the president in like manner offers up prayers and thanksgivings; and the people assent, saying Amen. Then there is distribution to each, and all partake of the elements that have been blessed; and those who are absent are brought elements by the deacons.
>
> And those who are well to do and willing give what each thinks fit. What is collected is deposited with the president, who gives aid to the orphans and widows and those who, through sickness or any other cause, are in want, and those who are in bonds, and the strangers sojourning among us, and this takes care of all who are in need.
>
> Justin: Apology, 67

Prayer

Lord, may our faith communities
become places of welcome, care and sharing. Amen.

JOB 3:20–26 — MARCH 11

Adversity

No matter where we are in the journey of life and faith, we are far from our home country, thus troubles and difficulties will continue to assail us.

St. Augustine cries out to God when adversities continue to come his way:

> Woe is me! Lord, have pity on me; my evil sorrows strive with my good joys, and on which side the victory lies, I do not know. Woe is me! Lord, have pity on me. Woe is me! Behold, I do not hide my wounds. You are the physician, I am the sick; you are merciful, I am miserable.
>
> Is not life on earth all trial? Who wishes for troubles and difficulties? You command them to be endured, not to be loved. None love what is endured, even though they love to endure. For though we rejoice that we endure, we would rather there was nothing for us to endure.
>
> In adversity, I long for prosperity; in prosperity, I fear adversity. What middle place is there, then, between these two, where human life is not all trial? There is woe in the prosperities of this world, and there is woe in the fear of adversity, and there is woe in the corruption of joy.
>
> There is woe in adversities of the world, and there is woe in the longing for prosperity. Because adversity itself is a hard thing, lest it shatter endurance, is not the life of man and woman upon earth all trial?
>
> *The Confessions of Saint Augustine*, 10.28

Meditation

Life is graced and difficult. We are blessed and wounded.
We achieve and we fail. We sin and are forgiven.
How do we live these tensions well?

LUKE 15:21–24   MARCH 12

The Return

We have all wandered off the path and found ourselves far from home. But we are always invited to return. It only takes an act of repentance and humility.

Jacopone da Todi, an early Franciscan and great poet, writes about coming home:

> I am not cruel or arrogant—why do you turn your back on me?
> I brought into being all other creatures
> That they might serve you, do your bidding;
> Why do you show no concern for me?
> As a father who loves an ungrateful son alternates threats
> And gentle counsel to turn him from his evil ways,
> Just so I act towards you, threatening Hell
> And promising Heaven, if only you will turn back to me.
> Flee no longer, child of my heart:
> Shielded from evil,
> All sins forgiven,
> I give you a kingdom as your inheritance . . .
> Long and bitter was the pilgrimage I made for you.
> Look here at my hands: see the price I paid for you.
> Let the ice in you begin to thaw,
> And your heart rejoice in your newfound riches.

Jacopone da Todi: The Lauds, 117

Prayer

Lord, may I know your welcoming heart and hear your loving call.
May I come home from my wandering. Heal me and grant me your peace.
Amen.

Genesis 1:1–2   March 13

God the Source of All Things

God, the uncreated One, creates and calls all things into being and sustains all things with great love and careful care. God is before all things but upholds all things in the vastness of his love.

St. Edmund Rich, in his *Mirror of Holy Church*, writes about God's amazing ways:

> God wished to show himself in four ways, two of them inward and two outward: inwardly by revelation and by reason, outwardly by Scripture and by his creatures. God shows himself by revelation when he appears to someone through inspiration or through miracles.
>
> He shows himself through reason to humanity's understanding in this way: we can well see the nature of our being, that is to say that we exist and that we have not always existed. And from that we each know well that there was a time when we began to be, and therefore that there was a time when we were not. But when we did not exist, then in no earthly fashion could we make ourselves.
>
> And we can see this in every creature, for each day we see some creatures departing, others coming. Because all things exist and do exist of themselves, it follows that there must be one thing which gives existence to all things, that is to say from which all things have their being. From this it follows that God, from whom all things have being, must be without beginning, for if he had had beginning from someone else, he would not have been the prime author and first beginning of all things.
>
> *The Mediaeval Mystics of England*, 133–34

Reflection

The movement of God is towards generativity and revelation. We, in our small way, should also be creative, productive and self-revealing.

MATTHEW 10:16   MARCH 14

Be Discerning

As Christians we are called neither to be rash nor reluctant, neither foolhardy nor hesitant. We are, instead, to be discerning and then willing to act on that wisdom with courage and commitment.

St. Gregory of Nyssa, the bishop of Nyssa, became one of the champions of Trinitarian orthodoxy in the church of the fourth century. He also wrote on spiritual and pastoral themes. Here is his reflection on virtue:

> This teaching lays down that virtue is discerned in the mean. Accordingly, all evil naturally operates in a deficiency of or an excess of virtue. In the case of courage, cowardice is the lack of virtue and rashness is its excess. What is pure in each of these is seen to lie between these corresponding evils and is virtue. In the same way, all other things which strive for the better also somehow take the middle road between the neighbouring evils.
>
> Wisdom holds to the mean between shrewdness and simplicity. Neither the wisdom of the serpent nor the simplicity of the dove is to be praised, if one should choose either of these with respect to itself alone. Rather it is the disposition which closely unites these two by the mean that is virtue. The person who lacks moderation is a libertine, and the one who goes beyond moderation has his or her conscience branded, as the Apostle says. For the one has given himself or herself up without restraint to pleasures, and the other defiles marriage as if it were adultery. The disposition observed in the mean between these two is moderation.
>
> *The Life of Moses*, 128

Thought

Those who are moralistic have a great ability to make rules and regulations, which are usually black and white.
But the life of love calls us to live in much more discerning ways.

1 TIMOTHY 4:4–5 — MARCH 15

Be Gentle with Yourself

While the life of faith is one of commitment and service, it is most basically a life of joy in the love of God. Therefore, be gentle with yourself and don't take every small thing too seriously.

Walter Hilton, the fourteenth-century English Christian mystic, has some good advice for us. He writes,

> Do then as I say: take your food as it comes, and make reasonable provision for it if necessary. Take it gladly as you need it, but be careful of the pleasure that comes with need. Eschew too much as well as too little, and when you have finished and there comes to your mind some remorse of conscience—that you have eaten either too much or too little—and it begins to weary you and distract you to overmuch bitterness, lift up the desire of your heart to your good Lord Jesus and acknowledge yourself as a wretch.... Ask him for forgiveness and say you want to amend it, and trust in forgiveness by his mercy.
>
> And when you have done so—the shorter the better—then leave off and spend no longer with it. Do not strive too hard, as if you wanted to destroy it utterly, for it is not worthwhile to do so and you shall never bring it about in this way; but promptly assign yourself to some other occupation of body or spirit for which you feel you are ready, so that you can advance more in other virtues such as humility and charity.
>
> *The Scale of Perfection,* 148

Reflection

We can get ourselves stuck around small issues of conscience.
Instead, we should confess and move on.
There are more important matters that should
capture our attention and imagination.
The foremost of these is love for God and service to others.

1 JOHN 5:6–12 MARCH 16

A Confession of Faith Concerning the Christ

Faith will draw us into a life of trust in God. But it also involves believing, living and proclaiming certain truths.

The Chalcedonian articulation of who this Jesus is includes the following statement:

> Wherefore, following the holy fathers and mothers, we all with one voice confess our Lord Jesus Christ one and the same Son, the same perfect in Godhead, the same perfect in personhood, truly God and truly person. The same consisting of a reasonable soul and a body, of one substance with the Father as touching the Godhead, the same of one substance with us as touching the personhood, like us in all things apart from sin.
>
> Begotten of the Father before the ages as touching the Godhead, the same in the last days, for us and for our salvation, born of the Virgin Mary, the *Theotocus*, as touching the personhood, one and the same Christ, Son, Lord, only-begotten, to be acknowledged in two natures without confusion, without change, without division, without separation.
>
> The distinction of the natures being in no way abolished because of the union, but rather the characteristic property of each nature being preserved, and concurring into one person and one subsistence, not as if Christ were parted or divided into two persons, but one and the same Son and only-begotten of God, Word, Lord, Jesus Christ; even as the Prophets from the beginning spoke concerning him, and our Lord Jesus Christ instructed us, and the creed that has been handed down to us.

Creeds, Councils, and Controversies, 337

Thought

While this kind of language seems heavy and wooden, we nevertheless all have to respond to the question that Jesus posed: "Who do you say that I am?"

2 CORINTHIANS 4:7   MARCH 17

Instruments in God's Hands

God has linked his sovereignty to human instrumentality. God is willing to use us as his channels of blessing and as his instruments for good.

The fourteenth-century Christian mystic Bridget of Sweden received a vision of the way in which God wants to use us for his purposes:

> The bride said to Christ, "Oh, my dearest God, what you do to me is a wonderful thing, for you make my body slumber and lift up my soul to see, hear, and feel spiritual things whenever you wish to do so. Your words are wonderfully sweet to my soul and more delicious to me than any food. They enter my soul and leave me both satisfied and hungry.
>
> "I am satisfied because I have no taste for anything else, but I crave them with holy hunger. Therefore, Lord, help me to do your will."
>
> Then Christ said, "I am acting like a king who sends wine to his servants and tells them to drink it because it is wholesome, it will heal sickness, and make the sorrowful glad and the healthy stronger. And the vessel in which it is sent is unsullied. In the same way, I am sending my words by you, a suitable vessel; you must therefore speak them boldly where and when my spirit bids you."
>
> Then the bride said, "I am a sinful creature and ignorant of such work." Christ answered, "Who would be surprised if a lord took some of his money or precious metal and made some of it into a crown, some into cups, some into rings for his own use? It is not surprising if I do the same thing with my servants and use them to make myself more respected and revered, in spite of the fact that by nature one has a better understanding than another. Therefore, hold yourself ready to do my will."
>
>   *Medieval Writings on Female Spirituality*, 148

Reflection

With different gifts given by the Spirit,
we have different callings and responsibilities.

PSALM 46:10-11   MARCH 18

The Practice of Solitude

We tend to be a very distracted people, and we have a lot to learn in the art of solitude. In the place of stillness, however, we so often find turmoil.

The unknown author of *The Cloud of Unknowing* has some advice for us regarding the practice of solitude:

> In spite of what I said earlier, I'll tell you some of what I know about these spiritual strategies for dealing with incessant thoughts. Try them out and improve on them, if you can do better.
>
> When distracting thoughts press down on you, when they stand between you and God and stubbornly demand your attention, pretend you don't even notice them. Try looking over their shoulders, as if you're searching for something else, and you are. That something else is God, hidden in a cloud of unknowing. Do this and I know the work of contemplation will start getting easier for you.
>
> When tried and understood, this spiritual technique is nothing but an intense longing for God, the desire to feel and see him as we can here. This longing is true love, and love always deserves the peace it wins.
>
> There is another trick you can try, if you want. When exhausted from fighting your thoughts, when you're unable to put them down, fall down before them and cower as a coward overcome in battle. Give up. Accept that it's foolish for you to fight them any longer. Do this, and you'll find that in the hands of your enemies, you are surrendering to God. Let yourself be defeated. Accept your failure. And always keep this plan in mind because when you try it, you'll discover that you melt like water. You become supple.
>
> *The Cloud of Unknowing with the Book of Privy Counsel*, 74–75

Thought

One further strategy is to embrace these thoughts—and the other is to bracket them.

MATTHEW 27:45-46 — MARCH 19

The Dark Night of the Soul

Believers throughout the ages have spoken about the experience of darkness or forsakenness in their relationship with God. During these times, they have had to walk the road of the absent presence of God.

The Franciscan Jacopone da Todi writes about this experience:

> No longer can I find that compassion
> That always led me back to the heavenly court.
> I hear the gate as it shuts,
> And ingratitude bars me entrance.
>
> Neither tears nor sighs nor prayer nor meditation
> Will prepare the way for my return.
> O my wretched and forlorn heart,
> No words can express your pain!
>
> I seek out your nativity, Lord,
> Seek out your suffering;
> There is no joy in the quest,
> For love has gone cold.
>
> Your providence is reason enough for loving you;
> I count your gifts, go over them one by one
> Trying to find my way back to you, but to no avail:
> You have hidden yourself from me.

Jacopone da Todi: The Lauds, 203-4

Reflection

Embrace the darkness. The light is even there.

1 CORINTHIANS 13:4–7　　　　　　　　　　MARCH 20

Christian Love

There are many kinds of love: love of family, that of friendship, and that of passion. There is also a way of love shaped by God's love for us in Christ. This is the love of worship, gratitude and service.

One of the earliest post-apostolic writings is that by Clement. In his *First Clement*, he writes about the nature of Christian love.

> Let the one who has love in Christ fulfill the commandments of Christ. Who can describe the bond of God's love? Who is able to explain the majesty of its beauty?
>
> The height to which this love leads is indescribable. Love unites us with God; love covers a multitude of sins; love endures all things, is patient in all things. There is nothing coarse, nothing arrogant in love.
>
> Love knows nothing of schisms, love leads no rebellions, love does everything in harmony.
>
> In love all the elect of God were made perfect; without love nothing is pleasing to God. In love the master received us.
>
> Because of the love that he had for us, Jesus Christ our Lord, in accordance with God's will, gave his blood for us, and his flesh for our flesh, and his life for our lives.
>
> *The Apostolic Fathers in English*, 65

Prayer

Lord, may I grow in the love you have poured into my life through Christ. Amen.

MATTHEW 6:7–15   MARCH 21

Prayer

Prayer is the language of the heart touched by God's grace. It is also the cry of the longing heart. And it is the language of worship and gratitude.

Julian of Norwich has this to say about prayer:

> Our Lord God's will is that we have true understanding about prayer, especially in three things. The first is to know by whom and how our prayer springs up. He shows us by whom when he says, "I am the ground," and he shows us how when by his goodness he says, "It is my will."
>
> The second is to know how we should use prayer. Our will should be joyfully turned to the will of the Lord. This is what he means when he says, "I make you to will it."
>
> The third is to know the fruit and purpose of our prayers. The fruit is that we will be united with our Lord and like him in all things. This is the purpose behind this loving lesson. He will help us, and we will make it so, as he says himself. Blessed may he be!
>
> For this is our Lord's will: that both our prayer and our trust will be large. We do not realize that our Lord is the ground on whom our prayer springs up. And we do not realize that our ability to pray itself is given us by the grace of his love. . . . I am sure that no one genuinely asks for mercy and grace without mercy and grace having already been given.
>
> *Revelations of Divine Love Shewed to a Devout Ankress,* 74–75

Prayer

Lord, may your goodness towards me script in me a longing to dwell in
your presence,
where I can be fully transparent and open. Amen.

MATTHEW 13:13–16   MARCH 22

An Inner Hearing

We may hear the voice of God to us through scripture, proclamation, the witness of others, and the power of the created world. But we also hear it in the very depths of our being.

St. Augustine, with poetic beauty, has this to say:

> If to any man or woman the tumult of the flesh were hushed, and the images of earth were hushed, and the waters and air were hushed, and the poles of heaven were hushed as well; indeed, if the very soul were hushed and were to overcome itself by not thinking about itself; if all dreams and imaginary revelations were hushed; if every tongue and every sign and every transient created thing were hushed—since, if any could hear, all these would say, "We did not create ourselves, but were created by him who abides forever." . . . If then he alone could speak, not by these things but by himself—not through any tongue of the flesh, nor angel's voice, nor sound of thunder, nor the dark riddle of a similitude—so that we might hear his word and hear him, in all these things that we love, we might hear his very self. . . . And then with swift thought, we might touch on that eternal wisdom which abides over all.
>
> *The Confessions of Saint Augustine*, 10.10

Meditation

Take some moments to be still.
Listen for the whispers from the edge of eternity.
Hear the voice of God.
Don't be afraid:
the word may already have arrived and is dwelling within you.

GALATIANS 5:1 — MARCH 23

Freedom in Christ

We have been set free from sin, the law and death. We have been set free for a life of worship, righteousness and service.

St. Bernard of Clairvaux writes about the nature of true freedom:

> The eternal law of righteousness ordains that whoever will not submit to God's sweet rule will suffer the bitter tyranny of self: but whoever wears the easy yoke and light burden of love (Matt 11:30) will escape the intolerable weight of his or her own self-will.
>
> Wonderfully and justly, that eternal law holds all rebels in submission, so that they are unable to escape from it. They are subject to God's power, yet deprived of happiness with him, unable to dwell with God in light and rest and everlasting glory. "O Lord my God, why do you not pardon my transgression and take away mine iniquity?" (Job 7:21). Then, freed from the weight of my own will, I can breathe easily under the light burden of love. I shall not be coerced by fear, nor allured by greedy desires; for I shall be led by the Spirit of God, the spirit of freedom by which your children live, which bears witness to my spirit that I am one of the children of God (Rom 8:16). So I will live under your law; and as you are, so shall I be in the world.
>
> *Bernard of Clairvaux: On Loving God*, ch. 13

Reflection

Why do we so readily want our own weary way, rather than the open spaces of God's love and will?

LUKE 1:35-38   MARCH 24

A Song to Mary

We bless and honor this woman of faith and obedience, who carried in her womb and heart the One who was the Savior of the world.

St. Anselm wrote a song to honor Mary, the mother of Jesus:

> He who could create all things from nothing
> would not remake his ruined creation without Mary.
> God, then, is the Father of the created world
> and Mary the mother of the re-created world.
> God is the Father by whom all things were given life,
> and Mary the mother through whom all things were given new life.
> For God begot the Son, through whom all things were made,
> and Mary gave birth to him as the Saviour of the world.
> Without God's Son, nothing could exist;
> without Mary's Son, nothing could be redeemed.
> Truly the Lord is with you,
> to whom the Lord granted that all nature
> should owe as much to you as to himself.
>
> *Anselm of Canterbury: Oratio 52*

A Song

To you, O Servant of Yahweh, we sing the songs of freedom and hope.

1 Samuel 2:1–3   March 25

A Vision of God

It is one thing to know God. It is quite another to receive a revelation of God's presence. This mystical experience grounds our faith in the very depths of our being.

St. Symeon, the New Theologian and Abbot of the Monastery of Saint Mamas, had various mystical experiences of God's presence. Of one of these he writes,

> Even I, who am of all most insignificant and useless, have received some of these gifts . . . by the grace of my Saviour, Jesus Christ. By grace I have received this grace (cf. John 1:16), by doing well I have received his kindness, by fire I have been requited with fire, by flame with flame.
>
> As I ascended, I was given other ascents. At the end of the ascent, I was given light, and by the light, an even greater light. In the midst thereof a sun shone brightly and from it a ray shone forth that filled all things.
>
> The object of my thought remained beyond understanding, and in this state I remained while I wept most sweetly and marveled at the ineffable. The divine mind conversed with my own mind and taught me, saying, "Do you realize what my power has done to you out of love for men and women, because of but a little faith and patience that strengthens your love? Behold, though you are subject to death, you have become immortal, and though you are ruled by corruption, you find yourself above it. You live in the world and yet you are with me; you are clothed with a body, and yet you are not weighed down by any of the pleasures of the body. You are puny in appearance, yet you see intellectually. It is in very deed I, who has brought you into being out of nothing."
>
> St. Symeon: The Discourses, 205

Reflection

The vision of God is not the same as a vision from God
that has something to do with one's life direction.
The former is the more grounding and significant.

PSALM 32:6–7   MARCH 26

A General Prayer

Prayer belongs to the personal and the public domain. We pray for ourselves and for others. But the prayers of others—within the community of faith—also carry us in our journey of life and faith.

The so-called *Divine Liturgy of James, the Holy Apostle and Brother of the Lord*, a document that comes from a much later time than the time of James, contains many corporate prayers for the faith community. Here is one:

> O God, who through your great and unspeakable love did send forth your only-begotten Son into the world, in order that he might turn back the lost sheep, turn not away us sinners, laying hold of you by this dread and bloodless sacrifice; for we trust not in our own righteousness, but in your good mercy, by which you purchased our race.
>
> We entreat and beseech your goodness that it may not be for condemnation to your people that this mystery for salvation has been administered by us, but for remission of sins, for renewal of souls and bodies, for pleasing you, our God and Father, in the mercy and love of your only-begotten Son, with whom you are blessed, together with your holy, good and quickening Spirit, now and always and forever.
>
> O Lord God, who did create us, and bring us into life, who has shown to us ways to salvation, who has granted to us a revelation of heavenly mysteries, who has appointed us to this ministry in the power of your Holy Spirit, grant that we may become servants . . . of your pure mysteries in the Eucharist . . . and send down in answer on us the grace of your Holy Spirit.

Ante-Nicene Fathers, vol. 7, 524–25

Reflection

More than ever, we need a praying church
that does not assume God's presence,
but earnestly seeks the presence and grace
of the Father, the Son and the Holy Spirit.

2 THESSALONIANS 2:13–17   MARCH 27

A Trinitarian Faith

The heart of the good news is that we are invited into the beautiful fellowship of the Father, the Son and the Holy Spirit. In that richness of being and relationship we can find our true home and purpose.

One of the early church fathers, St. Irenaeus, spells out the vision of a Trinitarian faith:

> And this is the drawing-up of our faith, the foundation of the building, and the consolidation of a way of life.
> God, the Father, uncreated, beyond grasp, invisible, one God, the maker of all; this is the first and foremost article of our faith.
> But the second article is the Word of God, the Son of God, Christ Jesus our Lord, who was shown forth by the prophets according to the design of their prophecy and according to the manner in which the Father disposed; and through him were made all things whatsoever.
> He also, *in the end of times,* for the recapitulation of all things, is become a man among all humankind, visible and tangible, in order to abolish death and bring to light life, and to bring about the communion of God and all humankind.
> And the third article is the Holy Spirit, through whom the prophets prophesied, and the patriarchs were taught about God, and the just were led in the path of justice, and who *in the end of times* has been poured forth in a new manner upon humanity over all the earth, renewing all humankind to God.
>
> *Proof of the Apostolic Preaching,* 51

Prayer

Lord, grant that your fullness of life may penetrate every part of my being and the whole life of the church. Amen.

SONG OF SOLOMON 7:10–12 MARCH 28

A Song of Love

Christianity is not, first and foremost, a religion of demand, but one of grace and love. Love is the source, focus and mission of our faith.

The medieval Beguine Hadewijch wrote many poems on love. Here is part of one of them:

> In all seasons new and old,
> If one is submissive to Love,
> In the hot summer, the cold winter,
> She will receive love from Love.
> She will satisfy with full service in encountering high Love;
> So she speedily becomes love with Love; that is bound to happen.
>
> Bitter and dark and desolate
> Are Love's ways in the beginning of love;
> Before anyone is perfect in Love's service,
> He/she often becomes desperate:
> Yet where she/he imagines losing, it is all gain. How can one experience this?
> By sparing neither much nor little, but giving oneself totally in love.

Hadewijch: The Complete Works, 183

Reflection

In the giving of love, nothing is lost—but all is gained.

PSALM 84:5–7   MARCH 29

Pilgrimage

We may have come home to Christ, but we are still on the pilgrim journey. That journey seeks to take us further into the ways of God and into service in our world.

The fourteenth-century English Christian mystic Walter Hilton speaks about the nature of our pilgrimage:

> Just as a true pilgrim going to Jerusalem leaves behind house and land, wife or husband and children, and becomes poor and bare of all that he or she has in order to travel light and without hindrance, so if you want to be a spiritual pilgrim, you are to strip yourself naked of all that you have—both good deeds and bad—and cast them all behind you. Thus you will become so poor in your own thinking that there can be no deed of your own that you want to lean upon for rest, but you are always desiring more grace of love, and always seeking the spiritual presence of Jesus.
>
> If you do so, you will resolve in your heart, wholly and fully, your desire to be at Jerusalem, and in no other place but there; and that is, you will set in your heart, wholly and fully, your will to have nothing but the love of Jesus and the spiritual sight of him, as far as he is pleased to show himself. It is for that end alone that you are made and redeemed, and that is your beginning and your end, your joy and your glory.
>
> Therefore, whatever you have, however rich you may be in the other works of body and spirit, unless you have this love that I speak of and know and feel that you have it, consider that you have nothing at all. Print this well on the desire of your soul, and hold firmly to it, and it will save you from all the perils of your journey, so that you will never perish.
>
> *The Scale of Perfection,* 2.2.3

Thought

To travel light does not mean that we are free from responsibilities, but rather from unnecessary burdens and worries.

EPHESIANS 5:18–20   MARCH 30

Songs of the Heart

The melody of the heart is not the call of demand, but the dance of grace. Through this grace we can both sing and serve.

During the twelfth century, St. Bernard of Clairvaux, became one of the key leaders in monastic renewal. He points to joy as a powerful force in the Christian life:

> Therefore, sing wisely, for you are joined in songs of praise with heavenly singers—since you, too, are fellow citizens with all the saints and members of God's household. As food is sweet to the palate, a psalm delights the heart. But the sincere and wise soul will chew the psalm with the "teeth" of its mind, for if it swallows it whole, without chewing, the palate will fail to taste the delicious flavour, sweeter even than honey that drips from the comb. Let us with the Apostles offer a honey-comb at the Lord's table in the heavenly banquet. As honey flows from the comb, so devotion should flow from your words. Otherwise, if you attempt to assimilate the words without the condiment of the Spirit's meaning, "the written letters will bring death."
>
> But if, like St. Paul, you sing praises with both the spirit and the mind, you will know the truth of Jesus' statement: "The words I have spoken to you are spirit, and they are life." You will also know the truth of the words of Wisdom: "My spirit is sweet above honey" (John 6:63, Sir. 24:20).
>
> *Bernard of Clairvaux: Song of Songs,* Sermon 7

A Song of Joy

"Deck myself, my soul, with gladness,
Leave the gloomy haunts of sadness,
Come into the daylight's splendor,
There with joy your praises render."

ACTS 13:43　　　　　　　　　　　　　　　MARCH 31

The Grace of God in Christ Jesus

Grace is God's unmerited favor, and it is the source out of which we live. It sustains us on our journeys, is food for our souls and marks us more than our careers or stations in life.

Julian of Norwich opens up for us a prayer of grace:

> Christ revealed our frailty and our falling,
> our trespasses and our humiliations.
> Christ also revealed his blessed power,
> his blessed wisdom and love.
> He protects us as tenderly and as sweetly,
> when we are in greatest need;
> He raises us in spirit
> and turns everything to glory and joy without ending.
> God is the ground and the substance, the very essence of nature,
> God is the true father and mother of natures.
> We are all bound to God by nature,
> and we are bound to God by grace.
> And this grace is for all the world,
> because it is our precious mother, Christ.

Celebrating Common Prayer: A Version of the Daily Office SSF, 236

Meditation

In the strength and warmth of God as father and mother,
we are kept and nurtured into a fullness of life that overflows to others.

April

Ephesians 6:11-13   April 1

Prayers of Protection

The persistent prayer of the Christian on pilgrimage is for light on the way, clarity in direction and protection on the journey.

In her letter to a priest, Hildegard of Bingen gives this pastoral advice and offers this prayer of protection to a troubled soul:

> O servant of God, you who are an ornament in Christ's service, do not fear the heaviness that rises in you on account of your terrifying dreams. . . . Your sleep is troubled, but your dreams very often are not true, because the ancient deceiver (although he does not harm your physical senses) troubles you by these deceptive dreams. It is by the dispensation of God that you are chastised by such an affliction, so that through this fear all your carnal thoughts will be sharply restrained.
>
> Every single night, place your hand on your heart, and with sincere devotion, read the gospel, "In the beginning was the Word" (John 1:1). And afterwards say these words: "Lord God almighty, who in your full goodness breathed the breath of life into me, I ask you through the holy garment of the gentle humanity of your Son (which he put on for my account) that you not suffer me to be torn apart by the bitterness of this great distress any longer, but through the love of your only begotten Son and your great mercy, free me from this tribulation, and defend me from all the snares of the spirits of the air.
>
> May the Holy Spirit make you a tabernacle of sanctification so that in the joys of supreme bliss you may live always with God.
>
> *The Personal Correspondence of Hildegard of Bingen*, 62-63

Prayer

In the safety of your love, O Lord,
I sleep protected by the grace of your strong Son, Jesus my Lord,
and in the comfort of the Holy Spirit.
Amen.

DEUTERONOMY 6:4–6   APRIL 2

The Contemplative Experience

The Christian life is not one of mere self-effort in religious matters. We base our faith on the belief that God draws near and reveals his presence. Living in the shadow of this revealed presence, our journey becomes a walk of faith, love and service.

The English Christian mystic Richard Rolle, in his *Ego Dormio, I Sleep and My Heart Wakes*, speaks of the contemplative experience:

> This . . . is called the contemplative life, the life which loves to be solitary, without ringing bells, or noise, or singing or shouting. When you first reach it, your spiritual eye is carried up into the glory of heaven, and there is enlightened by grace and set ablaze by the fire of Christ's love, so that you truly feel the burning of love in your heart, constantly lifting your mind toward God, filling you full of love and joy and sweetness, to such an extent that no illness nor mental agony nor humiliation nor harsh living conditions are able to distress you, but your life will change into joy.
>
> And then, because of the elevation of your heart, your prayer turns into joyful song and your thoughts into sweet sounds. Then Jesus is all your desire, all your delight, all your joy, all your consolation, all your strength, so that your song will always be about him, and in him all your rest. Then you may indeed say: "I sleep and my heart wakes: Who shall to my lover say, that for his love I long always?"
>
> *The English Writings*, 139–40

Reflection

So often the life of faith is mainly a matter of belief,
confined to the regions of the head.
But faith must also be a matter of the heart,
and in this region, the contemplative experience is central.

1 CORINTHIANS 2:14–16   APRIL 3

Discernment

> *One of the challenges in living the Christian life is not only to discern between good and evil, but also between good and good. For in all circumstances, our concern must be to do the will of God.*

Columbanus, in his *Monks' Rules*, has this to say about the need for discernment:

> Discernment is supremely necessary for monks. This is demonstrated by the mistake of many and the downfall of some, who begin without discernment, continue without a guiding knowledge, and thus cannot live a praiseworthy life.
>
> Just as error overtakes those who proceed without a path, so those who live without discernment cannot exercise restraint or self-control, and indulgence is contrary to the virtues, which lie between the extremes. The onset of indulgence is even more dangerous when our foes place the stumbling blocks of wickedness and various other temptations beside the straightway of discretion.
>
> Therefore, we must pray to God continually to illumine with the light of true discernment the virtuous pathway, which is surrounded on every side by the world's deep darkness, so that all who worship him may be able to come to him through this darkness without error. The word *discernment* came from distinguish, since in us it distinguishes between good and evil and between the moderate and the complete.
>
> *Monks' Rules*, 9

Prayer

Lord, give me the will to listen well, the heart to love well,
and the desire to do your will above all else.
For this I need your enlightening and empowering Spirit.
Amen.

1 PETER 1:15–16   APRIL 4

The Ascent to God

The great longing of the Christian saints throughout the ages has been the vision of God. This desire for God's presence is the heart of living the Christian life.

The great medieval Franciscan scholar Bonaventure, in his *Mind's Road to God*, has this to say about the ascent to God:

> Those who wish to ascend to God must avoid the sin that deforms nature. Through prayer, they must exercise the natural powers for regenerating grace. Through their way of life, they must strive toward the purification of justice. Through meditation, they must exercise the natural powers of illuminating knowledge. Through contemplation, they must exercise the natural powers for perfecting wisdom.
>
> Just as no one comes to wisdom except through grace, justice, and knowledge, so also no one comes to contemplation except through clear meditation, a holy way of life, and devout prayer.
>
> Grace is the foundation of the will's righteousness and the penetrating enlightenment of reason. Thus we must first pray; second, we must live a holy way of life; third, we must strive toward the reflection of truth and, by our striving, mount step by step until we come to "the high mountain, where we shall see the God of gods in Sion" (Ps 83:8).

The Mind's Road to God, 10

Reflection

"You are mine, I love and own you,
Light of joy
Ne'er shall I
From my heart dethrone you."

Hebrews 1:1–4 — April 5

Times of Preparation

In the biblical narratives we can clearly see that God works in history according to his own purposes. And at times it seems that God works ever so slowly and that times of preparation seem ever so long.

Bernard of Clairvaux alludes to the way that God prepared such a long time beforehand for the eventual coming of his Son. St. Bernard writes,

> The holy men who lived before the coming of Christ understood that God had in mind a plan to bring peace to the human race. "Surely the Lord God does nothing without revealing his secret to his servants, the prophets."
>
> What he did reveal, however, was obscure to many. For in those days, faith was a rare thing on the earth, and hope was only a faint impulse in the heart of those who looked forward to the deliverance of Israel. Those who foresaw proclaimed that Christ would come in the flesh and that with him would come peace. One of the prophets said: "He himself will be peace in our land when he comes."
>
> Enlightened from above, they confidently spread abroad the message that through this Christ, men and women would be restored to the favour of God. John, the fore-runner of the Lord, recognized that this prophecy would be fulfilled in his own time, and he declared: "Grace and truth have come through Jesus Christ."
>
> In our time, every Christian can discover by experience that this is true.
>
> *Bernard of Clairvaux: Song of Songs*, Sermon 2

Reflection

Waiting is a key dimension of Christian spirituality.
It is an acknowledgement that God has to initiate,
and we are merely followers.
What are you waiting and hoping for?

MARK 11:25 — APRIL 6

A Spirituality of Almsgiving

To give is never simply to give money. One can also give of one's time. One can give forgiveness. One can give oneself.

St. Augustine elaborates on a spirituality of almsgiving or generosity:

> Everyone who offers food to the hungry, drink to the thirsty, clothing to the naked, hospitality to the traveler, asylum to the fugitive, a visit to the sick or the prisoner, liberation to the captive, support to the weak, guidance to the blind, comfort to the sorrowful, medicine to the unwell, a path to the wanderer, advice to the uncertain, pardon to the sinner, or anything necessary to any person in need, is giving alms.
>
> So also, anyone who uses the whip to correct somebody, or restrains someone through discipline—and who at the same time forgives from the heart the sin by which he or she was hurt or offended, or prays that it may be forgiven—is giving alms.. This is not only the case in forgiveness and prayer, but also in rebuke and correction, for in these too, mercy is demonstrated.
>
> Many good things are offered to people who are unwilling to accept them, when the consideration is what is good for them, rather than what they desire. For many prove to be their own enemies, whereas their true friends are those whom they consider enemies—whom they mistakenly repay with evil the good that has been offered.
>
> Yet a Christian should not repay evil—even for evil. Thus there are many kinds of alms, and when we give them, we receive help for the forgiveness of our sins.

The Augustine Catechism, 99–100

Prayer

Lord, may a generosity of heart and hands always mark my life. Amen.

PSALM 92:1–4   APRIL 7

Prayer and Thanksgiving

While prayer is about bringing our needs to God, it is also about gratitude. Prayer is a life of seeing the goodness of God.

St. Basil, in one of his *Homilies*, speaks about a life of prayer:

> Prayer is a petition for good addressed by the pious to God. But we do not rigidly confine our petition to words. Nor yet do we imagine that God needs to be reminded by speech. He knows our needs even though we ask him not.
>
> What can I say then? . . . The strength of prayer lies rather in the purpose of our soul and in deeds of virtue reaching every part and moment of our life. "Whether you eat," it is said, "or drink, or whatever you do, do all to the glory of God."
>
> As you take your seat at table, pray. As you lift the loaf, offer thanks to the Giver. When you sustain your bodily weakness with wine, remember him who supplies you with this gift, to make your heart glad and to comfort your infirmity. Has your need for taking food passed away? Let not the thought of your Benefactor pass away too.
>
> As you are putting on your tunic, thank the Giver of it. As you wrap your cloak around you, feel yet greater love to God, who alike in summer and in winter has given us coverings convenient for us . . .
>
> Is the day done? Give thanks to him who has given us the sun for our daily work, and has provided for us a fire to light up the night, and to serve the rest of the needs of life. Let the night give the other occasions of prayer. When you look up to heaven and gaze at the beauty of the stars, pray to the Lord of the visible world. . . . When you see all nature sunk in sleep, then again worship him who gives us even against our wills release from the continuous strain of toil and by a short refreshment restores us once again to the vigour of our strength.
>
> *Nicene and Post-Nicene Fathers*, vol. 8, lxix

Thought

Thankfulness can be the melody of our life. When this is so, life overflows.

GALATIANS 6:8 — APRIL 8

The Renewing Work of the Spirit

The Spirit takes the good things of Christ and sculpts those into our hearts and minds. The Spirit ever renews and makes whole.

St. Symeon, the New Theologian, placed a great emphasis on the renewing work of the Spirit. He writes,

> Then, just as the one who has been physically stripped naked sees the wounds of his or her body, so the one who has been stripped spiritually may clearly see the passions that cling to his or her soul, such as ambition, avarice, rancour, hatred of brothers and sisters, envy, jealousy, contentiousness (cf. Phil 1:15), and all the rest.
>
> So men and women must apply the commandments to these passions as medicines, and trials as cautery, that they might be humbled and sorrowful, and fervently seek God's help. Then they will clearly see the grace of the Holy Spirit coming to them and tearing all these passions away, one after the other, and eliminating them until the Spirit has entirely freed their souls from them all.
>
> The coming of the Paraclete grants freedom to the soul, not merely in part, but completely and totally. Not only does it expel the passions mentioned above, but also all boredom, carelessness, slackness, and ignorance, all forgetfulness, gluttony, and love of pleasure. Thus the Spirit renews and restores men and women both spiritually and physically, so that they seem to be clothed, not with a corruptible and gross body (cf. Wis 9:15), but with one that is spiritual (cf. 1 Cor 15:44) and immaterial and even ready for the rapture (cf. 1 Thess 4:17).
>
> *St. Symeon: The Discourses,* 188–89

Reflection

The Spirit brings us to new life in Christ.
But the Spirit also deepens that life in us.

LUKE 1:50 — APRIL 9

God's Mercy

> *In being merciful God extends to us his grace, kindness and help. Mercy therefore restores, renews, strengthens and makes us whole.*

The English Christian mystic Julian of Norwich has this to say about the merciful nature of God:

> By our wretched sinning, we live contrary to the way of peace and love. For our sins, Christ expressed his loving compassion and pity. The foundation of mercy is love, and the working of mercy keeps us living in love.
>
> This was revealed to me in such a way that I could not separate mercy from love. Mercy is sweet and gracious as it compassionately works through love.
>
> Mercy keeps us and turns all things to good. Mercy, by love, allows us to fail, in some measure. And as much as we fail, that much we fall. And because we fall, we die. And we die because we fail to see and feel the God who is our very life.
>
> Our failure is dreadful, and our falling is shameful, and our dying is sorrowful. Yet in all this, the sweet eye of compassion and love never leaves us, and the working of mercy never ceases.
>
> *Revelations of Divine Love Shewed to a Devout Ankress*, 86

Reflection

Our relationship with God
is not first of all marked by our virtue and acts of goodness.
It is first and foremost marked by God's grace
and the love and mercy so continuously extended to us.

ISAIAH 65:24 — APRIL 10

A Cry to Yahweh

When you and I pray, we join the long thread throughout history of the women and men of faith who have cried out to God. Even now, we do not pray alone. Our voices mingle with many others who even now are seeking the face of God.

The fourteenth-century English Christian mystic Walter Hilton teaches us something about the art of prayer. He writes,

> Prayer is profitable, and a useful means of getting purity of heart through the destruction of sin and the reception of virtues. Not that you should by your prayer tell our Lord what you desire, for he knows all your needs well enough. But by your prayer make yourself able and ready like a clean vessel to receive the grace that our Lord will freely give you, and this cannot be felt until you are purified by the fire of desire in devout prayer. Although it is true that prayer is not the cause for which our Lord gives grace, nevertheless it is a way by which grace, freely given, comes to a soul . . .
>
> For prayer is nothing but a desire of the heart rising into God by its withdrawal from all earthly thoughts; and so it is compared to a fire, which of its own nature leaves the lowness of the earth and always goes up into the air. Just so, when desire in prayer has been touched and set alight by the spiritual fire which is God, it keeps rising naturally to him from whom it came.
>
> *The Scale of Perfection*, 97–98

Meditation

Be still and know your God.
By all means ask, but ask more to know the heart and ways of God,
than to ask for the things you think you need.

ISAIAH 45:15 — APRIL 11

The Hidden Face of God

While we may long to live in the presence of the living God, this God sometimes withdraws his consolation. Thus we may know God and yet feel abandoned.

Thomas à Kempis, who so much stresses the need to live in God's presence, knows something about the reality of the hidden face of God. He writes,

> Do not consider yourself forsaken if I send some temporary hardship, or withdraw the consolation you desire, for this is the way to the kingdom of heaven. Without a doubt, it is better for you and all of my servants to be tried in adversities than to have everything come out just as you wish.
>
> I know your secret thoughts, and I know that it is profitable for your salvation to lose hope and courage at times, so that you do not become arrogant by your success and think yourself to be better than you really are.
>
> Whatever I have given you, I can take away. And when it pleases me, I can restore it again.
>
> If I send you trouble or adversity, do not fret or become depressed, for I can raise you quickly up again and turn your sorrow into joy. I am no less just and worthy of praise when I deal with you in this way.
>
> *The Imitation of Christ (Croft)*, ch. 30

Reflection

God is not our Father Christmas. God is our Redeemer and Lord. And God has a way with us that we are invited to recognize and embrace. This is the way of love and purgation.

PSALM 3:3 — APRIL 12

God Our Protector

God sustains the world and our communities. God is the protector of all who call upon his name. God even cares for those who neglect him.

Drawn from the long oral tradition of Celtic prayers, gathered together in the *Carmina Gadelica*, is this prayer for God's protection:

> I am praying and appealing to God,
> The son of Mary and the Spirit of Truth,
> To aid me in distress of sea and land:
> May the Three succour me, may the Three shield me,
> May the Three watch me by day and by night.
>
> God and Jesus and the Spirit of cleansing
> Be shielding me, be possessing me, be aiding me,
> Be clearing my path and going before my soul,
> In hollow, on hill, on plain.
> On sea and land be the aiding of me.
>
> God and Jesus and the Holy Spirit
> Be shielding and saving me,
> As Three and as One,
> By my knee, by my back, by my side,
> Each step of the stormy world.

Carmina Gadelica, 173

Thought

In looking to God in all the circumstances of life,
we give God his rightful place.

JOHN 1:14 — APRIL 13

The Life of Christ

Christ is the Word made flesh. Christ is the revelation of the Father. Christ is the sin-bearer. Christ is the savior. Christ is the healer. In Christ we are safe. He will carry us into God's final future.

Tertullian (c. 160–c. 220), the African church father, was an early apologist who sought to explain and defend Christianity against critics and skeptics. In his *Apologeticus,* he makes this confession about Christ:

> From his lowly guise they took him to be merely a man; so it followed that, confronted by his power, they counted him a magician. For by his word he drove devils out of men and women, he gave light again to the blind, he cleansed lepers, he braced up the paralytic, and to crown all, he restored the dead to life. He made the very elements his servants, he controlled the storm, he walked on the sea—showing that he is the *Logos* of God, that is the Word, original and first-begotten, attended by Power and Reason, upheld by Spirit, the same Being who by his word still made as he made all things.
>
> His teaching, with its refutation of the instructors and chief men of the Jews, so incensed them (chiefly because of the vast multitudes which turned to him) that at last they brought him to Pontius Pilate, at that time Roman procurator of Syria, and by the fury of their petitions, they extorted Pilate to hand Jesus over to them to be crucified.
>
> He himself had foretold that they would do this, as had the prophets long before. Yet, nailed to the cross, he showed many signs by which his death was distinguished from others. For with a word of his own will, he dismissed his spirit—forestalling the work of the executor.
>
> *Tertullian: Apology and De Spectaculis,* 111

Reflection

He is the Word made flesh.
He is the Lord of Glory.

MATTHEW 18:10　　　　　　　　　　　　　　　APRIL 14

Despise Not the Day of Small Things

The Christian life is not formed primarily through grand events and momentous happenings, but rather by small steps in the right direction and great love expressed in small acts of faithfulness.

The well-known German Christian mystic Meister Eckhart has this to say about attentiveness to the small things:

> It often happens that what seems trivial to us is more important to God than what we think is important. Therefore, we ought to take everything God puts on us evenly, not comparing and wondering which is more important, or higher, or best.
>
> We ought simply to follow where God leads, that is, to do what we are most inclined to do, to go where we are repeatedly admonished to go—to where we feel the most drawn. If we do that, God gives us his greatest in our least and never fails.
>
> Now some people despise the little things of life. It is their mistake, for they thus prevent themselves from getting God's greatness out of these little things. God is every way, evenly in all ways, to the one who has the eyes to see.
>
> But sometimes it is hard to know whether one's inclinations come from God or not, but that can be decided this way: If you find yourself always possessed of a knowledge or intimation of God's will, which you obey before everything else, because you feel urged to obey it and the urge is frequent, then you may know that it is from God.

Meister Eckhart: A Modern Translation, 249

Thought

A willing heart that looks for God in all of life,
including the seeming insignificant,
is the gateway to knowing and doing what pleases the Lord of life.

LUKE 22:19–20　　　　　　　　　　　　　　　　　APRIL 15

Eucharistic Giving

In Christ we see the self-giving God: God as life for the world. In the Eucharistic celebration we are invited to receive this God and to offer our lives as well in the service of others.

St. Francis was enamored with the life and ways of Jesus. In the Lord's Supper he celebrates Jesus' self-giving:

> O admirable heights and sublime lowliness!
> O sublime humility! O humble sublimity!
> That the Lord of the universe, God and Son of God,
> so humbles himself that for our salvation
> He hides himself under the little form of bread!
> Look, brothers and sisters, at the humility of God
> And pour out your hearts before him!
> Humble yourselves, as well,
> That you may be exalted by him.
> Therefore, hold back nothing of yourselves for yourselves
> So that he who gives himself totally to you
> May receive you totally.

Francis and Clare: The Complete Works, 58

Reflection

The work of human hands and of the fruit of the earth,
The gift of the Great Giver,
Who gives himself in his gifts.

ACTS 9:3–6 — APRIL 16

Conversion

The turning of one's life in faith to God can be a most a dramatic experience. It can also be a quiet awakening to the love and grace of God in Christ through the winsome work of the Spirit.

St. Augustine's conversion was a gradual one that had a sudden culmination point. This is how he describes it:

> So I was speaking and weeping in the most bitter contrition of my heart, when, suddenly I heard from a neighbouring house a voice, as of boy or girl, I do not know, often repeating in a sing-song, "Take up and read; Take up and read." Instantly, my countenance altered, I began to think most intently, whether children were apt in any kind of play to sing such words; nor could I remember ever to have heard the like.
>
> So I checked the torrent of my tears, and got up; interpreting it to be no other than a command from God, to open the book, and read the first chapter I should find. For I had heard from Antony, that coming in during the reading of the gospel, he received the admonition, as if what was being read, was spoken to him: "*Go, sell all that you have, and give it to the poor, and you shall have treasure in heaven, and come follow me.*" And by such an oracle he was immediately converted to you.
>
> Eagerly then I returned to the place where Alypius was sitting, for there I had laid the volume of the Apostle, when I got up from there. I seized it, opened it, and in silence read that section, on which my eyes first fell: "*Not in rioting and drunkenness, not in chambering and wantoness, not in strife and envying; but put on the Lord Jesus Christ, and make no provision for the flesh, in concupiscence.*" I wished to read no further; nor did I need to, for instantly at the end of this sentence, by a light as it were of serenity infused into my heart, and all the darkness of doubt vanished.
>
> *The Confessions of Saint Augustine* (Pusey), 9.12

Reflection

The willingness to obey the promptings of the Spirit is to characterize our whole life.

ROMANS 7:24-25 — APRIL 17

Liberation through Christ

Jesus Christ is the New Adam and leader of the new humanity. Where the first Adam failed Christ is the great Repairer and Restorer and shows the new way.

Hildegard of Bingen, one of the great medieval Christian mystics, has this to say about the love and power of Christ's redemptive work. She writes,

> O strength of eternity, you ordained all things in your heart,
> By your word all things were created, as you willed.
> And your own Word put on flesh that was taken from Adam.
> In doing so, he cleansed us and freed us
> from the greatest suffering.
>
> O how great is the Saviour's kindness!
> He delivered all things by his incarnation,
> whom God breathed forth without the chains of sin.
> In doing so, he cleansed and freed us
> from the greatest suffering.

Symphonia, 99

Prayer

Jesus, Savior of the world, grant me
the grace, goodness, and fullness of your life. Amen.

ACTS 2:46-47   APRIL 18

Gather Together

While the church for many in the contemporary world has become an optional extra, in earlier times Christians gathered often. Their example is a challenge for us.

In the so-called *Constitutions of the Holy Apostles*, we gain a picture of the church as a gathered community:

> When you instruct the people, O bishop, command and exhort them to come constantly to church morning and evening every day, and by no means to forsake it on any account, but to assemble together continually; neither to diminish the church by withdrawing themselves, and causing the body of Christ to be without its members.
>
> For it is not only spoken concerning the priests, but let everyone of the laity hear it concerning himself or herself, considering that it is said by the Lord: "The one that is not with me is against me, and the one that gathers not with me scatters abroad." Do not, therefore, scatter yourselves abroad, who are the members of Christ, by not assembling together, since you have Christ as your head, according to his promise, present, and communicating to you.
>
> Be not careless of yourselves, neither deprive your Saviour of his own members, neither divide his body nor disperse his members, neither prefer the occasions of this life to the word of God. But assemble yourselves together every day, morning and evening, singing psalms and praying in the Lord's house: in the morning saying the sixty-second Psalm, and in the evening the hundred and fortieth, but principally on the Sabbath day. And on the day of our Lord's resurrection, which is the Lord's day, meet more diligently, sending praise to God that made the universe by Jesus, and sent him to us, and condescended to let him suffer, and raised him from the dead.
>
> *The Ante-Nicene Fathers*, vol. 7, 422-23

Thought

In the early history of Christianity,
the fellowship of the community of faith was an important theme.

1 CORINTHIANS 12:4–6   APRIL 19

Differing Tasks

> *In the wide scope of God's purposes in family, church and world, there are many different callings for the people of God. But all have to do with loving and serving well to the glory of God and the well-being of humanity.*

The fourteenth-century mystic St. Catherine of Siena wrote about a spirituality that plunges one into the depths of God in order to plumb the depths of the world's needs. Within this frame she writes about the importance of living out our differing callings:

> I have sent all of you into the vineyard of obedience to work in different ways. Each of you will be rewarded according to the measure of your love, not according to your work or the time spent. In other words, those who come early will not get more than those who come late, as it is said in the holy Gospel.
>
> My Truth gave you the example of those who were standing idle and were sent by the Lord to work in his vineyard. He gave as much to those who went out at dawn as to those who went out at the first hour, as much to those who went out at the third hour and to those who went out at the sixth and the ninth and near evening, as to the first. My Truth was showing you that you are rewarded not according to your work or your time but according to the measure of your love.
>
> Many are sent in their childhood to work in this vineyard. Some enter later, and some even in their old age. These last sometimes, because they see how short a time they have, come in with such burning love that they catch up with those who enter in their childhood and have walked slowly. It is from the love of obedience, then, that the soul receives her merit; it is there she fills her vessel in me, the sea of peace.
>
> *Dialogue of Catherine of Siena, 4.5.9*

Prayer

Lord, grant me a deep love for you and not simply a successful ministry.
Amen.

PROVERBS 3:34 — APRIL 20

Humility

The heart of humility is an openness to hear and do what God asks of us. It is the desire to please God and serve others above ourselves.

Bonaventure, in his *The Life of St. Francis*, speaks in lyrical language of Francis' quest for humility:

> Humility, the guardian and ornament
> of all virtues,
> had filled the man of God in copious abundance.
>
> In his own estimation he was nothing but a sinner,
> although in truth he was a resplendent mirror of all holiness.
>
> He strove to build himself up upon this virtue
> like an architect laying the foundations,
> for he learned this from Christ.
>
> He used to say that it was for this reason
> that the Son of God came down from the height of his Father's bosom
> to our lowly estate
> so that our Lord and Teacher might teach humility
> in both word and example.

The Life of St. Francis, 55

Reflection

Lay a deep foundation of your life in the love and grace of Christ. Such a life will bear fruit.

2 CORINTHIANS 13:5   APRIL 21

Self-Examination

Of all the ways that we live the spiritual disciplines, the most difficult and challenging is the art of self-examination. Though we may find it easier to pray and fast, we are called to confront ourselves in the light of God and embrace this form of death to self.

In *The Life of Antony*, St. Athanasius discusses this desert saint's advice about self-examination:

> Let us examine ourselves, and wherever we are lacking, let us hurry towards perfection. And may this remark serve as a precaution so that we might not sin. Let each one of us note and record our actions and the stirrings of our souls as though we were going to give an account to each other. And you can be sure that, being particularly ashamed to have them made known, we would stop sinning and even meditating on something evil.
>
> For who wants to be seen sinning? Or who, after sinning, would not prefer to lie, wanting it to remain unknown?
>
> So then, just as we would not practice fornication if we were observing each other directly, so also we will keep ourselves from impure thoughts if we record our thoughts as if reporting them to each other, for we would be ashamed to have these thoughts known.
>
> Let this record replace the eyes of our fellow ascetics, so that, blushing as much to write as to be seen, we might never be absorbed by evil things. Patterning ourselves in this way, we shall be able to enslave the body and also please the Lord and trample on the deceptions of the enemy.
>
> *The Life of Antony* and *The Letter to Marcellinus*, 73

Reflection

> Know my heart, O God.
> Renew my mind.
> Purge me within.

ROMANS 14:13 — APRIL 22

Don't Judge Others

Competition and comparison lie at the heart of the modern mindset, and many Christians readily compare themselves to others and think they are better. But what we are is by the grace of God, so there is no place for boasting or competition.

The unknown author of *The Cloud of Unknowing* warns us against making our Christian experience normative and judging others in its light:

> Those who habitually practice these exercises must never assume that other contemplatives share their same experiences. Those who see and experience the perfection of contemplation only after heavy toil may be easily deceived if they speak, think, or judge others according to their own experiences. Similarly, those who experience contemplation whenever they wish will be mistaken if they judge others by their experiences.
>
> Forget such comparisons, for we must not think in this way. It may be that in God's wisdom, those who struggle wearily in the beginning and only taste the fruits of contemplation occasionally may later experience them whenever they like.
>
> We have an example of this in Moses. On the mountain, he saw the form of the ark very rarely and only after heavy toil. But later on, when it was within the veil, he saw it as often as he liked.
>
> *The Cloud of Unknowing*, 259–60

Reflection

In the wisdom of God all are graced, gifted, and blessed by the same Spirit, but our lives unfold in different ways.
For some, the journey of faith seems a smooth path; for others, it is the rocky road.

Exodus 33:18–23 — April 23

The Vision of God

While in certain Christian circles the only mark of holiness is sacrificial service, the heartbeat of the Christian life is the vision of God that defines us and energizes our service.

Gregory the Great's *Dialogues* talk about God's saints in sixth-century Italy. Here is an excerpt from these writings:

> When the soul perceives a little of his light, it finds all creatures small indeed. The light of holy contemplation enlarges and expands the mind in God until it stands above the world. In fact, the soul that sees him rises even above itself, and as it is drawn upward in his light, all its inner powers unfold. Then, when it looks down from above, it sees how small everything is that was beyond its grasp before.
>
> Now, how else was it possible for this man or woman to behold the ball of fire and watch the angels on their return to heaven, except with light from God? Why should it surprise us, then, that she could see the whole world gathered up before her after this inner light had lifted her so far above the world? Of course, in saying that the world was gathered up before his eyes, I do not mean that heaven and earth grew small, but that his spirit was enlarged. Absorbed as he was in God, it was now easy for him to see all that lay beneath God. In the light outside that was shining before her eyes, there was a brightness which reached into her mind and lifted her spirit heavenward, showing her the insignificance of all that lies below.

Gregory the Great: Dialogues, 106

Prayer

Lord, may I see you more clearly with the eyes of faith.
And in your light may I see myself and the world in a truer perspective,
with greater love and with fuller engagement.
Amen.

PSALM 91:14   APRIL 24

God's Protection

In Celtic spirituality there is a profound sense of God's presence and light in all things, including nature. But there is at the same time a deep cry for God's protection in all things, including the forces of nature.

From the *Carmina Gadelica*, a compilation of ancient Celtic prayers, we read about this heart cry:

> God before me, God behind me,
> God above me, God below me;
> I on the path of God,
> God upon my track.
>
> Who is there on land?
> Who is there on wave?
> Who is there on billow?
> Who is there by door-post?
> Who is along with us? God and Lord.
>
> I am here abroad,
> I am here in need,
> I am here in pain,
> I am here in straights,
> I am here alone, O God aid me.

Carmina Gadelica, 319

Reflection

God is the Migrant God who is with us in all our life's journeys.

LEVITICUS 19:16   APRIL 25

Avoid Slandering

Though we are called to love, do good and build up other people, so often we pull people down. One way we do this is when we speak ill of others and slander them.

The unknown author of the late first-century or early second-century *The Shepherd of Hermas* gives this advice to post-apostolic Christians:

> First of all, believe that God is One, who created all things and set them in order, who took what did not exist and brought it into being, who comprehends all things, though he himself is incomprehensible.
>
> Believe him, therefore, and fear him, and fearing him, exercise self-control. Observe these things, and you will cast off all wickedness from yourself and will clothe yourself with every virtue of righteousness, and you will live unto God.
>
> Remain simple and innocent, and you will be as little children who do not know the wickedness that destroys human life. First of all, do not speak evil of anyone and do not take pleasure in listening to a slanderer. Otherwise, you will be responsible for the sin of the one speaking evil, for if you believe the slander that you hear, you will hold a grudge against your brother or sister. In this way, you will become responsible for the sin of the one who speaks the evil.
>
> Slander is evil; it is a restless demon, never at peace, but always at home with dissension. Refrain from it, therefore, and you shall have success at all times with everyone.
>
> Clothe yourself with reverence, which has no evil stumbling-block, but makes everything smooth and joyful.

The Shepherd of Hermas, Mandate 1–2

Thought

To think well of another is to celebrate God's work in their lives.

EPHESIANS 2:19–22 — APRIL 26

Grounded in the Grace of God

To live the Christian life well, one must be grounded in the grace of God in Christ and be living life in faith, obedience and service.

The fourteenth-century Christian mystic Jan van Ruysbroeck, in his book *The Sparkling Stone*, writes about becoming a good person of holiness and faithfulness. He writes,

> Hear now three things that constitute a good man or woman. The first is a clean conscience without reproach of mortal sin. And therefore whoever wishes to become a good person must examine and prove such due discernment, from that time onward when he or she could first have committed sin.
>
> The second thing that pertains to a good person is that he or she must in all things be obedient to God, and to holy church, and to proper convictions. And to each of these three there must be equal obedience: so shall the person live without care and doubt, and shall ever abide without inward reproach in all his or her deeds.
>
> The third thing that behoves every good person is that in all deeds, he or she should have in mind, above all else, the glory of God. And if it happens that by reason of business or the multiplicity of works, this man or woman has not always God before his or her eyes, yet at least there should be established within the intention and desire to live according to the dearest will of God.

The Sparkling Stone, ch. 1

Reflection

To live the Christian life well is a heart matter,
for it calls us to desire to please God both in our inner being and in the things we do.

1 JOHN 2:12-14 — APRIL 27

Phases in the Christian Life

Just as there are stages or phases in our psycho-social development, so there are phases in our spiritual growth and development. But none of these stages constitute a higher spirituality, just a greater manifestation of God's grace in one's life.

Hildegard of Bingen, in a letter to a priest, had this to say about this topic:

> When a person is in the first age (as at Prime), when as a child he has taken up holiness, let him not speak on his own authority but rather listen to the masters and teachers, and, in this way, he will bind the bellowing and wailing devil.
>
> But in the second age (as at Terce), in youth, let her continue to contain her sanctity in silence, and remain quiet. Let her seek out with full solicitude and absolute devotion that which is good, lest she fall into pride, and, in this way, she will kill the devil.
>
> In the third age (as at Sext), let him no longer be silent, but let him humbly seek out from his master what ought to be sought, because that age is not lacking in lasciviousness, and, therefore, the demons of this group seem to be dead.
>
> In the fourth age (as at None), when a woman is inspired by God, let her seek counsel from the masters and wise men and women, for then she is weak in the heat of the virility of the flesh, and let her give thanks to God.
>
> For the first age is naturally impatient.... The second age believes that the fear of the Lord is not necessary.... The third age gladly has the fear of the Lord, and, therefore, let it be joyous in its sanctity.... The fourth age lifts up sighs to God, but joy must also be offered to him in all things.
>
> *The Letters of Hildegard of Bingen*, vol. 3, 97

Prayer

Lord, grant that in every phase of my faith journey you will keep me, and my heart will remain turned towards you. Amen.

1 PETER 2:9 — APRIL 28

The Light of Christ

The heart of Christian experience is to be enlightened through the Spirit with the light of Christ. Christ reveals himself, and we are amazed and forever changed.

St. Augustine writes about this transformation:

> Proceed with your confession, O my faith. Say to the Lord, "Holy, holy, holy, O Lord my God, in your name we have been baptized, in the name of the Father, Son, and Holy Spirit." In your name, we baptize others, in the name of the Father, the Son, and the Holy Spirit.
>
> For even among us, God in Christ made "heaven and earth," that is, the spiritual and carnal people of his church. And before this earth of ours received "the form of doctrine," it was "invisible and without form," and we were covered by the darkness of ignorance. For you corrected both man and woman for their iniquity, and your judgments are like a great abyss to them.
>
> But because your Spirit was moving over the waters, your mercy did not forsake our misery, and you said, "Let there be light; repent, for the kingdom of heaven is at hand. Repent, and let there be light."
>
> And because our soul was troubled within us, we remembered you, O Lord, from the land of Jordan, and out of that mountain—which was equal unto you, but which became little for our sakes—we became displeased with our darkness, and we turned to you, "and there was light." And behold, we were previously in darkness, but now we are light in the Lord.

Confessions of St. Augustine, 415

Reflection

Christ is received by faith, but he comes to us by revelation. And this may well occur when, by his Spirit, we are moved to repentance and renewal.

PHILIPPIANS 4:6 — APRIL 29

Prayer for All

A life of prayer is not restricted to one's personal concerns and one's intimate circle. It is an ever-widening circle that seeks to bring all to the heart of God's concern.

St. Anselm of Canterbury speaks about the wide spaces of prayer:

> O hear me as one mighty and merciful;
> and grant to my friends and to my enemies,
> not only what I have prayed, but by your mercy,
> whatever you know will be helpful for everyone,
> both living and dead,
> according to your will.
>
> Do not hear me according to the desires of my heart
> or the requests of my lips,
> but as you know and will that I should wish and ask,
> O Saviour of the world,
> who with the Father and the Holy Spirit
> lives and reigns, everlasting God, world without end. Amen.

The Devotions of Saint Anselm, 133–34

Reflection

Encircled in your love, O God of life,
may that love flow
to others,
both friends and enemies.

DEUTERONOMY 29:29 — APRIL 30

Things That Are Hidden and Revealed

The more we know God the more we realize how little in fact we know. God will always be the mysterious One whom we love, worship, and serve.

The English Christian mystic Julian of Norwich speaks about what God has made known and what God has hidden from us. She writes,

> He gave me understanding in two parts. The first part concerns our Saviour and our salvation. There is no mystery about this part—it is clear, beautiful, splendid, and abundant. Everyone of present and future goodwill is included in it. To it we are bound, and to it we are drawn to God; in it we are advised, and in it we are instructed, inwardly by the Holy Spirit, and outwardly through the same grace by the Holy Church. In this, our Lord intends us to be occupied: delighting in himself, as he delights in us. The more fully we make this truth our own, with reverent humility, the more thanks we get from him, and the greater is our gain. Thus, so to speak, we enjoy our share of our Lord.
>
> The other part is completely hidden from us, for it deals with all those things that do not concern our salvation. It is our Lord's own private matter, and it is the royal prerogative of God to be undisturbed in that which is his own business. It is not for his or her servant, obedient and reverent, to pry at all in these secrets. . . . I am sure that if we realised how much it would please him and benefit ourselves to refrain from this prying, we would stop.
>
> The desire of the saints in heaven is only to know such things as our Lord wills to show them. Their love and their longing likewise are ruled by the Lord's will.
>
> *Showings*, ch. 48

Reflection

In Scripture, nature, and in human experience,
there is enough for us to ponder for many lifetimes.

May

LUKE 9:23   MAY 1

Cross Bearers

We are most fundamentally cross bearers because the cross of Christ has forever marked us in redemption and healing. But we are also called to suffer with and for Christ and thus carry the cross in some small way.

Thomas à Kempis makes it clear that the cross is central to the Christian life. He writes,

> Do you know of any saint who, during his or her life, was without the cross and some affliction? Our Lord Jesus Christ himself did not live one hour of his life without suffering: "It was fitting that Christ should suffer and rise again from the dead and so to enter his glory." So why would you seek a way other than this royal way, which is the way of the holy cross?
>
> The whole life of Christ was a cross and a martyrdom, and yet you seek rest and joy? You err, yes you err, if you seek anything other than trials and tribulations, for this whole mortal life is full of miseries and surrounded by crosses. The higher we advance in spirit, the heavier will be the crosses that we bear, because the pain of exile from God increases in proportion to our love for God.
>
> Though we are afflicted in many ways, we are not without some comfort, because we recognize the great profit which we reap by bearing the cross.
>
> *My Imitation of Christ*, 147–48

Prayer

Lord, may I be united to you and your purposes and thus experience your death and resurrection in my life, love and service. Amen.

EPHESIANS 2:4–5   MAY 2

God's Drawing Love

Yes, surely, we must make a faith response to God. And though we are called to a life of worship, repentance and service, it is always God's prior love for us that moves and draws us.

St. Bernard of Clairvaux, in his *On Loving God*, speaks of God as the source of our love. He writes,

> I have said already that the motive for loving God is God himself. And I spoke truly, for he is both the cause and the final object of our love. He provides the occasion for love, and he creates the affection of love, and he himself fulfils love's desire. Because love is his natural due, hope in him is natural, since our present love would be foolish if did we not hope to love him perfectly some day.
>
> Our love is both prepared and rewarded by his love. Out of his great tenderness, he loves us first. Then we are bound to repay him with love, and we are permitted to cherish exultant hopes in him. Though he is rich to all who call upon him, he has no gift better than himself. He gives himself as a prize and reward. He is the refreshment of the holy soul and the ransom of those in captivity.
>
> The Lord is good to all who wait for him. So what will he be to those who gain his presence? But here is a wonderful paradox: no one can seek the Lord who has not already found him.

On Loving God, ch. 7

Thought

God is the source of all things
and the spring from which our love issues forth.

LUKE 9:1–6 — MAY 3

The Sent Ones

Cross-cultural Christian workers know something of leaving home and loved ones and going to distant places for the sake of the gospel. But we are all sent ones, even to the neighbor across the street.

St. Francis, in his *Rule* for his community of brothers, had this to say about the call to itinerancy and mutual care. He writes,

> The friars should not possess anything for themselves, neither a house, nor a place, nor anything else. As strangers and pilgrims in this world, who serve God in poverty and humility, they should beg for alms confidently, without being ashamed, because God made himself poor for us in this world.
>
> This is the pinnacle of the most exalted poverty, which has made you, my dearest brothers, heirs and kings of the kingdom of heaven, poor in temporal things but rich in virtue. This should be your portion, because it leads to the land of the living (Ps 142:5). And to this poverty, my beloved brothers, you must cling with all your heart, and you must never wish to have anything else under heaven, for the sake of our Lord Jesus Christ.
>
> Wherever the friars meet one another, they should show that they are members of the same family. And they should have no hesitation in making known their needs to one another. For if a mother loves and cares for her child in the flesh, a friar should certainly love and care for his spiritual brother all the more tenderly. If a friar falls ill, the others are bound to look after him, just as they would like to be looked after themselves.

The Rule of St. Francis, ch. 6

Reflection

To be the sent ones should not lead to individual scattering, but to a community in mission.

PSALM 16:9 — MAY 4

Rest

Rest is both physical and spiritual. We need to rest our bodies with the blessing of sleep. But we also need the gift of inner peace.

A Celtic prayer from the *Carmina Gadelica* is a longing for the blessing of rest:

> In the name of the Lord Jesus,
> And of the Spirit of healing balm,
> In the name of the Father of Israel,
> I lay me down to rest.
>
> If there be evil threat or quirk,
> Or covert act intent on me,
> God free me and encompass me,
> And drive from me my enemy.
>
> In the name of the Father precious,
> And of the Spirit of healing balm,
> In the name of the Lord Jesus,
> I lay me down to rest.

Carmina Gadelica, 97

Reflection

> I am placing my being,
> my plans,
> my hopes,
> into thy keeping, O God.

2 KINGS 6:8–10   MAY 5

Advice to Rulers

> *The God of the Bible is concerned about the political sphere. In the Old Testament, prophets guided kings. Ever since, Christians have raised their voice in calling rulers to fidelity and justice.*

The medieval Christian mystic Hildegard of Bingen was an advisor to kings. In a letter to Henry II, king of England, she had this to say:

> Yours are the gifts of giving: it is by ruling and defending, protecting and providing, that you may reach heaven. But a bird, as black as can be, comes to you from the North, and says: "You have the power to do whatever you want. So do this and do that, make this excuse and that excuse. It does not profit you to have regard for justice; for if you are always attentive to her, you will not be a master but a slave."
>
> Yet you should not listen to the thief that gives you that advice, for he was the thief who stripped you of great glory in your infancy, when your beauty was first created from ashes and you drew your first breath of life.
>
> Instead, look more attentively upon your Father, who made you. For your mind is well disposed, so that you readily do good, except when the immoral habits of others overwhelm you and you become entangled in them for a time. Shun this with all your might, beloved son of God, and call upon your Father, since willingly he stretches out his hand to help you.
>
> Now, live forever, and remain in eternal happiness.
>
> *Mystical Writings*, 140

Reflection

A faith that only knows spiritual matters is a denuded faith.
A full-orbed faith must be robust enough to address all the issues of life, including the economic and political spheres.

PSALM 90:9–10   MAY 6

Grieving Loss

Even for a life of faith in the midst of community, we are alone with our own struggles and difficulties. We are invited to embrace these in humility. To do otherwise will usher us into the blame game. Instead of embracing what comes our way, we will blame God or others.

In St. Basil's *Letter XXX* to Eusebius, bishop of Samosata, he speaks about his grief:

> If I should relate at length all the reasons for my being detained at home, even though I am eager to set out to see your reverence, I should traverse an interminable length of narrative. I pass over a succession of bodily ills, a tedious winter, vexatious affairs of business.... And now, as the result of my sins, I have been bereft of the solace that I possessed, my mother.
>
> Pray, do not deride me for bewailing my orphanhood at this time of life, but forgive me for not having the patience to endure separation from a soul whose like I do not behold among those who are left behind.
>
> My ill-health has now returned again, and again I lie on my bed, tossing about on the anchorage of my little remaining strength, and ready at almost every hour to accept the inevitable end of my life.

Saint Basil, The Letters, vol. 1, 175

Reflection

A life of gaining and getting
is stripped bare.
Naked, but in faith and trust
we return to the God
who gives, takes away, and gives again.

PSALM 31:19 — MAY 7

Basking in God's Goodness

Our achievements do not give significant shape to our identity as Christians, but rather the fact that we are graced by the goodness of God.

Julian of Norwich, in one of her reflections on a vision of the goodness of God, has these words of encouragement:

> To know the goodness of God is the highest prayer of all, and it is a prayer that comes down to the lowest part of our need. It quickens our soul, and brings it to life, and makes it grow in grace and virtue.
>
> Grace, which is always ready to help, is the nearest aid. For this is the same grace that the soul seeks and will continue to seek until we know truly that he has united us to himself. He does not despise what he has made, nor does he disdain to serve us, however lowly our natural need may be, for he loves the soul that he has made in his own likeness.
>
> Just as the body is clothed in garments, and the flesh in skin, and the bones in flesh, and the heart in the body, so are we, soul and body, clothed in the goodness of God. Yes, and even more, for all bodily things may decay and wear away, but the goodness of God is ever whole.
>
> *Revelations of Divine Love* (Warrack), ch. 6

Prayer

Lord, even in difficult times,
may I bask in the abundance of your goodness.
Amen.

PSALM 146:5–7   MAY 8

The Challenges of the Ascetic Life

The ascetic life is no picnic. Men and women of old were willing to embrace great hardship in the desert, where they prayed, sought to deepen their union with God, and wrestled with the spiritual forces of darkness. We know little of such a life of commitment.

St. Jerome, in a letter to Heliodorus, a former soldier turned ascetic, challenges him to continue in this journey of faith. Heliodorus leaves this form of life and later becomes a bishop. But here is Jerome's challenge:

> What keeps you in the world, my brother, you who are above the world? How long shall gloomy roofs oppress you? How long shall smoky cities immure [confine] you? Believe me, I have more light than you. Sweet it is to lay aside the weight of the body and to soar into the pure bright ether.
>
> Do you dread poverty? Christ calls you blessed. Does toil frighten you? No athlete is crowned but in the sweat of his brow. Are you anxious as regards food? Faith fears no famine. Do you dread the bare ground for limbs wasted with fasting? The Lord lies there beside you.
>
> Do you recoil from an unwashed head and uncombed hair? Christ is your head. Does the boundless solitude of the desert terrify you? In the spirit you may always walk in paradise. . . . Is your skin rough and scaly because you no longer bathe? He that is once washed in Christ need not wash again . . .
>
> "The sufferings of this present time are not worthy to be compared with the glory . . . which shall be revealed to us."
>
> *The Letters of St. Jerome, Letter XIV to Heliodorus*, 10

Reflection

We too are invited into the "desert" to practice forms of asceticism for the sake of the kingdom of God.

PSALM 17:6 MAY 9

Prayer for God's Presence

The God that we seek is the God that we both know and yet continue to long for. One's cry is ever: show me your love and presence, O God.

Thomas à Kempis gives us this heart prayer:

> O, eternal light, transcending all created light, send down your lightning from on high and penetrate the recesses of my heart! Make my spirit pure, joyous, enlightened and alive, so that with all its powers and with boundless joy, it may cling to you.
>
> When will that blessed and longed for hour come, when you will satisfy me with your presence and be all in all to me? As long as your presence is withheld, my joy will not be full.
>
> Sorrowfully, the "old man" still lives in me; he is neither wholly crucified, nor utterly dead. He still battles strongly against the spirit, stirs up civil war, and does not allow my soul to be at peace.
>
> But you, who control the power of the sea and calm the surge of its waves, rise up, aid me. Scatter those who seek war. Crush them by your might.
>
> Show me, I beg, your mighty works, and let your right hand be glorified, for there is no other hope or refuge for me, save in you, Lord, my God.
>
> *The Imitation of Christ* (Blaiklock), 141

Thought

As we pray, we recognize our true nature and the grace of God, who renews us with his life-giving Spirit.

GALATIANS 1:11–17   MAY 10

God Calling

It is one thing to believe that there is a God. It is a whole other thing to be called by God. In this we see that God is personal and that God has a purpose for our life.

St. Cuthbert, the Northumbrian saint, speaks about the call of God:

> Hear my voice when I call, O Lord;
> Be merciful to me and answer me.
> My heart says of you, 'Seek his face!'
> Your face, Lord, will I seek.
> Do not hide your face from me,
> Do not turn your servant away in anger;
> You have been my helper…
>
> Lord, I have heard your voice
> Calling at a distance.
> Guide my steps to you, Lord,
> Guide my steps to you.
> Lord, I have heard your voice
> Calling at a distance.
> Guard my way to you, Lord,
> Guard my way to you
>
> *Celtic Daily Prayer*, 172–73

Reflection

In the call of God the whole fabric of one's life is woven.

MATTHEW 7:24-27 — MAY 11

Let the Good Flourish

We are capable of great good and much mischief. The God who is good and full of love seeks to nourish the good in each of us.

Hildegard, the abbess of the Benedictine community at Rupertsberg, near Bingen, has this advice for a lay person who is seeking wisdom:

> O child of God (for such you are because he formed you in the first man and woman, just as he has established you in his providence), although you are in the dark prison of this life, God has granted you this gift: the ability to know and to choose both what is good for you, and what is harmful. Therefore, hear what I saw and heard about you in a true vision.
>
> I saw a white cloud, devoid of any light, and it was joined to another stormy cloud, above which appeared tongues of fire penetrating both those clouds. This white cloud signifies those good desires which you frequently have, and which you refuse to give up, while the stormy cloud denotes the busyness of your office that threatens to overwhelm you. As a result, you are so engrossed that you cannot do the good works that are the radiance of good desires.
>
> By the tongues of fire I understood that because of the good desires which he loves in you, God enkindles you with the fire of the Holy Spirit to do good works. Therefore, with the plough of the fear of God, which pierces all sins to overcome them, plough up the field of your self-will, taking note how the vile weeds have grown up there in such great luxuriance that you are scarcely able to sow your seeds in any place.... Therefore, for the love of Christ, give up that stubborn part of your will which does not contribute to the refreshment of your soul ...
>
> *The Letters of Hildegard of Bingen*, vol. 3, 146

Thought

Goodness and virtue do not automatically grow in us;
rather, they need to be nurtured so that they can grow in the love of God
through the Spirit.

DEUTERONOMY 10:17   MAY 12

God's Greatness

We acknowledge God's greatness and power in the creation—but it is the greatness of his love that draws and conquers us.

St. Basil, in his homilies compiled in the *Hexaemeron*, has this to say about God's majesty:

> But enough on the greatness of the sun and moon. May he who has given us intelligence to recognize in the smallest objects of creation the great wisdom of the Contriver make us find in the heavenly bodies a still higher idea of their Creator.
>
> However, compared with their Author, the sun and moon are but a fly and an ant.
>
> The whole universe cannot give us a right idea of the greatness of God; and it is only by signs, weak and slight in themselves, often by the help of the smallest insects and of the least plants, that we raise ourselves to him.
>
> Content with these words let us offer our thanks, I to him who has given me the ministry of the Word, you to him who feeds you with spiritual food; who, even at this moment, makes you find in my weak voice the strength of barley bread.
>
> May he feed you forever, and in proportion to your faith grant you the manifestation of the Spirit in Jesus Christ our Lord, to whom be glory and power forever and ever. Amen.
>
> *Nicene and Post-Nicene Fathers*, vol. 8, 89

Reflection

We will always have to embrace the mystery of the being of God.
But God has revealed himself
and by way of analogy we may apprehend something of who this God is.

PSALM 51:1–2   MAY 13

Prayer of Repentance

Whatever may be true of us in the long journey of faith, we will never outgrow our need for confession and repentance.

In the Prayers of Moucan, which possibly go back to the eighth century, we have an expression of the deeply penitential tradition of Celtic spirituality:

> Father, I have sinned against heaven and before you,
> > Have mercy upon me and hear me.
> I am now not worthy to be called your child, come to my aid, O God.
> > Make me like one of your hired servants,
> > Forgive me and spare me my sins.
> Because I greatly hunger for you, wipe out the wickedness of my sin.
> > Show favour to me, Lord, a sinner,
> > Snatch my soul from the hand of hell.
> > Remember me, Lord, in your kingdom . . .
> And do not remove your Holy Spirit from me . . .
> To you I flee, most Holy Father, and I have no refuge but you . . .
> Lord God, the power of my salvation, do not utterly abandon me.
>
> *Celtic Spirituality*, 302–3

Reflection

In the confession of sins lies our true freedom.

1 JOHN 4:7-12 — MAY 14

The Nature of Christian Love

The way of self-giving love finds its source in the God who first loved us. Thus our love is the overflow of God's good gifts to us.

The medieval cardinal Nicholas of Cusa, in a letter to Abbot Kaspar Ayndorffer of the Benedictine monastery of Tegernsee, in Bavaria, has this to say about the nature of love:

> Love of the good presents the good as not yet grasped, for the spirit's motion that is love would cease if it attained its goal. It is always moved to attain more, and because the good is infinite, the spirit will never cease being moved forward. Therefore, the loving spirit can never stop, because of the lovableness of the one loved cannot be attained.
>
> The loving person is swept up, but not without any knowledge. Knowledge is perceived from adhering to God—"My soul," says the prophet, "has adhered to you; your right hand has received me" (Ps 62:9).
>
> Because this is the gospel, that is, attaining by means of faith while in the world, there is no love of God that sweeps the lover up into God apart from belief in Christ who has revealed what he saw when he was with the Father. Namely, there is an immortal life which we can attain through the joining of the divine life to pure human nature in the Son of God and of Man.

The Essential Writings of Christian Mysticism, 271

Reflection

"Come down, O Love divine,
Seek thou this soul of mine,
And visit it with thine own ardor glowing;
O Comforter, draw near,
Within my heart appear
And kindle it, thy flame bestowing."

JOB 11:7 — MAY 15

The Depths of God

We know God through his words and his works—but God is nevertheless beyond us. Yet God is still the very ground of our being.

Meister Eckhart is known as the ontological spiritual mystic. This is because he reflected deeply on the being of God as the ground for our being. He writes,

> I have spoken of a power in the soul. This power does not grasp at God because he is good, nor because he is the truth, but it delves deeply and ceaselessly, seeking to grasp God in his unity and uniqueness. It grasps God in his wilderness, his desert, his own ground.
>
> The soul does not rest content with anything, but further seeks to discover God in his Godhead and in the singularity of his nature.
>
> Now it is said that there is no greater unity than that of the three persons in God. It might also be said that there is no greater unity than that between God and the soul. When the soul receives a kiss from the Godhead, it stands in absolute perfection and blessedness as it is embraced by unity.
>
> . . . When God sees a creature, he bestows being upon it, and when a creature sees God, it receives its being from him.
>
> *Meister Eckhart: Selected Writings,* 174

Reflection

In Christ through the Spirit, God has made his home in us.

1 JOHN 3:18 — MAY 16

A Severe Love

God's love in Christ is no cheap love, for it is a love that gives all. We, too, are called to this way of loving. Love, while beautiful, is severe, for it calls us to self-giving, surrender and suffering.

Hadewijch, possibly the greatest Dutch poet of the Middle Ages, has this to say about the nature of love:

> But we who are so shallow, of frivolous mind,
> Find the fears of Love harsh;
> We are inconstant with small gains;
> Therefore we are deprived of Love's clear truth
> I know (although I know not all the joys
> That one experiences in Love's wealth,
> Still enlightened reason teaches all this)
> How to correspond with Love to the full.
> Reason does not teach this truth:
> No task too hard, and all is prepared anew.

Hadewijch: The Complete Works, 73

Reflection

Love brings its beauty and its gifts. It also brings its demands.

1 Peter 5:10 — May 17

Recovery

In the journey of faith we do become discouraged and we can lose our way. We need to be found again. We need to be restored.

In the sayings of the Desert Fathers and Mothers there is the story of abbot Antony and his renewal:

> Once when Antony was living in the desert, his soul was troubled by boredom and irritation. He said to God, "Lord, I want to be made whole and my thoughts do not let me. What am I to do about this trouble, how shall I be cured?"
>
> After a while, he got up and went outside. He saw someone like himself sitting and working, then standing up to pray; then sitting down again to make a plait of palm leaves and standing up again to pray.
>
> It was an angel of the Lord sent to correct Antony and make him vigilant. He heard the voice of the angel saying, "Do this and you will be cured."
>
> When he heard it, he was very glad and recovered his confidence. He did what the angel had done and found the salvation that he was seeking.
>
> *The Desert Fathers: Sayings of the Early Christian Monks*, 60

Prayer

Lord, I do not find the journey of faith easy.
I do get confused and I do lose my way from time to time.
Please find me again and restore me. I don't mind how you will do this.
Amen.

GALATIANS 6:14-15 — MAY 18

A New World Waiting to Be Born

The Christian longs for heaven, but not only for the future heaven. The Christian also longs for the heaven of God's present kingdom. This is the grace of God's love, rule and justice amongst us.

The monastic writer John Cassian speaks of the need to bring "heaven" to earth. He writes,

> What you call works of religion and mercy are needed in this life, as long as inequalities and diverse conditions still prevail. We would not have to perform these works if it were not for the large proportion of poor, needy, and sick, whose plight is brought about by the wickedness of those who have grasped and kept for their own use—without even using them—what the common Creator granted to all.
>
> As long as this inequality lasts in this world, this sort of work will be necessary and important to anyone who practices it, for it brings about a good purpose and the pious reward of an eternal inheritance. But all this will cease in the life to come, when equality will reign, and when there will no longer be the injustice that makes these works necessary. Everyone will pass from these many practical works to the love of God and to the contemplation of heavenly things with a continually pure heart. Men and women who devote themselves to the knowledge of God and to purifying their hearts have chosen to give themselves up to this one task. While they still live in the flesh, they give themselves to the service that they will continue when their corruption has been laid aside, when they come to the promise of the Lord, the Saviour, which says, "Blessed are the pure in heart, for they shall see God."
>
> *The Conferences of John Cassian,* 1.10

Prayer

Lord, may we live in the present in joyful anticipation of what your final kingdom will be like. Amen.

ROMANS 5:15 MAY 19

The Abundant Grace of God

> *The Christian life is to be lived out of a profound sense of God's abiding love for humanity, but also his love for each one of us personally. Well loved, we can rejoice in this goodness and be grateful all the days of our lives.*

The medieval Christian mystic Jan van Ruysbroeck, in his *Sparkling Stone*, writes as follows about this God of grace:

> And therefore we should all conceive of God in this way: First of all that, of his free goodness, he calls and invites all men and women, without distinction, to union with himself; both the good and the wicked, without exception. Secondly, we should thus comprehend the goodness of God; how he through grace flows forth toward all men and women who are obedient to the call of God.
>
> Thirdly, we should find and understand clearly in ourselves that we can become one life and one spirit with God when we renounce ourselves in every way, and follow the grace of God to the height whereto it would guide us. For the grace of God works according to order in every man and woman, after the measure and the way in which he or she is able to receive it. And thereby, through the universal working of the grace of God, all sinners, if they desire it, receive the discernment and strength which are needful, that they may leave sin and turn toward virtue.
>
> And, through that hidden cooperation of the grace of God, every good man or woman can overcome all sins, and can resist all temptations, and can fulfil all virtues, and can persevere in the highest perfection, if in all things he or she is submissive to the grace of God.
>
> *The Sparkling Stone*, ch. 5

Reflection

The grace of God, in the power of the Spirit,
is what can sustain us in every sphere of life.

JOHN 10:14–16 MAY 20

The Good Shepherd

The image of Christ as shepherd speaks of a caring, protecting, and nurturing God. This is the God who is close and who is neither arbitrary nor remote. We are safe with such a God.

In St. Basil's *The Letters,* XLVI, he paints a picture of this winsome Christ:

> While it is still possible, let us raise ourselves from the fall, and not despair of ourselves, so that we can become free from sin.
>
> Jesus Christ came into the world to save sinners. "Come, let us adore and fall down and weep before him." The Word calls us to repentance, crying aloud: "Come to me, all you who labour and are burdened, and I will refresh you."
>
> There is a way of salvation, if we are willing. Death swallows us up in his might, but rest and know that God has wiped tears from the face of every penitent.
>
> The Lord is faithful in all his words. He does not lie when he says: "If your sins are scarlet, they shall be made white as snow; and if they be red as crimson, they shall be white as wool." The great physician of souls is ready to cure your ill; for he is the liberator, not of you alone, but of all who have been enslaved by sin.
>
> His sweet and saving lips have said: "Those who are in health do not need a physician, but those who are ill. I did not come to call the just, but sinners to repentance."
>
> *Saint Basil: The Letters,* vol. 1, 307

Reflection

He is the shepherd who seeks us out.
The shepherd who finds us.
The One who heals us.
The One who brings us home.

ROMANS 15:4   MAY 21

Reading Scripture

We believe in the Word made flesh, Jesus Christ. We are enlightened by the life-giving Spirit. And through both, we are drawn to reflect on Scripture to gain the wisdom of God.

In *Exposition of the Orthodox Faith*, John of Damascus (c. 675–c. 749), a Greek theologian and doctor of the church, speaks about the importance of being guided and sustained by Scripture.

> To search the Scriptures is a beautiful and profitable work for the soul. For just as a tree that is planted by channels of waters will be enriched and will produce fruit in its season, so the soul that is watered by the divine Scriptures will yield orthodox belief and be adorned with evergreen leafage, which are actions that are pleasing to God.
>
> Through the Holy Scriptures, we are trained to action that is pleasing to God and to untroubled contemplation . . .
>
> So let us knock at that very fair garden of the Scriptures, so fragrant and sweet and blooming, with its varied sounds of spiritual and divinely inspired birds ringing all around our ears, laying hold of our hearts, comforting the mourner, pacifying the angry and filling him and her with everlasting joy. This will set our minds on the gold-gleaming brilliant back of divine love . . . [through] the only-begotten Son . . . to the Father of Lights.
>
> *Nicene and Post-Nicene Fathers*, vol. 9, 89

Reflection

In the light of your Word I will walk.
In it I hear your voice calling.
It is the voice of love.
It is the way of life.
It makes the old new.
It restores a broken world.

PSALM 42:8   MAY 22

A Night Prayer

At the start of day with the song of birds, we want to lift our voices to the God of life. And in the evening we wish to sleep in the blessing of God's care.

In the Celtic prayers of the *Carmina Gadelica* there is this night prayer:

> I am lying down tonight as befits
> In the fellowship of Christ, Son of the virgin of ringlets.
> In the fellowship of the gracious Father of glory,
> In the fellowship of the Spirit of powerful aid.
>
> I am lying down tonight with God,
> And God tonight will lie down with me,
> I will not lie down tonight with sin, nor shall
> Sin nor sin's shadow lie down with me.
>
> I am lying down tonight with the Holy Spirit
> And the Holy Spirit this night will lie down with me,
> I will lie down this night with the Three of my love,
> And the Three of my love will lie down with me.

Carmina Gadelica, 83

Reflection

You give rest and protection.
Even while I sleep your care is for me.
You are the God of my life.
I am so blessed.

John 16:12–15   May 23

The Guiding Spirit

> *The Spirit is God's presence with us in the present. The Spirit is with us in this pilgrim journey of faith. The Spirit is given to sustain, lead and empower us. Blessed be the Spirit! And blessed are those who seek the close company of the Spirit!*

The early church father Tertullian speaks about the role of the Spirit in guiding those who belong to Christ:

> Actually the reason why the Lord sent the Paraclete was, that, since human mediocrity was unable to take in all things at once, discipline should, little by little, be directed, ordained and brought to perfection by that Vicar of the Lord, the Holy Spirit.
>
> "Still," he said, "I have many things to say to you, but you are not yet able to bear them: when that Spirit of Truth comes, he will lead you into all truth, and will report to you the things to come" (John 16:12–13).
>
> Thus he declared the work of the Spirit. This, then, is the Paraclete's guiding office: the direction of discipline, the revelation of the Scriptures, the reformation of the intellect, the advancement towards the "better things."
>
> *The Holy Spirit, Message of the Church Fathers*, vol. 3, 53

Reflection

We need to be sustained.
We need to be guided.
But we also need to be led forward in the
purposes of God in our time.

ROMANS 5:5 — MAY 24

The Goodness of Love

To receive love and to give love is one of the basic rhythms of life, providing of course that such love is not for self-gain, but is truly for the sake of the other. This kind of love is most clearly mirrored in Christ's love for us.

St. Clement, an early church father, in his letter *I Clement*, XLIX, speaks about this:

> Let those who have the love in Christ perform the commandments of Christ.
> Who is able to explain the bond of the love of God? Who can speak of the greatness of its beauty? The height to which love lifts us cannot be expressed.
> Love unites us to God. Love covers a multitude of sins. Love bears all things and endures all things.
> There is nothing immoral nor haughty in love. Love does not admit divisions, nor does it make offenses. Rather, love does all things in harmony.
> Without love, nothing is pleasing to God.
> In love, the master received us; because of his love for us, Jesus Christ our Lord gave his blood for us, by the will of God. He offered his flesh for our flesh, his soul for our souls.
>
> *The Apostolic Fathers*, vol. 1, 94–95

Reflection

Begotten in love.
Sustained in love.
Fruitful in love.

GALATIANS 6:1 — MAY 25

The Art of Gentleness

It is a strange irony that the Christian faith, which is based on the generous love of God, has Christians often dealing harshly with those who fail in some way.

In the writings of the Desert Fathers and Desert Mothers, we have this story of forgiving love:

> When Isaac of the Thebaid visited a community, he saw that one of the brothers was sinful and passed judgement on him. But when Abbot Isaac was returning to his cell in the desert, the angel of the Lord came and stood in front of the door of his cell, saying, 'I will not let you go in.'
>
> He asked, "Why not?" The angel of the Lord replied, "God sent me to ask you, Where do you command me to send that sinful brother whom you judged?"
>
> At once Isaac repented, saying, "I have sinned, forgive me."
>
> The angel said, "Get up, God has forgiven you. In the future, take care not to judge anyone before God has judged him."

The Desert Fathers: Sayings of the Early Christian Monks, 84

Reflection

"Thrice holy—Father, Spirit, Son,
Mysterious Godhead, Three in One,
Before your throne we sinners bend;
Grace, pardon, life to us extend."

2 SAMUEL 9:7 — MAY 26

Acts of Charity

Charity expressed in acts of kindness is to be freely extended to a person in need. Such acts bless the recipient, but they also reflect our humanity. Above all, such acts are a small expression of God's great generosity.

Deogratias, the bishop of Carthage, extended great kindness to captives brought from Rome to Carthage by the conquering Vandals:

> No sooner had he been made bishop than, since our sins demanded it, Gaiseric, in the fifteenth year of his reign, captured Rome, that once noble and famous city; and, at the same time, brought captive from thence the riches of many kings, with their peoples.
>
> When the multitude of captives reached the shore of Africa, the Vandals and Moors divided up the vast crowds of people; and, as is the way with barbarians, separated husbands from wives and children from parents. Immediately Deogratias, so full of God and so dear to him, set about to sell all the gold and silver vessels of service, and set them free from enslavement to the barbarians, in order that marriage might remain unbroken and children be restored to their parents.
>
> And since there were no places big enough to accommodate so large a multitude, he assigned two famous churches, the *Basilica Fausti* and the *Basilica Novarum,* furnishing them with beds and bedding, and arranging day by day how much each person should receive in proportion to his or her need.

Creeds, Councils, and Controversies, 360

Reflection

The holy things set aside for the service of God
may be used for the well-being of humanity.

GALATIANS 2:19–20　　　　　　　　　　　　　MAY 27

Identifying with the Crucified Christ

> *By faith we join with the crucified Christ to receive his gifts of salvation and healing. But we are also called to identify with the crucified Christ in worship and service.*

The fifteenth-century English laywoman Margery Kempe was a Christian visionary whose mystical experiences of the crucified Christ inspired popular religiosity. Here is part of an account of a vision she had in the Church of the Holy Sepulcher in Jerusalem and as they walked the *via dolorosa*.

> They were let in at evensong on one day and remained until evensong of the next day. Then the friars lifted up a cross and led the pilgrims to the places where our Lord suffered his passion, every man and woman bearing a wax candle in one's hand. And the friars always, as they went about, told them what our Lord suffered in every place.
>
> The aforesaid creature [Margery] wept and sobbed plenteously as if she had seen our Lord with her bodily eyes suffering his passion at that time. And when she came up on to the Mount of Calvary, she fell down because she could not stand or kneel ... and cried with a loud voice as though her heart would have burst apart. For in the city of her soul, she saw truly and vividly how our Lord was crucified. Before her face, she saw and heard the mourning of our Lady, of St. John and Mary Magdalene, and of many others that loved our Lord.
>
> She had such deep compassion and such great pain, at seeing our Lord's pain, that she could not keep herself from crying and roaring, even if she should have died for it.
>
> *The Book of Margery Kempe*, 104

Prayer

Lord, may I enter into your sufferings
and be purged by your grace.
Amen.

COLOSSIANS 2:2   MAY 28

Encouragement

While we are responsible for our journey in the life of faith, we do need encouragement and companions on the journey.

St. Francis, in a word of encouragement to St. Clare and her sisters, had this to say:

> Listen, little poor ones called by the Lord,
> Who have come together from many parts and provinces:
> Live always in truth, that you may die in obedience.
> Do not look at the life outside, for that of the Spirit is better.
>
> I beg you through great love, to use with discretion
> The alms which the Lord gives you.
> Those who are weighed down by sickness
> And the others who are wearied because of them,
> All of you: bear it in peace.
>
> For you will sell this fatigue at a very high price
> And each one of you will be crowned queen
> In heaven with the Virgin Mary.

Francis and Clare: The Complete Works, 40–41

Reflection

While our service is not done to receive rewards,
we will receive God's benediction.

JOHN 14:15-17   MAY 29

The God Within

The heart of the Christian faith is not belief in a God "out there," removed and distant. It is faith in the God within, the God who has drawn near to us in the Spirit.

The English medieval mystic, Walter Hilton, has this to say about the God within:

> This word *within* should be understood in the same way. It is commonly said that a soul should see our Lord *within all things*, and *within itself*. It is true that our Lord is *within* all creatures, but not in the way that a kernel is hidden within the shell of a nut, nor as a little bodily thing is contained within a bigger one.
>
> But he is within all creatures, holding and preserving them in their being, through the subtlety and power of his own blessed nature and invisible purity. For just as a thing that is most precious and most pure is hidden away deep within the interior, in the same way the nature of God, which is most precious, most pure, most righteous, and furthest from the material nature, is hidden within all things.
>
> Therefore, anyone who will seek God within must first forget all material things, including his or her own body, for all these things are on the outside. And they must also forget thinking about their own souls, but think instead on the uncreated nature, which is Jesus, who made them, gives life to them, holds them, and gives them reason, memory and love. Jesus is within them through his power and divine nature. This is what the soul must do when grace touches it, or else it will be of little use to seek Jesus or to find him within oneself or within all creatures.
>
> *The Scale (or Ladder) of Perfection*, 2.3.3

Thought

That God has made his home with us is a miracle and a mystery.
But we can live this mystery well
when we live all of life out of the presence of God.

JOHN 15:1–5　　　　　　　　　　　　　　　　　MAY 30

Pruning

The Christian life is about growth into Christ, growth in love and growth in service. But growth always involves pruning.

St. Catherine of Siena speaks about God's pruning work in us:

> Do you know what course I follow, once my servants have completely given themselves to the teaching of the gentle loving Word? I prune them, so that they will bear much fruit—cultivated fruit, not wild. Just as the gardener prunes the branch that is joined to the vine so that it will yield more and better wine, but cuts off and throws into the fire the branch that is barren, so do I the true gardener act.
>
> When my servants remain united to me I prune them with great suffering so that they will bear more and better fruit, and virtue will be proved in them. But those who bear no fruit are cut off and thrown into the fire.
>
> These are the true workers. They till their souls well, uprooting every selfish love, cultivating the soil of their love in me. They feed and tend the growth of the seed of grace that they received in holy baptism. And as they till their own vineyards, so they till their neighbours' as well, for they cannot do the one without the other ...
>
> You, then, are my workers. You have come from me, the supreme eternal gardener, and I have engrafted you onto the vine by making myself one with you.
>
> *Catherine of Siena: The Dialogue*, 24

Reflection

God is Savior and Lord and has his purposes with us,
even our growth and sanctification.
In this, God's heavy but gracious hand may be upon us.

HOSEA 2:19–20 MAY 31

Betrothed to Christ

Christ is our Savior, but he is also our "mother" in that he brings us forth to new life. And he is our "spouse" since we are bound to him in love.

The medieval Christian mystic Hildegard of Bingen expresses our being united to Christ in this way:

> Now, we call out to you,
> Bridegroom, Consoler,
> To you who redeemed us on the cross.
>
> Through your blood,
> We have been joined to you in betrothal,
> Refusing a husband,
> And choosing you, O Son of God.
>
> O most beautiful form,
> O sweetest fragrance
> Of the most delectable delights,
> We always sigh for you
> In this tear-filled exile.
> When can we see you?
> When can we stay with you?

The Personal Correspondence of Hildegard of Bingen, 170–71

Reflection

We are bound to you, O Christ, in faith and love.
May your Spirit ever sustain us in this special bond.

June

To Live in Wonder

God's deeds of creation and redemption are the wonders God has shown his people. And in the light of such wonders we wonder what God will yet do. Thus we live in hope and expectation.

Richard of St. Victor, in his *Mystical Ark*, has this to say about the grace and power of wonder:

> Now that these things have been said concerning the ecstasy of mind, which rises up from the greatness of devotion, it seems necessary to speak about that which is accustomed to rise up from the greatness of wonder. Who does not know that wonder takes its beginning when we discern something beyond hope and above expectation? And so when something begins to be seen that is scarcely possible to believe, the newness of the vision and of a thing that is scarcely believable is accustomed to lead to wonder of mind.
>
> Therefore pay attention to how suitably that ecstasy of mind, which takes its origin from wonder, is indicated in the place where it is said: "Who is she who comes forth like the dawn rising?" (Song 6:9). What is the dawn except new light mixed with darkness? And, I ask, from where does wonder come, except from an unexpected and incredible manifestation?
>
> And so wonder itself has sudden light mixed with darkness, a light of vision together with remnants of incredulity and the darkness of uncertainty. So in a marvellous manner, the mind undoubtedly sees what it is scarcely able to believe. But the more greatly we marvel at the newness of a thing, the more carefully we pay attention to it. The more attentively we look, the more fully we come to know.
>
> *The Twelve Patriarchs, The Mystical Ark, Book Three of the Trinity*, 322

Reflection

In the ordinariness of our mundane world,
we urgently need to recover our imagination based on the grace, love, and mercy of God.
In living this way, wonder will rise like morning mist.

JOHN 5:21   JUNE 2

The Great Life-Giver

Christ is the gift of God's new creation, the new Adam, the leader of the new humanity, the savior, healer and life-giver. In him we find life.

Bonaventure, in his *Tree of Life*, speaks of our attraction to Christ:

> Believing, hoping and loving
> With my whole heart, with my whole mind
> And with my whole strength,
> May I be carried to you, beloved Jesus,
> As the goal of all things,
> Because you alone are sufficient,
> You alone are good and pleasing to those who seek you and love your name.
> For you, my good Jesus, are the redeemer of the lost,
> The saviour of the redeemed, the hope of exiles,
> The strength of labourers, the sweet solace of anguished spirits,
> The crown and imperial dignity of the triumphant,
> The unique reward and joy of all the citizens of heaven,
> The renowned offspring of the supreme God . . . the abundant fountain of all graces.

The Soul's Journey into God, The Tree of Life, The Life of St. Francis, 173

Reflection

> You, O Lord, are not the carer for the special.
> You are the lover of all.
> Especially those at the margins of life,
> Can find solace with you.

EPHESIANS 1:17   JUNE 3

Intimacy with God

Intimacy with God is never simply a human project of attainment, even though we are called to seek God and to worship and obey him. Intimacy is much more the gift of the God who draws near.

Meister Eckhart, in his *Talks of Instruction*, speaks of God as everywhere and as close:

> Whoever has God truly as a companion is with him in all places, both on the street and among people, as well as in church or in the desert or in a monastic cell. . . . Why is this so? It is because such people possess God alone, keeping their gaze fixed upon God, and thus all things become God for them.
>
> Such people bear God in all their deeds and in all the places they go, and it is God alone who is the author of all their deeds . . .
>
> If we keep our eyes fixed on God alone, then truly he must work in us, and nothing, neither crowd nor any place, can hinder him in this. And so nothing will be able to hinder us, if we desire and seek God alone, and take pleasure in nothing else.

Quoted in Christian Mystics:
Their Lives and Legacies throughout the Ages, 110

Reflection

"God himself is present, let us now adore him
As with awe we now come before him.
God is in our midst, now in hearts keep silence,
Worshipping in deepest reverence."

JOHN 1:14   JUNE 4

The Incarnation

In the incarnation we bow before the mystery of the transcendent God, who not only draws close to us in acts of mercy and care, but becomes one of us in Christ through the Spirit. This radical identification is repeated in a small way when Christ comes to dwell within us and is furthered when, through prayer and service, Christ comes home in the lives of others.

In Meister Eckhart's *German Works*, he reflects on the great mystery of the incarnation:

> The greatest good that God ever performed for us was that he became man.
>
> I ought to tell a story now that is very apposite here. There was a rich husband and wife. Then the wife suffered a misfortune through which she lost an eye, and she was much distressed by this. Then her husband came to her and said: "Madam, why are you so distressed? You should not distress yourself so, because you have lost your eye."
>
> Then she said: "Sir, I am not distressing myself about the fact that I have lost my eye; what distresses me is that it seems to me that you will love me less because of it." Then he said: "Madam, I do love you." Not long after that, he gouged out one of his own eyes and came to his wife and said: "Madam, to make you believe that I love you, I have made myself like you; now I too have only one eye."
>
> This represents man, who could scarcely believe that God loved him so much, until God gouged out one of his own eyes and took upon himself human nature. This is what "being made flesh" (John 1:14) is. The mother of our Lord said: "How should this happen?" Then the angel said: "The Holy Spirit will come down from above into you" (Luke 1:34–35), from the highest throne, from the Father of eternal light.
>
> Meister Eckhart: The Essential Sermons, Commentaries, Treatises and Defense, 193

Reflection

So achingly close.
One of us.
But with power to save us.

PHILIPPIANS 4:8–9   JUNE 5

The Spiritual Virtues

The great challenge lies not only in the doing of good, but in becoming good. Growth in the spiritual virtues is a growth in the grace of God.

St. Francis of Assisi has written in praise of certain virtues that should adorn a Christian's life:

> The man or woman who possesses one of the virtues and does not offend the others possesses them all, but he or she who violates even one possesses none at all and violates them all.
>
> Each virtue routs vice and sin, covering them with confusion. Holy wisdom confounds Satan and all his malice. Pure holy simplicity confounds all the wisdom of this world and of the body. Holy poverty confounds cupidity, avarice and the cares of this life.
>
> Holy humility confounds all arrogance, all who live for this world, and likewise all the things that are of the world. Holy charity confounds all temptations of the flesh, the devil, and all fear of the flesh.
>
> Holy obedience confounds all corporal and carnal desires and keeps the body mortified, so that men and women may obey the spirit and obey their brothers and sisters, and be subject and submissive to all humankind—and not to men and women alone, but also to all animals and wild beasts, so that they can do with humankind what they will, so far as it is permitted to them by the Lord on high. Thanks be to God. Amen.
>
> *Late Medieval Mysticism*, 122

Reflection

"And all people of tender heart
Forgiving others, take your part, O sing ye, alleluia.
You who long pain and sorrow bear,
praise God and on him cast your care;
O praise him, O praise him, alleluia, alleluia, alleluia."

JOHN 15:16   JUNE 6

The Fruit of Christ's Passion

Christ's suffering and death on our behalf, for he was the sinless one, has brought us forgiveness and new life. May we who now bear the fruit of Christ's passion bear also the wounds of others to bring them life and hope.

St. Bernard of Clairvaux writes about the fruits of Christ's passion:

> We recognize the symbols of the Passion as the fruit of past ages—all the fruit that grew during the reign of sin and death (Gal 4:4). But in the new springtime of regenerating grace, the glory of the resurrection—fresh flowers of a later age—will come forth. Their fruit will be the general resurrection, which will be given without measure when time is no more. And so it is written, "The winter is past, the rain is over and gone, the flowers appear on the earth" (Song 2:11–12). This signifies that summer returns with him who dissolves icy death into the spring of a new life and says, "Behold, I make all things new" (Rev 21:5). His body was sown in the grave and blossomed anew in the resurrection (1 Cor 15:42). In the same way, our valleys and fields, which were barren and frozen and seemed dead, will glow with reviving life and warmth.
>
> The Father of Christ, who makes all things new, is well pleased with the freshness of those flowers and fruits and the beauty of the field that breathes forth such a heavenly fragrance. He says in benediction, "See, the smell of my Son is like the smell of a field that the Lord has blessed" (Gen 27:27). Blessed to overflowing, indeed, since we have all received of his fullness.
>
> *On Loving God*, ch. 3

Reflection

Christ renews humanity and the church and the whole creation.
In the new heavens and earth, this renewal will come to its completeness.

JOHN 6:35 — JUNE 7

Word and Sacrament

The word brings light in understanding and direction. It shows us the way. The Eucharist is the food that nourishes us in the journey of faith. Jesus is both the Living Word and the Living Bread.

Possibly one of the best-known writers on Christian spirituality, Thomas à Kempis, has this to say about word and sacrament:

> In this life, there are two things necessary to me above all others. Without them, this wretched life would be beyond bearing. Held in the prison of this body, I confess that I need two things: namely food and light.
>
> And so, in my weakness, you have given me your sacred body for the refreshment of my mind and body, and you have set your word as a lamp for my feet. Without these two, I could not live, for the word of God is light to my soul, and your sacrament is the bread of life.
>
> These can also be called two tables, placed on either side of the treasury of the holy church. One table is the holy altar, which holds the bread, the precious body of Christ. The other table is the divine law, which contains the holy doctrines that teach right faith and steadfastly lead us through the veil to the holy of holies.
>
> Thanks be to you, Lord Jesus, light of eternal light, for the table of holy doctrine, which you have provided for us through your servants, the prophets, the apostles and other teachers.
>
> *The Imitation of Christ* (Blaiklock), 209–10

Prayer

Lord, you accompany us and go before us with good gifts:
the gift of your Spirit, your word, and the sacraments.
We are blessed indeed!
We are sustained!
We are enriched!
Thank you. Amen.

EPHESIANS 3:14–19   JUNE 8

A Song of Our True Nature

We are not what we are but what we hope to be. Our true nature lies in what we hope for. And what we hope for has already been made manifest in the life of Jesus Christ.

Julian of Norwich sings this song of hope:

> Christ revealed our frailty and our falling,
> Our trespasses and our humiliations.
>
> Christ also revealed his blessed power,
> His blessed wisdom and love.
>
> He protects us as tenderly and as sweetly
> When we are in greatest need;
> He raises us in spirit
> And turns everything to glory and joy without ending.
>
> God is the ground and substance,
> The very essence of nature,
> God is the true father and mother of natures.
>
> We are all bound to God by nature,
> And we are all bound to God by grace.
> And this grace is for all the world,
> Because it is our precious mother, Christ.

Celebrating Common Prayer: A Version of the Daily Office SSF, 236

Reflection

Being bound to God is our greatest freedom.

2 CORINTHIANS 4:16–18   JUNE 9

Following the Suffering Christ

We would like to follow the Christ who showers us with benefits, but this Christ also calls us to suffering—not suffering of our own making, but suffering for the sake of the Kingdom of God.

In Meister Eckhart's *Book of Comfort*, he brings us this challenge in following Christ:

> There is still another consolation. St. Paul says that God chastises all whom he takes and receives as children. Thus it follows that to be a child of God, we should also suffer. Because the Son of God could not suffer in his godhead and in eternity, the heavenly Father sent him into time to become human so that he could suffer.
>
> If, then, you would like to be God's child and yet not suffer, you are very wrong. It is written in the Book of Wisdom that God examines and searches the just child as gold is proved in the burning of the furnace.
>
> When a king or prince trusts a knight well, he sends him into the combat. I have seen a lord who, when he had accepted someone among his followers, would send him out into the night and then attack him himself and fight with him. And once it happened that he was nearly killed by someone he meant to try in this way . . .
>
> We read that in the desert, St. Anthony had to suffer particularly bad temptations from the evil spirits, and when he had conquered his suffering, our Lord appeared visibly and joyfully. Then St. Anthony said: "Ah, dear Lord, where were you just now when I needed you so much?" Our Lord replied: "I was here, just as I am now, but I greatly desired to see how good you were."

Meister Eckhart, from Whom God Hid Nothing, 41

Reflection

Whatever God may have in mind
with our experience of life's difficulties, they come.
And testing and trials are part of the Christian's journey.
These things certainly shape us.

Proverbs 2:1–8 — June 10

Seeking Wisdom

The path of wisdom is no easy road. It is a journey to the heart of God through the pain of the world. It involves the inner transformations of the heart.

Bonaventure, in his *Mind's Road to God*, challenges us with the following:

> Therefore, first of all, I invite the reader to groaning prayer through Christ crucified, whose blood purges us from the stains of vices. I do so lest the reader think that reading is sufficient without heavenly anointing, or thinking without devotion, or investigating without admiration, or mere observation without rejoicing, or effort without piety, or knowledge without charity, intelligence without humility, endeavour without divine grace, the soul as mirror without divinely inspired wisdom.
>
> Therefore I am setting forth the following insights to those who have been prepared by divine grace, to the humble and faithful, to those with compunction and devotion, to those anointed "with the oil of gladness" (Ps 44:8), to the lovers of divine wisdom who are enflamed with its desire, to those wanting to be free to magnify the Lord, to be in awe of him, and even to taste him.
>
> I am suggesting that the mirror of the world, set forth outside, counts for little or nothing unless the mirror of our mind has been cleansed and polished. Rouse yourself up, then, child of God, first to the biting goad of conscience, before you lift your eyes up to the rays of wisdom reflected in its mirrors, lest by looking at these rays you perhaps fall into a deeper pit of darkness.
>
> *The Mind's Road to God*, 4–5

Prayer

Lord, inscribe your word in my heart and mind,
and may I see all things in its light.

Song of Solomon 8:6–7 — June 11

A Song to Love

> *While violence so often seems to reign in our world, and indifference is so often the habit we wear, the goodness of love can undo and outlast all things.*

The medieval mystic Marguerite Porete, who was burned at the stake in the Place de Greve for heresy, celebrated the power of love and its movement to union. In *The Mirror of Simple Souls* she writes,

> This Soul, says Love, swims in the sea of joy, that is, in the sea of delights that stream from divine influences. She feels no joy, for she herself is joy. She swims and drowns in joy, for she dwells in joy without feeling any joy.
>
> Joy is in her in such a way that she herself is joy, by the power of joy that has changed her into itself. Now the will of the beloved and the will of the Soul are turned into one, like fire and flame, for Love has turned the Soul entirely into himself.
>
> Ah, sweetest pure divine Love, says the Soul, what a sweet union this is, that has changed me into the thing that I love more than myself! I who can love so little have lost my own name for the sake of Love. Thus I am changed into the thing that I love more than myself, that is, into Love, for Love is all I love.
>
> *The Mirror of Simple Souls*, 48–49

Reflection

"O Love, how deep, how broad, how high!
It fills the heart with ecstasy
That God, the Son of God, should take
Our mortal form for mortal's sake."

MATTHEW 6:9–13   JUNE 12

The Lord's Prayer

> *In saying the Lord's prayer we are acknowledging a common Father, a common life and common needs. This prayer binds us together.*

St. John Chrysostom, in one of his homilies on Matthew's Gospel, has this to say about a dimension of the Lord's Prayer:

> Christ teaches, moreover, to make our prayer common, on behalf of our brothers and sisters also. For he does not say, "my Father, who art in heaven," but, "our Father," offering up his supplications for the body in common, and nowhere looking to his own, but everywhere to his neighbour's good.
>
> And by this he at once takes away hatred, quells pride, and casts out envy. And by this he also brings in the mother of all good things, which is charity, exterminating the inequality of human things, and showing how far the equality reaches between the king and the poor man, for if at least in those things which are greatest and most indispensable, we are all of us companions.
>
> For what harm comes to our kindred below, when in that which is on high we are all of us knit together, and no one ought to have more than another—neither the rich more than the poor, nor the master than the servant, neither the ruler than the subject, nor the king than the common soldier, nor the skilful than the unlearned?
>
> For to all he has given one nobility, having vouchsafed to be called the Father of all alike.
>
> *Nicene and Post-Nicene Fathers*, vol. 10, 134

Reflection

The grace of God in Christ is the great leveller. We are all its beneficiaries. Therefore, we are one, and beyond all social distinctions.

ROMANS 14:19 — JUNE 13

At Peace with One Another

Our relationship with God is to work itself out in our relationships with each other. One can't truly be at peace with God while not at peace with others.

One of the sayings of the Desert Fathers makes an important point regarding relationships in the faith community:

> Two hermits lived together for many years without a quarrel. One said to the other, "Let's have a quarrel with each other as other men do." The other answered, "I don't know how a quarrel happens."
>
> The first said, "Look here, I put a brick between us and say, 'That's mine.' Then you say, 'No, it's mine.' That's how you begin a quarrel."
>
> So they put the brick between them, and one of them said, "That's mine." The other said, "No; it's mine." He answered, "Yes it's yours. Take it away."
>
> They were unable to argue with each other.
>
> *The Desert Fathers: Sayings of the Early Christian Monks*, 182

Thought

If I hold what I have
With open hand,
I may freely give.
And another may freely take.

PSALM 90:10   JUNE 14

Our Troubled Existence

While some may hope that Christianity will give them the final answers and safety, the Christian journey calls us to something else. This is the journey of faith in the midst of life's difficulties and challenges.

St. Anselm gives this testimony about the challenge of a life of faith:

> Alas, unfortunate that I am,
> One of the miserable children of Eve, separated from God.
> What have I undertaken? What have I actually done?
> Where was I going? Where have I come to?
> To what was I aspiring? For what do I yearn?
> I sought goodness, and there is only confusion.
> I yearned for God, and I got in my own way.
> I sought peace within myself,
> and I have found tribulation and sadness in my heart of hearts.
> I wished to laugh for the joy in my soul,
> and the sobbing of my heart made me cry out.
> I hoped for gladness, but my sighs came thick and fast.

St. Anselm: The Major Works, 86

Reflection

The Christian's journey of faith is no smooth road.
And it is no continual picnic.
It is a journey of faith and failure, and of goodness and challenge.

MATTHEW 25:42-43 — JUNE 15

Care for the Sick

The Early Christians not only cared for their own who had needs or were sick, but they also cared for the needs of others. In this, they demonstrated the power of love and God's concern for all humanity.

St. Benedict, in his *Rule*, has this to say about care for the sick within the faith community:

> Care of the sick must rank above and before all else, so that the sick may be truly served as Christ. For he said: "I was sick and you visited me," and "What you did for one of these least brothers you did for me."
>
> Let the sick, on their part, remember that they are being served to honour God, and let them not distress their brothers and sisters who serve them by making excessive demands. Nevertheless, sick brothers and sisters must be patiently borne, for serving them leads to a greater reward. Consequently, the abbot should be extremely careful that the sick do not suffer neglect.
>
> Let a separate room be designated for the sick, and let them be served by an attendant who is God-fearing, attentive and concerned. The sick may take baths whenever it is advisable, but the healthy, and especially the young, should receive permission less readily. Moreover, to regain their strength, the sick who are very weak may eat meat, but when their health improves, they should abstain from meat as usual.
>
> The abbot must take the greatest care that cellarers and those who serve the sick do not neglect them, for the shortcomings of the disciples are his responsibility.
>
> *The Rule of Saint Benedict*, 38–39

Reflection

Our piety towards God must be matched
with our love and care for others.

ROMANS 1:18-23   JUNE 16

Life without God

The heart of the Christian story is to live with God as the centre of our lives. A de-throned God leads to a lost and warped life.

St. Catherine of Siena has this to say about living without God:

> Without me they could never be satisfied, even if they possessed the whole world. For created things are less than the human person. They were made for you, not you for them, and so they can never satisfy you. Only I can satisfy you. . . . Caught in such blindness, they are forever toiling but never satisfied. They long for what they cannot have because they will not ask it of me, though I could satisfy them.
>
> Do you want me to tell you why they suffer? You know that love always brings suffering if what a person has identified with is lost. These souls, in one way or another, have identified with the earth in their love, and so they have in fact become earth themselves. Some have identified with their wealth, some with their status, some with their children. Some lose me in their slavery to creatures. Some in their great indecency make brute beasts of their bodies. And so in one way and another they hunger for and feed on earth.
>
> They would like to be stable but are not. Indeed, they are passing as the wind, for either they themselves fail through death or my will deprives them of the very things they loved. They suffer unbearable pain in their loss. And the more disordered their love in possessing, the greater is their grief in loss. Had they held these things as lent to them, rather than as their own, they could let them go without pain. They suffer, because they do not have what they long for. For, as I told you, the world cannot satisfy them, and not being satisfied, they suffer.
>
> *Catherine of Siena: The Dialogue*, 98-99

Prayer

Lord, help me to live in the light of your grace
and not in the things I have or in what I may achieve. Amen.

PHILIPPIANS 1:29–30   JUNE 17

One with the Suffering Christ

Christ invites us to embrace his grace and blessings and his way of life. He invites us to enter in, to draw close, to be conformed to his likeness, to imitate him. Thus we are invited into his resurrection and his suffering.

Hadewijch, the thirteenth-century Beguine, speaks in her Letters of joining with Christ in his sufferings:

> Nowadays this is the way everyone loves himself or herself; people wish to live with God in consolations and repose, in wealth and power, and to share the fruition of his glory. We all indeed wish to be God with God, but God knows there are few of us who want to live as persons with his humanity, or want to carry his cross with him, or want to hang on the cross with him and pay humanity's debt to the full.
>
> Indeed, we can rightly discern this regarding ourselves, because we are not able to hold out against suffering in all respects. An unexpected sorrow, though slight, goes to our heart—or a slander, or a lie people tell about us, or someone's robbing us of our honor, or our rest, or our own will. How quickly and deeply any of this wounds us all! . . .
>
> By this we show plainly that we do not live with Christ as he lived; neither do we forsake all as Christ did; nor are we forsaken by all as Christ was. We can discern this in many ways: for we strain every nerve in our own interests . . . and we gladly seize our outward and inward advantages.
>
> *Hadewijch: The Complete Works*, 61

Reflection

I want my life and yours.
I want my benefit and your honor.
I have much to learn to be wholly yours.

Proverbs 2:7-8   June 18

God Our Protector

> *The faith community looks to God for grace but also for protection. Our prayer is always, Lord, guard our footsteps and keep us in your ways.*

One of the ancient Celtic prayers acknowledges God's sovereignty and cries out for God's protection:

> My God and my chief, I seek you in the morning.
> My God and my chief, I seek you this night.
> I am giving you my mind, I am giving you my will.
> I am giving you my wish,
> My soul everlasting and my body.
>
> May you be chieftain over me,
> May you be master unto me,
> May you be shepherd over me,
> May you be guardian unto me,
> May you be herdsman over me,
> May you be guide unto me,
> May you be with me, O chief of chiefs,
> Father everlasting and God of the heavens.
>
> *The Celtic Vision*, 30

Thought

To live and work and rest in the sheltering presence of the God of grace is to be sustained and protected in the love of the great Lover.

1 PETER 2:24–25 JUNE 19

The Power of the Cross of Christ

The cross of Christ seems to be Christ's failure, for he dies like a criminal. But his death has been the gateway of life for all who look to him for the forgiveness of sins, healing and the power to live a new life.

St. Irenaeus, in his *Demonstration of the Apostolic Preaching*, speaks about the significance of the cross of Christ:

> And the sin that came by the tree was undone by the tree of obedience. When out of obedience to God the Son of man was nailed to the tree, he put away the knowledge of evil and ushered in and established the knowledge of the good. Now evil is disobedience to God, and obedience to God is good.
>
> Therefore the word spoken by the prophet Isaiah announced beforehand that which was to come . . . "I refuse not, and gain nothing; I gave my back to scourging and my cheeks to smiting, and I did not turn my face away from the shame of spitting."
>
> So by obedience unto death, as he hung on the tree, he put away the old disobedience that was wrought in the tree. He is the Word of God Almighty, who in his invisible form is both in our midst and extended throughout the whole world, encompassing its length and breadth and height and depth. And by the Word of God, the whole universe is ordered and administered. In this universe, the Son of God was crucified, and the shape of his cross was imprinted on the whole universe, setting upon all visible things the sharing of his cross . . . in order to summon all that are scattered in every quarter to the knowledge of the Father.
>
> St. Irenaeus: *The Demonstration of the Apostolic Preaching*, 100–2

Reflection

Through the cross of Christ, a whole new humanity can emerge. He is the New Adam of us all.

GENESIS 1:27 　　　　　　　　　　　　　JUNE 20

Made in God's Image

At the heart of the biblical story lies the idea that in our seeking God, we are already on the way, because God has already drawn close to us in the creation.

St. Columbanus, in his *Sermons*, has this to say about God's work in us:

> What does the human race have in common with God? What does earth have in common with spirit? For God is spirit. It is a great honour that God bestowed on men and women the image of his eternity and the likeness of his character. Our likeness to God, if we can preserve it, is a great distinction, but it is a great damnation to defile the image of God.
>
> For if we prostitute what we have received from the breath of God and corrupt the blessing of our nature, then we distort our likeness to God and destroy its image within us. Yet if we use the virtues planted within our souls to a proper end, then we will be like God.
>
> So whatever virtues God sowed in us in our original state, he taught us in the commandments to restore them to him. This is the first: to love our Lord with the whole heart (cf. Matt 22:37), since he first loved us (cf. 1 John 4:10) from the beginning and before we were. For to love God is to restore his image.
>
> But they love God who observe his commands, for he said: "If you love me, keep my commands" (John 14:15). This is his commandment, a mutual love, according to the saying: "This is my command, that you love one another, as I have also loved you" (John 15:12). But true love is not in word only, but also in deed and in truth.
>
> *Sermons*, 11.1

Prayer

Lord, give me the grace of your Son and the power of your Spirit to live fully your mark upon my life—a mark present in my very humanity.
Amen.

JOHN 15:14–15   JUNE 21

Friendship with God

Grace moves us from enmity to friendship with God. This friendship is never our right, but is ever only God's surprising gift.

Julian of Norwich has this to say about our friendship with God:

> The greatest honour that a noble king or lord may give to a poor servant is to be friendly to him or her, sincerely and joyfully, both privately and in public. The poor man or woman might think, "How might this noble lord be kinder or honor me more than to show someone as simple as me this marvelous friendship? Indeed, it brings me more joy and pleasure than if he were to give me great gifts but present them in a haughty manner." It is the same way with the Lord Jesus and us. For as I see it, we have no greater joy than that he, who is the highest and mightiest, noblest and worthiest is also the lowest and meekest, friendliest and most considerate. Truly, this marvelous joy will be ours when we see him.
>
> His will for us is that we should seek him and trust him, rejoice and delight in him, as he comforts and consoles us with his grace and help until it becomes our true reality. For the fullest joy that we shall have, as I see it, is the marvelous consideration and friendliness of our Father, who is our Maker, in our Lord Jesus Christ, who is our brother and our Saviour.
>
> *Revelations of Divine Love* (Warrack), ch. 7

Prayer

Lord, may I ever live, serve, and dance
in the joy of this friendship.
Amen.

1 CORINTHIANS 15:42-44 JUNE 22

The Renewal of All Things

The Christian hope is the resurrection, in which all things will be made new. It is only then that all things will truly be well, whole and restored.

St. Augustine speaks of the restoration of what has been deformed or incomplete:

> Hence in the first place arises a question about abortive conceptions, which have indeed been born in the mother's womb, but not so born that they could be born again. For if we shall decide that these are to rise again, we cannot object to any conclusion that may be drawn in regard to those which are fully formed.
>
> Now who is there that is not rather disposed to think that unformed abortions perish, like seeds that have never fructified? But who will dare to deny, though he may dare to affirm that at the resurrection every defect in the form shall be supplied, so that the perfection which time would have brought shall not be wanting, any more than the blemishes which time did bring shall be present. In this way, the nature shall neither want anything suitable and in harmony with it that length of days would have added, nor be debased by the presence of anything of an opposite kind that length of days has added; but that what is not yet complete shall be completed, just as what has been injured shall be renewed.
>
> *Enchiridion on Faith, Hope, and Love*, 100-1

Reflection

We end our days not in completeness
But in imperfection and brokenness.
And so we trust that God will make all things new,
As we surrender ourselves to our last breath.

2 CORINTHIANS 4:7–12   JUNE 23

In the Midst of Great Trials

Faith is not well forged in the setting of a comfortable life, but is more truly shaped in the midst of difficulties and trials. Our ancient fore-fathers and mothers in the faith knew about this.

St. Basil, in one of his letters to the Alexandrians, has these words of consolation:

> I have already heard of the persecution in Alexandria and the rest of Egypt, and, as might be expected, I am deeply affected. I have observed the ingenuity of the devil's mode of warfare. When he saw that the church increased under the persecution of enemies and flourished all the more, he changed his plan. He no longer carries on an open warfare, but lays secret snares against us, hiding his hostility under the name which they bear, in order that we may both suffer like our fathers and mothers, and, at the same time, seem not to suffer for Christ's sake, because our persecutors too bear the name of Christians.
>
> With these thoughts for a long time, we sat still, dazed at the news of what had happened, for, in sober earnest, both our ears tingled on hearing of the shameless and inhuman heresy of your persecutors. They have reverenced neither age, nor services to society, nor people's affection. They have inflicted torture, ignominy and exile; they have plundered all the property they could find; they were careless alike of human condemnation and of the awful retribution to come at the hands of the righteous Judge.
>
> All this has amazed me and all but driven me out of my senses. To my reflections have been added this thought, too: can the Lord have wholly abandoned his churches? Has the last hour come, and is "the falling away" thus coming upon us, that now the lawless one "may be revealed, the son of perdition who opposes and exalts himself above all that is called God and is worshipped?"
>
> But if the temptation is for a season, bear it, you noble athletes of Christ. If the world is being delivered to complete and final destruction, let us not lose heart for the present, but let us await the revelation from heaven, and the manifestation of our great God and Saviour Jesus Christ.

Nicene and Post-Nicene Fathers, vol. 8, 203

MATTHEW 5:48   JUNE 24

Deification

The ancient Christian saying, God became man so that humans may become God, is a far too ambitious statement. Yet, we are to become more god-like through God's indwelling presence.

The unknown author of *The Cloud of Unknowing* talks about becoming god-like through the grace of Christ:

> When contemplation makes you one with God in spirit, love, and will, you're "above" yourself because you've only reached that state by grace and not by your own efforts. You're also "under" God then, even though contemplative prayer makes you one with God in spirit, no longer two. In this unity, which is the height of contemplation, you can be thought of as godlike, as Scripture says (John 10:34; Ps 82:6). Still, you're below God because he's naturally eternal and you're not. God has no beginning, but there was a time when you didn't even exist. You were nothing, and after you were made by God's power and God's love, you willfully chose sin, making yourself worse than nothing. We deserve no mercy, but through his grace, we are made godly. Our souls are joined to him in spirit with no separation, both here and in heaven's joy, forever. This is how, though you're one with him in grace, you're still infinitely inferior to him in nature.

The Cloud of Unknowing and Book of Privy Counsel, 150

Reflection

We are invited into a process of "Christification,"
in order that we may live a cruciform lifestyle to the glory of God
and the service of our neighbor.

PROVERBS 28:27   JUNE 25

Care for the Poor

> *Everywhere in the biblical story there is the call to care for the poor. This call is not to do a bit of charity, but for a life of generosity.*

St. John Chrysostom is well known for his commitment to orthodoxy, but he is equally the champion of *orthopraxis:* the doing of good, especially to the poor. Here is what he has to say:

> Let us, I say, suppose there are two persons (and I do not now speak of injuriousness, but as yet of honest wealth). And of these two, let the one get together money and sail on the sea, till the land, and find many other ways of merchandise. Although I know not quite, whether, by so doing, he can make honest gains; nevertheless let it . . . be granted that his gains are gotten with honesty . . . and that in all things connected with his wealth, there has been no injustice.
>
> But let the other one, possessing as much, sell fields, sell houses, and vessels of gold and silver, and give to the poor; let her supply what is needed, heal the sick, free such as are in straits; some let her deliver from bonds; others let her release that are in mines; these let her bring back from the noose; those, who are captives, let her rescue them from their punishment.
>
> Of whose side then would you be? And we have not as yet spoken of the future, but as yet of what is here. Of whose part then would you be? His that is gathering gold, or hers that is doing away with calamities? With him that is purchasing fields, or with her who is making herself a harbour of refuge for the human race?
>
> *Nicene and Post-Nicene Fathers*, vol. 10, 166

Thought

The practice of generosity and justice,
is a reflection of the generosity at the heart of the Trinity.

EZEKIEL 3:1–3　　　　　　　　　　　　　　　　　　JUNE 26

Tasting the Word

> *It is a well-known fact that contemporary Christians no longer seriously read Scripture. Yet we are invited to read it, meditate on it and absorb God's wisdom into the very fabric of our being.*

Bonaventure, in his witness to the life of St. Francis, has this to say about a love for Scripture:

> It was his habit to say the Psalms with his mind and spirit so attentive that he seemed to see God present before his eyes. When the name of the Lord occurred in the Psalms, he seemed to taste its sweetness on his very lips. He desired to honour reverently the name of the Lord, not only in thought, but also whenever it was spoken or written. At times, he would persuade the brothers to collect all papers with writing upon them and to place them in a clean place, so that if the sacred name happened to be written there, it would not be walked upon. When he uttered or heard the name of Jesus, he was filled with inner joy and seemed outwardly altered, as if a honey-sweet taste had soothed his palate, or he had some melodious sound his ear.
>
> *The Little Flowers and the Life of St. Francis, with the Mirror of Perfection*, 368

Reflection

"The rolling sun, the changing light,
And night and day, your power confess;
But the blessed volume of your word
Reveals your justice and your grace."

2 SAMUEL 22:29 — JUNE 27

Living in God's Dark Light

The most basic movement in the Christian life is from darkness to light, from sin into God's forgiveness. But there is also another movement, from grace and enlightenment into mystery.

The English mystic Walter Hilton has this to say about the blessedness of living in God's darkness:

> This darkness and night is so good and restful, even though it is short, for it consists only of a blind desiring and longing after the love of Jesus. How good, then, and how blessed it is to *feel* his love and to be illuminated with his blessed invisible light in order to see the truth. This is the light that a soul receives when the night passes and the day springs.
>
> As I see it, this was the night that the prophet meant when he said, "My soul has desired you in the night." As I have said before, it is much better to be hidden in this dark night and not looking at the world, even though it is painful, than to be out enjoying the false pleasures of this world, which seem to shine with such comfort to those who are blind to the knowledge of spiritual light.
>
> For when you are in this darkness, you are much nearer to Jerusalem than when you were in the midst of false light. Therefore, apply your heart fully to the stirrings of grace. Dwell in this darkness and try to become acquainted with it. It will soon become restful to you, and the true light of spiritual knowing shall rise to you: not all at once, but secretly, little by little.
>
> *The Scale (or Ladder) of Perfection,* 2.2.6

Reflection

In the false light of worldliness lies deception;
in the light of God's darkness lies wisdom.

PSALM 8:1-4   JUNE 28

God's Revelation

The God who is complete in fullness as Trinity is the God who nevertheless wishes to be known. As so in nature, Scripture, the affairs of human life, and in the mysterious workings of the Holy Spirit, God's will and way can be discerned in faith, hope, and love.

St. Augustine writes about God's ways of making himself known through the faith community:

> As a skin, you stretched out the firmament of your book, placing your words over us, in harmony, by the ministry of mortal men and women. By their deaths, the firmament of the authority in your words through them was elevated and stretched over all that lay below. While they lived, their authority did not reach as high, nor extend as far. You had not yet stretched out the heaven like a tent; you had not yet spread the fame of their death throughout the world.
>
> Let us see, O Lord, "the heavens, the work of your fingers" and clear away from our eyes the fog with which you have covered them. Your works declare your testimony, which gives wisdom even to the little ones. O my God, out of the mouths of babes and sucklings, perfect your praise. For we know no other book that so destroys our pride or breaks down those who resist reconciliation with you by justifying their sins.
>
> O Lord, I do not know any other writings so pure, none that have so powerfully persuaded me to confession and bent my neck to your yoke, inviting me to worship you for worship's sake alone. Help me in my submission to understand these words, O good Father, since you have established these things for those who submit to them.

Confessions, 268–69

Prayer

O Lord, speak to me in whatever you wish
in order that I may live in your presence and to your glory.
Amen.

ACTS 26:15–18 JUNE 29

Good and Evil

> *In the biblical narrative God alone is seen as good and the source of all good. What springs from the Evil One is a diversion that spawns barrenness.*

Hildegard of Bingen, in her *Causes and Cures*, has this to say about the work of God and that of Satan:

> But because Lucifer in his perverse will wished to elevate himself to nothingness, all that he wished to create was indeed nothing, and he fell into it and could not stand since he had no ground beneath him. Indeed, he had no height above him and no depth below him to prevent him from falling. But now, as he stretched forth to grasp at nothing, the inception of this action of stretching forth produced evil, and the evil caught fire within itself—although without any light or brightness and inflamed by his envy of God—and it rotated like a wheel turned only itself, and showed burning darkness within itself.
>
> In this way, good and evil fell apart: good did not touch evil, nor evil good. But God himself remained whole and perfect like a wheel; he remained the Father in goodness, because his fatherhood is full of his goodness. Therefore his fatherhood is very just and fully good, and at once both strong and stable; and seen in this measure, it is conceived as a wheel. Now this wheel is in some place, and there is something inside the wheel.
>
> Human creature, take a careful look at humankind! Each human being contains heaven and earth and all of creation, and yet remains one whole figure, and within every human being all things lie concealed.
>
> *Hildegard of Bingen: Selected Writings*, 94–95

Reflection

God's work is generative. It brings forth life and sustains all things. The work of the Evil One is degenerative. It brings forth chaos and death.

1 TIMOTHY 6:6–10 JUNE 30

Practices in the Community of Faith

Brought together in the love of Christ, Christians are called to practices that build up the community of faith and that express generosity and care.

The unknown author of the early Christian writing called the *Didache* challenges us about certain spiritual practices:

> My child, remember night and day the one who speaks the word of God to you, and honor him or her as you do the Lord. For wherever the lord's reign is spoken, there is the Lord. And seek out day by day the faces of the saints so that you may rest upon their words. Do not cause division, but rather seek to make peace between those who argue with one another. Judge righteously, and do not show favoritism when reproving transgressions. Do not waver in your decision making. Do not stretch forth of your hands to receive and then draw them back when it is time to give. If you earn anything by working with your hands, you shall give a portion for your sins. Do not hesitate to give, nor complain when you give, for you will know who is faithful to reward those who have been hired. Do not turn away from someone in need, but share everything with your brothers and sisters, and do not say that anything is your own. For if you share in what is immortal, how much more will you share in things that are mortal?
>
> *Didache*, ch. 4

Reflection

> Spiritual practices that build up the community of faith
>   are not certain bursts of enthusiasm,
>   but rather a way of life crafted in our very being.

July

GALATIANS 5:22–25   JULY 1

Living the Christian Virtues

The goal of being a Christian is to be Christlike. Christian virtues, therefore, are qualities and aspirations that are oriented towards Christ, flow from Christ and express Christ in our violent and unjust world.

St. Francis of Assisi, in his writing *The Admonitions*, spells out a vision of the virtuous person:

> Where there is charity and wisdom,
> there is neither fear nor ignorance.
> Where there is patience and humility,
> there is neither anger nor disturbance.
> Where there is poverty with joy,
> there is neither covetousness nor avarice.
> Where there is inner peace and meditation,
> there is neither anxiousness nor dissipation.
> Where there is fear of the Lord to guard the house,
> there the enemy cannot gain entry.
> Where there is mercy and discernment,
> there is neither excess nor hardness of heart.
>
> *The Admonitions of St. Francis*, XXVII

Reflection

Shaped by the Gospel
In the love of God
A way of life emerges
That spreads goodness
Rather than death-dealing practices.

ACTS 2:42–47   JULY 2

Christian Community

> *If the people of God are truly to be an icon of the Trinity, then they are called to a community where life and spirituality, celebration and service, and communion and sharing are intertwining themes.*

St. Basil, in his *Longer Rules*, has this to say about the power and witness of community:

> "I have learned," he says, "that a life lived in common with others is more useful for many purposes. In the first place, even in the matter of bodily needs, no man is sufficient to himself, but we require each other's aid in the provision of such things as are necessary to life. . . . In the solitary life what we have is useless to anyone else, and what we ourselves want cannot be supplied. . . . And further, the law of the love of Christ does not permit each one of us to regard his own things alone. For 'Love seeks not her own.' The life of complete seclusion has only one aim, that each may serve his own needs. But this is plainly opposed to the law of charity which the Apostle fulfilled, who sought not his own profit, but the profit of many, that they might be saved."

St. Basil and His Rule, 41

Reflection

In a life together the manifold love of God the Father,
the grace of Christ,
and the power of Spirit can most clearly shine forth.

PROVERBS 4:6   JULY 3

Love's Pain

There is great joy in love, but love also calls us to great suffering—suffering on behalf of the one whom one loves. This suffering for the sake of love produces true wisdom and compassion.

The thirteenth-century Christian mystic and poet Hadewijch celebrates the nature of love:

> God grant success to those who strive
> To please the will of love,
> Who for her sake gladly receive
> Great burdens and heavy weights,
> And who always endure on her account many sufferings,
> Of which they judge love worthy,
> I truly wish they should yet behold
> The wonders of love's wisdom.

Hadewijch: The Complete Works, 221

Prayer

O Lord, in your gift of love
you have wounded and bound me
to your will and way.
Help me to frolic in love's joy
and bear love's burdens.
Amen.

PSALM 119:13-16   JULY 4

Reading and Meditating on Scripture

The Word of God points us to the Living Word, Jesus Christ, who is the gateway into a life shaped by scripture and the creative sculpting of the Holy Spirit.

John Cassian, the great fifth-century writer on the monastic way of life, challenges us about reading Scripture:

> Therefore the series of holy scriptures should be diligently committed to memory and repeated ceaselessly. This continual meditation will bring two benefits. First, while the attention of the mind is occupied with reading and preparing the lessons, it cannot be snared by bad thoughts. Second, when we strive to commit the scriptures to memory through frequent repetition, we do not have the time to understand them, but once we are free from the distractions of all we do and see, particularly as we reflect on them in silence during our night-time meditation, we can ponder and understand them more fully.
>
> When we are at rest, plunged into the stupor of sleep, the most secret meanings are revealed to us, even though we did not even remotely conceive of these while we were awake.
>
> As our souls are renewed by this study, scripture will begin to take on a new face, and the beauty of the holier meanings will grow within us.
>
> *The Conferences of John Cassian,* 14.10–11

Thought

We are invited to read the word of God, but it should also read us.

PSALM 91:9–12   JULY 5

God's Beneficence

In the biblical story God's power and transcendence is such that he nevertheless is mindful of us, and his goodness and protection is ever towards all he has created.

Meilyr Son of Gwalchmai's poem "Ode to God" speaks of God's power and goodness:

> And may heaven's King protect me from error;
> May his gift and his understanding cure my faults.
> May God, who is flawless, not destroy me;
> Undarkened is the mind that praises him,
> Undeceived is the love that loves him,
> Unblemished glory for all who believe in him.
>
> May God, creator and ruler, guide me till judgment,
> May he desire the ways of sinlessness for me,
> And may it be his majestic desire to give me
> Bright gifts that can purify me:
> May rites of remission accompany my end,
> And gifts of counsel guide me.

Celtic Spirituality, 280

Prayer

May God uphold me.
May Christ enfold me.
May the Spirit renew me.
May friends accompany me.
May the community of faith nurture me.

God's Strange Ways

God is wholly other and therefore mysterious in his being and unfathomable in his ways. We entrust ourselves to him, but his ways with us will always be a journey of faith.

St. John Chrysostom describes something of God's mysterious way with us. He writes,

> Knowing therefore that God is more tenderly loving than all physicians, do not enquire too curiously concerning his treatment, nor demand an account of it from him, but whether he is pleased to let us go free or whether he punishes, let us offer ourselves alike. For he seeks by means of each to lead us back to health, and to communion with himself, and he knows our several needs, and what is expedient for each one, and how and in what manner we ought to be saved, and along that path he leads us.
>
> Let us then follow wherever he bids us, and let us not too carefully consider whether he commands us to go by a smooth and easy path, or by a difficult and rugged one, as is the case of the paralytic. It was one species of benefit, indeed, that his soul should be purged by the long duration of his suffering, being delivered to the fiery trial of affliction as to a kind of furnace; but it was another benefit no less than this that God was present with him in the midst of the trials, and afforded him great consolation. He it was who strengthened him, upheld him, stretched forth a hand to him, and suffered him not to fall.
>
> *Nicene and Post-Nicene Fathers*, vol. 9, 212

Reflection

That God does all things well in his wondrous and difficult ways with us calls us to the most precarious journey of faith.

PROVERBS 30:8   JULY 7

Moderation

Sometimes religion is seen as a form of extremism. Sometimes it is seen as puerile and anemic. But religious experience should express itself as passion in moderation within the framework of love.

The unknown author of *The Cloud of Unknowing* has this to say about moderation:

> Now if you ask me what discretion you should exercise in the work of contemplation, my answer is, "None whatever!" In everything else you do, you have to use your own discretion, as, for example, in the matter of food and drink and sleep and keeping warm or cool, the time you spend in praying or reading and your conversations with your fellow Christians. In all these you have to use discretion, so that they are neither too much nor too little. But in this work, cast discretion to the wind! I want you to never give this work up as long as you live.
>
> I am not saying you will always come to it fresh, for that can never be. Sometimes illness, or some other affliction of body or soul, or some other natural necessity will hinder you and prevent you from contemplating. But you should always be at this work, both "on duty" and "off," in intention if not in reality. For the love of God, avoid illness as much as you can, so that as much as possible you are not responsible for any weakness. I tell you the truth when I say that this work demands great serenity and an integrated and pure disposition in soul and in body.
>
> So for the love of God, control your body and soul alike with great care and keep as fit as you can.
>
> *The Cloud of Unknowing and Other Works*, 108–9

Reflection

Love of God, self, and neighbor nurtured in prayer
can be a sustainable love.

ZEPHANIAH 2:3 — JULY 8

God's Call to Humility

Our culture calls us to self-assertion and achievement. Scripture calls us to creativity and action from a posture of having first listened to the voice of God. This willingness to listen is the heartbeat of humility.

St. Gregory VII, the eleventh-century pope, wrote the following about humility in a letter to the Bishop of Metz:

> We refer to those kings and emperors who have been swollen by worldly glory and do not rule for God but for themselves. Because it is the duty of our office to exhort and admonish each person according to rank or dignity, God's grace impels us to arm emperors, kings and other princes with the weapons of humility so that they may be able to subdue the waves and floods of pride. For we know that earthly glory and worldly cares induce pride, especially those who are in authority, so that they neglect humility and seek their own glory, always desiring to dominate their brothers and sisters. Therefore, when kings and emperors exalt themselves and delight in their own glory, it is beneficial for them to seek a means of humbling themselves and recognizing that what they have been rejoicing in should be feared above all else. Let them diligently consider the perils of royal and imperial dignity. For few who enjoy it are saved; and those who, through the mercy of God, come to salvation are not as glorified in the holy church and in the judgment of the Holy Spirit as many poor people.

Letter of Gregory VII to Bishop Hermann of Metz, March 15, 1081

Reflection

The grace of God does not recognize status,
but only the seeking heart marked by humility.

ISAIAH 53:4-6 — JULY 9

Identifying with the Suffering Christ

While the mystics often gazed at an image of the suffering Christ, and in this way sought identification, there are other ways to identify with Christ. One way is to enter into a radical identification with Christ's way and thus incur suffering as he did.

Julian of Norwich writes of a vision of the suffering Christ:

> This revelation of Christ's pain filled me full of pains. Though I know that he suffered only once, it seemed to be his will to show it to me and to fill my mind with it, as I had asked.
>
> While Christ was present to me, I felt no pain except for Christ's pains. And I thought to myself that I had little known the pain I had asked for; and wretch that I am, I regretted it, thinking that if I had known what it would be, I should have hesitated asking for it.
>
> For it seemed to me that my pains exceeded any mortal death. I wondered if there was any pain in hell like this pain. And my reason answered, "Hell is a different pain, for in it there is despair. But of all the pains that lead to salvation, this is the greatest: to see the lover suffer. How could any pain be greater than to see him suffer, who is all my life, my bliss, and all my joy?"
>
> Here I felt unshakably that I loved Christ so much more than myself, and that no pain could be compared with the sorrow I felt in seeing him in pain.
>
> *Showings*, 209

Prayer

Lord, your suffering was for the life of the world.
Help me, blessed by your suffering,
to suffer for others so that your renewing life may come to them.
Amen.

PROVERBS 19:11 — JULY 10

Long-Suffering and Patience

In our modern world we know little of patience. Things have to happen immediately. Though in the journey of faith there may be dramatic moments, so much of the journey is a slow unfolding.

One of the Desert Fathers gave this advice to a fellow monk about the long journey of faith:

> Theodore of Pherme was once consulted by a hermit brother who was troubled in his solitude. Theodore advised him to try returning to cenobitic [monastic] life for the sake of humility and obedience.
>
> But the brother returned and confessed that he was no more at peace with others as when alone.
>
> A conversation ensued, with Theodore asking the young brother: "If you are not at peace whether you are alone or with others, why have you become a monk? Is it not to suffer trials? Tell me, how many years have you worn the habit?"
>
> He replied, "For eight years."
>
> Then the old man said to him, "I have worn the habit seventy years and not for one day have I found peace. Do you expect to obtain peace in eight years?"
>
> "The Desert Fathers and Mothers on Solitude," 92–93

Reflection

There is no conclusion in the life of faith.
There are only ongoing cries for mercy.
There is no perfection in this life.
There is only the triumph of grace.

EXODUS 13:21   JULY 11

God the Guide

Life's journey is precarious. A lot happens that is outside of our control. Things happen to us that we least expect. Thus we need God to protect us and guide us through rough waters and on rocky roads.

Here is a prayer from the Celtic tradition in the *Carmina Gadelica* that speaks about God as guide:

> Be a smooth way before me,
> Be a guiding star above me,
> Be a keen eye behind me,
> This day, this night, forever.
>
> I am weary and forlorn,
> Lead me to the land of the angels;
> I think it is time I went for a space
> To the court of Christ, to the place of heaven;
>
> If only you, O God of life,
> Be at peace with me, be my support,
> Be to me a star, be to me as a helm,
> From my lying down in peace to my rising anew.

The Celtic Vision, 150

Thought

We tell God our needs. But in faith we also tell God what we believe he will do for us.

2 CORINTHIANS 3:17-18 — JULY 12

A Fuller Spirituality

We can so easily settle for less in the spiritual life. We seem to be drawn to mediocrity. But the Spirit always seeks to draw us into a fuller life in Christ.

The English mystic Richard Rolle, in *I Sleep and the Soul Wakes*, has this to say about growing into a fuller spirituality:

> But when you have lived fully by the commandments of God and have strictly kept yourself from all mortal sins and have pleased God in that degree of love, then decide that you will love God yet more and do better for your soul and become perfect. Then you will enter the second degree of love, which is to give up the whole world, your father and mother and all your relatives, to follow Christ in poverty.
>
> In this second degree, you must make every effort to be pure in heart and chaste in body, dedicating yourself to simplicity, endurance and obedience, to see how beautiful you can make your soul with virtue, detesting all moral weakness, so that all your life will become spiritual instead of physical.
>
> Do not speak harm about those around you, nor return any unkind word for another, but tolerate everything patiently in your heart without showing any anger. In this way, you will experience peace, interior and exterior, and will come to a spiritual life, which you will find sweeter than anything on earth.
>
> *The English Writings*, 136

Thought

Growth in spirituality is the work of the Spirit, is birthed in grace, and is the effort of seeking to please God with a grateful heart.

ACTS 7:59-60   JULY 13

The Power of Forgiveness

To forgive those who have wronged us is to resonate with the heartbeat of Christ. The power of forgiveness frees the perpetrator for repentance and opens the recipient to grace and healing.

St. Anselm, in his reflection on Stephen's martyrdom, utters this prayer:

> When those who in their folly were your enemies
> pressed upon you, O friend of God,
> this is what the truth of scripture testifies—
> on your knees you cried with a loud voice, "Lord, lay it not to their charge."
> O heart, rich with the treasures of charity,
> from which when it was afflicted, such copious mercy poured!
> O mind, vehemently ablaze with love,
> filled with the oil of charity,
> from which when it was in tribulation such sparks shone,
> sweetly burning and burning with sweetness!
> O honeycomb, rich with the honey of love, from which when it was pressed
> such rich and joyous drops were distilled!

The Prayers and Meditations of Saint Anselm with the Proslogion, 178

Reflection

The blessing of forgiveness
Is the gift
To live again
In joy and freedom.

1 THESSALONIANS 5:16–18   JULY 14

A Life of Prayer

Prayer is a form of surrender to the mystery of God's existence and God's way with us. As such, prayer is a life of faith, the cry of the heart, a longing for what is yet possible in the Spirit.

Jacques de Vitry, in his biography *The Life of St. Mary of Oignies*, speaks of Mary's life of prayer:

> When she had debilitated her body by fasting, her spirit was freed and fattened with prayer. The more she weakened her body by fasting, the more her soul was strengthened by the Lord. She obtained so many special graces from the Lord that day and night her spirit did not relax from prayer. She prayed without ceasing, crying to the Lord with a silent heart, or expressing the longings of her heart in words, sending up the fragrant smoke of her prayers continually to the altar of the Lord. As she worked with her hands, clasping the spindle with her fingers, a psalter was placed before her so that she could lovingly recite psalms to the Lord.
>
> In this way, she fastened her heart to God with strong nails in order to keep it from wandering astray. And when she prayed for someone in particular, the Lord replied to her in her spirit. For her spirit was fastened to the Lord with the fat of devotion, and she grew sleek in prayer when the Lord granted her petitions, and she often knew whether the Lord had heard her or not by the elevation or depression of her spirit.

The Life of Marie d'Oignies, 25–26

Reflection

Prayer on behalf of others is a grace that benefits others through the quiet hiddenness of the person called to such self-sacrifice. Such prayers are part of the hidden mystery of human affairs.

DEUTERONOMY 10:12-13 — JULY 15

The Paths of Love

The way of love is no smooth path. It is full of hope, but marked with disappointments. It is strong in its commitment, but it wavers with the vicissitudes of life. It is full of kindness, but has to drink the bitter cup of suffering.

The medieval mystic and poet Hadewijch writes about the nature of love:

> Sometimes burning and sometimes cold,
> Sometimes timid and sometimes bold,
> The whims of love are manifold . . .
>
> Sometimes gracious and sometimes cruel,
> Sometimes far and sometimes near . . .
> Sometimes light, and sometimes heavy,
> Sometimes sombre and sometimes bright.
>
> In freeing consolation, in stifling anguish,
> In taking and in giving,
> Thus live the spirits
> Who wander here below,
> Along the paths of love.

> Quoted in *Christian Mystics:
> Their Lives and Legacies throughout the Ages*, 100

Prayer

Lord, help me to live the joys and the burdens of love.
Amen.

1 TIMOTHY 4:9–10 — JULY 16

The Way of Christ

Christianity in history has not always had a good track record. There have been times of intolerance and acts of violence. If only we had followed the way of Christ, these things would not have happened.

Hippolytus, one of the key theologians of the third century, in his *Treatise on Christ and the Antichrist*, has this to say about the way of Jesus:

> Do you wish then to know in what manner the Word of God, who was again the Son of God, as he was of old the Word, communicated his revelations to the blessed prophets in former times? Well, as the Word shows his compassion and his denial of all respect of persons by all the saints, he enlightens them and adapts them to that which is advantageous for us, like a skilful physician, understanding the weakness of men and women. The ignorant he loves to teach, and the erring he turns again to his own true way. And by those who live by faith, he is easily found; and to those of pure eye and holy heart, who desire to knock at the door, he opens immediately, for he regards none of his servants as unworthy of the divine mysteries.
>
> He does not esteem the rich man more highly than the poor, nor does he despise the poor man for his poverty. He does not disdain the barbarian, nor does he set the eunuch aside as no man. He does not hate the female on account of the woman's act of disobedience in the beginning, nor does he reject the male on account of man's transgression. But he seeks all, and desires to save all, wishing to make all the children of God, and calling all the saints unto one perfect Son of Man.
>
> *The Ante-Nicene Fathers*, vol. 5, 205

Reflection

In the wide love of Christ all can find healing and shelter.

1 KINGS 19:11–13   JULY 17

God the Divine Whisperer

God speaks to us in many ways. While we may expect that God should shout at us, God far more often whispers his wisdom to us.

Gregory the Great, in his commentary on Job, points out something of God's way of gaining our attention:

> At one time he pierces us with love and at another time with terror. Sometimes he shows us how little the present reality of things is and lifts up our hearts to desire the eternal world. Sometimes he first points out the things of eternity so that in time all worldly things may become worthless in our eyes. Sometimes he discloses our evil deeds and then leads us to feel sorrow for the evil deeds of others. Sometimes he shows us the evil deeds of others and pierces us with compunction, thereby reforming our own wickedness. Thus to "hear the veins of divine whispering by stealth" is to know the gentle and secret methods of divine inspiration.
>
> Yet we may interpret "the veins of whispering" in another way. For the one who "whispers" is speaking in secret, imitating a voice. Therefore, as long as we are threatened by the corruptions of the flesh, we cannot behold the brightness of the divine power as it abides unchanging in itself. For in the eyes of our weakness, we cannot endure the brilliant luster that shines from the ray of God's eternal being. When the Almighty shows himself to us by the chinks of contemplation, he does not speak to us, but rather whispers. Though he does not make himself fully known, he reveals something of himself to the human mind.
>
> *The Book of Morals*, 5.51–52

Reflection

God's way with us is through his love
and must be received in faith and wonder.

PHILIPPIANS 3:10-11   JULY 18

Following Christ

While we may often think that following Christ is a perilous duty, it is, instead, an act of love and a source of joy.

Bonaventure, in his *Life of St. Francis*, spells out something of St. Francis' inspiration in following Christ:

> In the fervent fire of his charity
> he strove to emulate
> the glorious triumph of the holy martyrs
> in whom
> the flame of love could not be extinguished
> nor courage be weakened.
> Set on fire, therefore, by that perfect charity
> which drives out fear,
> he longed to offer to the Lord his own life as a living sacrifice
> in the flames of martyrdom
> so he might repay Christ, who died for us,
> and inspire others to divine love.
>
> *The Life of St. Francis, 97–98*

Meditation

Where in my life lie the seeds of holy passion that need to spring up in the following of Christ and in the service of his reign of peace.

EZEKIEL 34:7-11   JULY 19

Servants of the People of God

> *It matters little whether one's title is priest, prophet, pastor, elder, or bishop. All of us are part of the one people of God. No one is higher or greater than the other in the community of faith. But all are called to serve and be a blessing in the household of faith.*

St. Catherine of Siena spells out the calling and responsibility of those who are called to leadership in the church. She casts this in the voice of Christ speaking:

> So you see, the soul's powers have taken on the qualities of the sun. In other words, once these powers have been filled and clothed with me, the true sun, they behave as the sun does. The sun warms and enlightens, and with its heat makes the earth bring forth fruit. So also these gentle ministers of mine, whom I chose and anointed and sent into the mystical body of holy church to be stewards of me, the sun, that is, of the body and blood of my only-begotten Son, along with the other sacraments that draw life from this blood.
>
> They administer it both actually and spiritually by giving off within the mystical body of the holy church the brightness of supernatural learning, the colour of a holy and honourable life in following the teaching of my truth, and the warmth of blazing charity. Thus with their warmth they cause barren souls to bring forth fruit and enlighten them with the brightness of learning. By their holy and well-ordered lives they drive out the dark shadows of deadly sin and unfaithfulness, and they set in order the lives of those who had been living disordered lives in the darkness of sin and the cold that came of their lack of charity. So see how these ministers of mine are suns, because they have taken on the qualities of me, the true sun.
>
> *Dialogue of Catherine of Siena*, 4.4.28

Prayer

Lord, may all your people be penetrated by your light and grace,
and may we radiate your beauty and goodness.
May this be especially true of all in positions of leadership in your church.
Amen.

PSALM 4:4 — JULY 20

Self-Insight

Insight into the ways of God is related to self-insight. While God may reveal himself to us, we need to embrace that revelation by acknowledging our own need, blindness and brokenness.

The unknown author of the *Theologica Germanica* has this to say about the importance of self-insight:

> Therefore, although it is good and profitable that we should ask and learn and know what good and holy men and women have wrought and suffered, and likewise what God has willed and wrought in and through them, yet were it a thousand times better that we should, in ourselves, learn and perceive and understand who we are, how and what our life is, what God is in us and how he works in us, and to what ends he will or will not make use of us.
>
> For wholly to know oneself in the truth is above all learning: it is the highest learning. If you know yourself well, you are better and more praiseworthy before God than if you did not know yourself, but knew the course of the heavens and all planets and stars, the virtue of all herbs, and the bodily and intellectual frame of all humankind, the nature of all beasts, and had further all the arts of all who are in heaven and on earth.
>
> For it is said, there came a voice from heaven, saying, "Humankind, know yourself."
>
> *Late Medieval Mysticism*, 330

Reflection

The light of God is a two-way mirror.
I see the God of all grace.
I see myself as welcomed home.
I see God's smiling face.

1 CORINTHIANS 12:4–11   JULY 21

The Gift-Giving Spirit

> *The greatest gift is the Holy Spirit. The life-giving and empowering Spirit does not come empty handed, but bears graces and gifts for us. These gifts are not badges of our spirituality, but rather blessings that enable us to bless others.*

St. Cyril of Jerusalem sounds like a contemporary Pentecostal when he speaks about the gifts of the Spirit. Yet he speaks of how the Spirit enables Christians to suffer for Christ, a theme that is surely lacking in many of our churches. He writes,

> Thus also the Holy Spirit, being one and of one nature and indivisible, divides his grace to each "according to his will" (1 Cor 12:11).
>
> As the dry tree, after partaking of water, puts forth shoots, so also the soul in sin, when it has been made worthy of the Holy Spirit through repentance, brings forth clusters of righteousness.
>
> Though the Spirit is one in nature, he works many virtues by the will of God and in the name of Christ. He employs the tongue of one person for wisdom; the soul of another he enlightens by prophecy; to another he gives power to drive away devils; to another he gives interpretation of the divine scriptures.
>
> He strengthens one person's self-control; he teaches another to give alms; . . . another he trains for martyrdom.
>
> *The Holy Spirit. Message of the Church Fathers*, vol. 3, 94

Reflection

The gift of Father and Son.
The in-dwelling companion.
The beautifier and empowerer.

EXODUS 23:20   JULY 22

A Guardian Angel

In our so-called sophisticated and rationalistic world, both demons and angels have been eliminated from our consciousness and world. But angels are there to assist us. So maybe we should once again open the windows of our heart.

One of the prayers from the *Carmina Gadelica* is a prayer to Michael of the Angels:

> O Michael of the angels
> And the righteous in heaven,
> Shield my soul
> With the shade of your wing;
> Shield my soul on earth and in heaven;
>
> From foes upon the earth,
> From foes beneath the earth,
> From foes in concealment
> Protect and encircle my soul beneath your wing,
> Oh, my soul, with the shade of your wing!

The Celtic Vision, 204

Reflection

You are my true home
O Father, Son and Spirit.
In the beauty of your love
I am loved
And I can love.

LEVITICUS 19:16 JULY 23

Slandering

It is easy to speak badly about other people. Worse, we can defame others and besmudge their names and reputations. Instead, we should speak well of others.

St. John Chrysostom, in one of his homilies, addresses the issue of slander:

> For it is not those that are slandered, but the slanderers, that need to be anxious and to tremble. For the former are not constrained to answer for themselves touching the evil things which are said of them, but the latter will, for the evil they have spoken; and over these impends the whole danger.
>
> So that the persons censured should be without anxiety, not being to give account of the evil that others have said; but the censurers have cause to be in anxiety, and to tremble, as being themselves to be dragged before the judgment seat on that account.
>
> For this is indeed a diabolical snare, and a sin having in it no pleasure, but harm only. Yes, and such a one is laying up an evil treasure in his or her soul. And if the one that has an evil humour within does first reap the fruits of the malady, much more the one that is treasuring up within what is more bitter than bile, for wickedness will suffer the utmost evils, gathering unto himself or herself a grievous disease. . . . Thus the plotter destroys himself or herself first.
>
> *Nicene and Post-Nicene Fathers*, vol. 10, 270

Prayer

Lord, grant me a good, loving, forgiving, and generous heart.
Help me to speak about others out of such a heart, or let me fall silent.
Amen.

PSALM 145:3 — JULY 24

God's Beauty and Greatness

The greatness and power of God is a greatness that gives and a power that empowers. Both are expressed in a beauty that cares and fructifies. Therefore God is not to be feared. Rather, we can bask in God's love.

Hilary of Poitiers (c. 300–c. 367) became bishop of Poitiers in 350. His main writing is on the Trinity, where he touches on God's beauty and greatness.

> But if we can estimate this beauty of the universe by natural instinct ... must not the Lord of this universal beauty be recognized as the most beautiful amidst all the beauty that surrounds him? For even though the splendour of his eternal glory overwhelms our minds, we cannot fail to recognize that he is beautiful ...
>
> Thus my mind, filled with the fruits of reflection and the teachings of Scripture, rests with assurance, as on some peaceful watchtower ... in the conviction that his greatness is too vast for our comprehension, but not for our faith.
>
> *Nicene and Post-Nicene Fathers*, vol. 9, 42

Reflection

God's greatness and power
spoke a world into being.
God's searching love
became the Man of Nazareth.
God's beauty
is the unbounded Spirit.

MARK 14:3–9   JULY 25

Loving the Jesus Who Forgives

We do not come to Jesus to become heroic followers. Rather, we come to Jesus to be forgiven sinners. We follow the One who heals us. We serve the One who makes us whole.

Bonaventure, in his *Tree of Life*, invites us into this kind of following of Jesus:

> Like Matthew, therefore
> follow this most devoted shepherd;
> like Zacchaeus
> receive him with hospitality;
> like the sinful woman
> anoint him with ointment
> and wash his feet with your tears,
> and wipe them with your hair
> and caress them with your kisses,
> so that finally,
> with the woman presented to him for judgment,
> you may deserve to hear
> the sentence of forgiveness:
> "Has no one condemned you? Neither will I condemn you.
> Go, and sin no more."

The Soul's Journey into God, The Tree of Life, The Life of St. Francis, 137

Reflection

We come to Christ as sinners seeking forgiveness,
the blind seeking sight, the broken seeking healing, and the wayward coming home.

1 CORINTHIANS 12:4–6   JULY 26

God's Varied Ways of Working

In the creation we see God's amazing creativity and diversity. In human affairs God works in multiple ways. And in the community of faith, God has imparted varied gifts and uses us in a variety of ways.

The fourteenth-century Christian mystic, Bridget of Sweden, in her *Liber Celestis*, has this to say about God's differing ways of working:

> Nevertheless I will receive anyone who turns humbly to me, and anyone who does the work of righteousness shall gain me. For it is right that the house which the king will enter should be cleaned, and a glass cleaned so that the drink will show through it; and the more quickly wheat is separated from chaff the sooner the bread will be made.
>
> And then, just as summer follows winter, so I shall send comfort after tribulation to those who are humble and long for heavenly things. And I shall treat some according to the proverb: "Smite someone on the neck and he or she will run," for tribulation will make a man or woman exert himself or herself.
>
> And I will treat some according to the saying: "Open your mouth and I will fill it." And to some I will say, "Come, you simple laity, and I will give you such words and such wisdom that the greatest speakers will not be able to stand up to you." And I have done thus in these days. And great men and women have suddenly passed away because they would not do my bidding.

Medieval Writings on Female Spirituality, 161

Prayer

Lord, grant that in all your ways with me,
I may in faith and trust believe that you know the way I should go
and you know what is best for me.
Amen.

2 Timothy 4:9–11   July 27

Consolation

The Christian journey is not a solo walk, but is about having companions on the journey. Not only has God promised to be with us, but we also need our brothers and sisters to be there for us.

St. Basil, in one of his letters, speaks about the importance of human encouragement and support:

> May the Lord, who brought me prompt help in my afflictions, grant you the help of the refreshment with which you have refreshed me by writing to me, rewarding you for your consolation of my humble self with the real and great gladness of the Spirit. For I was indeed downcast in soul when I saw in the great multitude the almost brutish and unreasonable insensibility of the people . . . and the unsatisfactory nature of their leaders.
>
> But I saw your letter; I saw the treasure of love which it contained; then I knew that he who ordains all our lives had made some sweet consolation shine on me in the bitterness of my life. I therefore salute your holiness in return, and exhort you not to cease to pray for my unhappy life, that I may never, drowned in the unrealities of this world, forget God, "who raises up the poor out of the dust," that I may never be lifted up with pride and fall into the condemnation of the devil; that I may never be found by the Lord neglectful of my stewardship and asleep; never discharging it amiss, and wounding the conscience of my fellow-servants; and, never companying with the drunken, suffer the pains threatened in God's just judgment against wicked stewards.
>
> I beg you, therefore, in all your prayers, to pray God that I may be watchful in all things; that I may be no shame or disgrace to the name of Christ, in the revelation of the secrets of my heart, in the great day of the appearing of our Saviour Jesus Christ.

Nicene and Post-Nicene Fathers of the Christian Church, vol. 8, 252–53

Thought

In the communion of the saints and the community of faith
lie the setting of our safety.

LUKE 4:1–2   JULY 28

The Desert

In Christian spirituality the desert is a desolate and empty place that operates as a metaphor highlighting the call to emptiness and surrender.

The thirteenth-century German Christian mystic St. Mechthild of Magdeburg expresses this movement toward emptiness in the following ways:

> You must love nothingness,
> You must flee something,
> You must remain alone
> And go to nobody.
>
> You must be very active
> And free of all things.
> You must deliver the captives
> And force those who are free.
>
> You must comfort the sick
> And yet have nothing for yourself.
> You must drink the water of suffering
> And light the fire of love with the wood of virtues.
> Thus you live in the true desert.

> Quoted in *Christian Mystics:
> Their Lives and Legacies Throughout the Ages*, 94

Reflection

The desert as a spiritual state is not escape from the issues of our time.
Rather, the desert is a movement towards emptiness
in order to see more clearly
and thus engage our broken world.

JOB 6:14 — JULY 29

Friendship

Friendship is a gift and a vocation. It is a gift in that the magic of such a relationship happens. It is a vocation in that friendship needs to be cared for like a garden in full bloom.

The twelfth-century English Christian mystic Aelred of Rievaulx wrote on the Cistercian understanding of friendship:

> Through the perfection of charity, we have perfect love for those who are a burden and a bore to us. Although we consider their interests honestly, without pretense or hypocrisy, but truthfully and voluntarily, we do not invite them into the intimacies of friendship.
>
> In friendship, we join honesty with kindness, truth with joy, sweetness with good will, and affection with kind action. All this begins with Christ, is advanced through Christ, and is perfected in Christ. The ascent does not seem too steep or unnatural from the Christ who inspires us to love a friend to the Christ who offers himself to us as a friend to love, so that tenderness will yield tenderness, sweetness will yield sweetness, and affection will yield affection. Thus a friend who clings to a friend in the spirit of Christ becomes *one heart and one soul* with him (Acts 4:32), and the two spirits meet, lend and unite.
>
> Ascending the steps of love to friendship with Christ, a friend becomes one with him through the one kiss of the spirit (1 Cor 6:17).
>
> *Aelred of Rievaulx: Spiritual Friendship,* 75

Meditation

Friendship with Christ deepens all human friendship.
Human friendship is a school master leading us to Christ.

1 Samuel 2:22-24 — July 30

Discipline

A life well lived is a life with joy, inspiration and discipline. While discipline can be learned in later life, it is best forged in one's younger years. Thus we have a responsibility for all those who are learning this gentle art.

The unknown author of *The Shepherd of Hermas* has this to say about discipline in the home:

> But out of fondness for your children, you did not admonish your family, but allowed it to become terribly corrupt. Therefore the Lord is angry with you. But he will heal all the past sins that have been committed in your family; for because of their sins and iniquities, you have been corrupted by the affairs of this world.
>
> But the great mercy of the Lord had pity on you and your family and will strengthen you and establish you in his glory. Only do not be careless, but take courage and strengthen your family. For just as the blacksmith completes the task he wants to do by hammering his work, so also the righteous word repeated daily conquers all evil. Therefore, do not cease to instruct your children, for I know that if they repent with all their heart, they will be written in the books of life with the saints.
>
> *The Shepherd of Hermas,* Vision 1

Reflection

Gentleness and strength
are the ways
that guide the young
to shape their life
in structures
that are pathways to creativity and joy.

ROMANS 13:1–7   JULY 31

A Call to Political Leaders

> *The idea that Christians should not be concerned about politics is clearly far off the mark. God's grace can bring goodness to every sphere of life, and political leaders are called, like the rest of us, to hear and live the gospel.*

St. Francis, in *A Letter to the Rulers of the Peoples*, shows his concern for political leaders:

> To all mayors and consuls, judges and governors throughout the world, and to all others who may receive these letters, Brother Francis, your little and contemptible servant, wishes health and peace to you.
>
> Consider and see that the day of death draws near (Gen 47:39). I ask you, therefore, with as much reverence as I can, not to forget the Lord nor turn away from his commandments because of the cares and preoccupations of this world. For all those who forget him and turn away from his commandments are cursed (cf. Ps 118:21) and will be forgotten by him (Ezek 33:13). And when the day of death comes, everything that they think they have will be taken away from them (cf. Luke 8:18). And the wiser and more powerful they have been in this world, the greater will be their punishment.
>
> Therefore, I strongly advise you, my lords, to put aside all cares and preoccupations and to receive joyfully the most holy body and blood of our Lord Jesus Christ in holy remembrance of him. And great honour should be rendered to the Lord by the people entrusted to you, so that every evening, through a town crier or some other sign, you may announce that praises and thanks will be given to the Lord God Almighty from all the people.
>
> *The Writings of St. Francis of Assisi*, 125–26

Prayer

Lord, may those in authority follow the paths of goodness and justice. And may something of your kingdom come even through them.
Amen.

August

ROMANS 6:8   AUGUST 1

God's Restoration

> *The three great themes of the biblical narrative are creation, fall and recreation. But God's restorative work does not simply bring back what was lost in the fall. Rather, this work is even more glorious because it has gone through the eye of suffering.*

Julian of Norwich speaks about God's restorative work:

> We know in our faith, and believe in our teaching and preaching of the holy church, that the entire blessed Trinity created humankind in his image and to his likeness. In the same way, we know that when man and woman fell so deeply and wretchedly by sin, there was no other help to restore them accept through him who created them.
>
> And he who created humankind for love, by the same love wished to restore them, not only to their former bliss, but to one even greater.
>
> And just as we were created like the Trinity in our first creation, our Maker wished that we would be like Jesus Christ our Saviour, in heaven forever as a result of our re-creation.
>
> *A Lesson of Love*, 27

Reflection

A wounded person
Made whole
Has a way of being and seeing
That a well person
Knows nothing about.

JEREMIAH 29:12 — AUGUST 2

The Meaning of Prayer

Prayer is a way of life, the constant opening of ourselves to the God who sustains us and journeys with us. Prayer is the desire for intimacy with the God who is our very life.

John Cassian has this to say about prayer:

> In prayers we offer or promise something to God. The Greek term means "vow." Greek has "I shall offer my vows to the Lord" and in Latin it is, "I shall do what I have promised to the Lord" (Ps 117:14). . . . In Ecclesiastes we read: "If you have made a promise to God do not delay in fulfilling it" (5:3). The Greek has "If you are to pray to the Lord, do not delay about it."
>
> This is how each of us must do this. We pray when we renounce this world, when we undertake to die to all the world's deeds and mode of living and to serve the Lord with all our heart's zeal. We pray when we promise to despise worldly glory and earth's riches and to cling to the Lord with contrite hearts and poverty of spirit.
>
> We pray when we promise to put on the purest bodily chastity and unswerving patience, or when we vow to drag completely from our hearts the root of anger and the gleam which is the harbinger of death.
>
> And if we are brought down by laziness, if we return to our old sinful ways because of not doing at all what we promised, we shall have to answer for our prayers and our commitments, and it will be said of us, "Better not to promise than to promise and not deliver." As the Greek would have it, "It is better that you do not pray than that, having prayed, you do not do as you had undertaken" (Eccl 5:4).
>
> *John Cassian: Conferences*, 108–9

Thought

Prayer is a form of promise. It is a word and a deed.

ACTS 9:17–19　　　　　　　　　　　　　　　　　　AUGUST 3

Baptism

In baptism we receive the mark and the reminder that we have laid aside our old way of living and have entered into a new life where Christ is the centre. Through his death we have entered a new life in the power of the Spirit.

St. John Chrysostom, in his *Instructions to Catechumens*, explains the significance of baptism in the Christian life:

> But, if you will, let us discourse about the name which this mystical cleansing bears: for its name is not one, but very many and varied. For this purification is called the laver (washbasin) of regeneration. "He saved us," St. Paul said, "through the laver of regeneration, and renewing of the Holy Spirit" (Titus 3:5).
>
> This mystical cleansing is also called illumination, and this St. Paul again has called it, "For call to remembrance the former days in which after you were illuminated you endured a great conflict of sufferings" (Heb 10:32). And again, "For it is impossible for those who were once illuminated, and have tasted of the heavenly gift, and then fall away, to renew them again unto repentance" (Heb 6:4).
>
> This cleansing is also called baptism: "For as many of you as were baptized into Christ did put on Christ" (Gal 3:27). It is also called burial: "For we were buried," says St. Paul, "with him, through baptism, into death" (Rom 6:4). It is also called circumcision: "In whom you were also circumcised, with a circumcision not made with hands, in the putting off of the body of the sins of the flesh" (Col 2:11).
>
> And it is called a cross: "Our old self was crucified with him that the body of sin might be done away" (Rom 6:6).
>
> *Nicene and Post-Nicene Fathers*, vol. 9, 160–61

Reflection

In baptism we are identified with Christ
and with the faith community to enter its joys and bear its sufferings.

SONG OF SOLOMON 1:15–17　　　　　　　　AUGUST 4

Appreciation

Sometimes one gains the impression that Christianity is all about a narrow grayness of life. But Christianity, with its theme of humans as the imago Deo, are called to celebrate beauty.

One of the Desert Fathers shared this story:

> Some of the other bishops asked my superior, Nonnus, whether he had any edifying comments for them, and without delay our holy bishop began to tell them something for the instruction and salvation of all who were listening. As we were all listening with enjoyment to his holy teaching, suddenly there passed by in front of us the foremost actress of Antioch, the star of the local theatre. She was seated on a donkey and accompanied by a great and fanciful procession. She seemed to be clothed in nothing but gold and pearls and other precious stones. Even her feet were covered with gold and pearls. The male and female slaves accompanying her were extravagantly clothed in costly garments, and the torcs [metal neck rings] round their necks were all of gold. Some of them went before, others followed after.
>
> The worldly crowd could not get enough of their beauty and attractiveness. As they passed by us the air was filled with the scent of musk and other most delicious perfumes, but when the bishops saw her passing by so immodestly, with her head bare, and the outlines of her body clearly visible, nothing over her shoulders as well as her head, and yet the object of such adulation, they all fell silent, groaned and sighed, and averted their eyes as if being forced to witness some grave sin.
>
> The most blessed Nonnus, however, looked at her long and hard, and even after she had passed by he looked after her for as long as she remained in sight. Not till then did he turn round and speak to the other bishops. "Weren't you delighted to see such beauty as hers?"

The Life of St. Pelagia the Harlot, ch. 2–3

Reflection

Love of beauty, wherever that is found,
need not become lust—and therefore should be celebrated.

John 21:9–14 — August 5

Invitation to Breakfast

Manna in the desert. Eucharist in the community of faith. Hospitality to the stranger. These are all signs of the God of great generosity.

The unknown author of *The Voyage of Brendan* speaks about this hospitality:

> St. Brendan ordered the serving brother to serve the meal that God had sent them. Without delay, the table was laid with napkins and with white loaves and fish for each brother. When all had been laid out, St. Brendan blessed the food and said to his brothers: "Let us give praise to the God of heaven, who provides food for all his creatures." Then the brothers ate and drank as much as they pleased, giving thanks to the Lord. When the meal was finished and they had concluded the divine office, St. Brendan said: "Go to your rest now. Here are well-made beds for each of you. Rest your bodies, which have been over-wearied by labour during our voyage."
>
> When the brothers had gone to sleep, St. Brendan saw a demon, in the guise of a little Ethiopian boy, holding a bridle-bit in his hands and beckoning towards him. St. Brendan rose from his bed and remained all night in prayer.
>
> When morning came, the brothers rushed through the divine office, as they wished to take to their boat again. Then they found the table already laid for their meal, as on the previous day. And so for three days and nights, God provided food for his servants.
>
> *The Voyage of St. Brendan the Abbot, 6–7*

Prayer

Lord, may I live my life with others and in dependence on your provision,
both spiritually and practically.
Amen.

MATTHEW 25:44–45   AUGUST 6

Practical Care

The heartbeat of the Christian life is a life of prayer and of practical service. Combining heart and hand, Christian love seeks to bring goodness and help to those in need.

St. Gregory of Nazianzus speaks in glowing terms of St. Basil's hospital in Caesarea:

> My subject is the most wonderful of all, the short road to salvation, the easiest ascent to heaven. There is no longer before our eyes that terrible and piteous spectacle of men and women who are living corpses, the greater part of whose limbs have mortified, driven away from their cities and homes and public places and fountains, and even from their dearest ones, recognizable by their names rather than their features. They are no longer brought before us at our gatherings and meetings, in our common intercourse and union, no longer the objects of hatred, instead of pity, on account of their disease; composers of piteous songs, if any of them have their voice still left to them.
>
> Why should I try to express in tragic style all our experiences, when no language can be adequate to their hard lot? He however it was, who took the lead in pressing upon men and women that they ought not to despise their fellow humankind, nor to dishonour Christ, the one head of all, by their inhuman treatment of them; but to use the misfortunes of others as an opportunity of firmly establishing their own lot, and to lend to God that mercy of which they stand in need at his hands . . .
>
> Taking the lead in approaching to tend them, as a consequence of Basil's philosophy . . . the effect produced is to be seen not only in the city, but in the country and beyond, and even the leaders of society have vied with one another in their philanthropy and magnanimity towards them. Others have had their cooks, and splendid tables, and the dainties of confectioners, and exquisite carriages, and soft, flowing robes; [but] Basil's care was for the sick, and the relief of their wounds, and the imitation of Christ, by cleansing leprosy, not by word, but in deed.
>
> Gregory Nazianzen: Oration, 43.6

Thought

When following the way of Christ,
Christianity becomes a healing presence in the world.

JOHN 17:11 — AUGUST 7

Protection in the Power of the Gospels

Christians also experience calamities, difficulties, and sickness. But their trust is not simply that God will spare them from these things, but rather when they come that God will sustain them in the midst of life's trials.

In the long tradition of Celtic prayers collected in the *Carmina Gadelica*, there is this prayer for protection:

> I set the keeping of Christ about you,
> I set the guarding of God with you,
> To possess you, to protect you
> From drowning, from danger, from loss,
> From drowning, from danger, from loss.
>
> The Gospel of the God of grace,
> Be from your summit to your sole;
> The Gospel of Christ, King of salvation,
> Be as a mantle to your body,
> Be as a mantle to your body.
>
> *Carmina Gadelica*, 193

Reflection

> In the trials of life
> Hold me, O gracious God.
> Give me the grace,
> That I may fall into your hands.

DEUTERONOMY 33:12 AUGUST 8

Beloved of God

In the long history of Christian spirituality, there have been women and men who have spoken of a profound relationship with God. This poses a challenge to us in the modern world, when our faith seems to be so fragile.

The Christian mystic Mechthild of Magdeburg, in her *Flowing Light of the Godhead*, speaks of such intimacy with God:

> When the poor soul comes to Court, she is wise and well-behaved; she gazes merrily upon her Creator. How joyfully she is received! She is silent, though her longing to praise him is immeasurable.
>
> Then, with great love, he shows her his divine heart. It is like red-gold that burns in a great fire of coals. Then he puts her soul into his glowing heart, so that the mighty ruler and the humble maidservant embrace and are united like water and wine. Then she is overcome and altogether helpless. And he is sick with love for her, as he was from the beginning, for nothing can either be added to him or taken away from him.
>
> Then she says, "Lord, you are comfort, my desire, my flowing spring, my sun, and I am your mirror." This is the presentation at court of the loving soul, who cannot be without God.

Ecstatic Confessions: The Heart of Mysticism, 51

Prayer

O mysterious and shadowy One, purify my heart
so that I may see you more clearly.

ISAIAH 55:6 — AUGUST 9

The Seeking Heart

God is never our automatic possession. God is the One who is found by the seeking heart, which has been moved by the grace of the seeking God.

St. Anselm in the *Proslogion* writes about the seeking heart:

> Lord, I am bowed down so far that I can only look downwards;
> raise me up, that I may look upwards.
> "My sins are heaped up over my head,"
> they cover me and "like a heavy load" crush me down.
> Save me, unburden me,
> "lest the pit close its mouth over me."
> Let me discern your light,
> whether it be from afar or from the depths.
>
> Teach me to seek you,
> and reveal yourself to me as I seek,
> for I cannot seek you if you do not teach me how,
> and I cannot find you unless you reveal yourself.
> Let me seek you by desiring you;
> and desire you by seeking you;
> let me find you by loving you;
> and love you by finding you.

St. Anselm: The Major Works, 86–87

Reflection

In seeking you, O God,
I find the object of all my longing.
In being found by you, O my God,
I find my greatest homecoming.

Psalm 89:11 — August 10

Contemplating Creation

The great contemplative tradition of the Christian church has always emphasized the contemplation of God, Scripture, the neighbor and nature. In fact, this tradition suggests that all things should come under the contemplative gaze of faith and love.

St. John Chrysostom speaks to us in his *Homily* about the contemplation of nature:

> But in addition to what has been said, follow me while I enumerate the meadows, the gardens, the various tribes of flowers, all sorts of herbs and their uses, odours, forms, disposition—even their very names—along with the trees that are fruitful and those that are barren, the nature of metals and of animals—those in the sea, or on the land, those that swim, and those that traverse the air—the mountains, the forests, the groves, the meadow below and the meadow above—for there is a meadow on earth and a meadow too in the sky—where there are the various flowers of the stars, the rose below and the rainbow above!
>
> Would you have me point out also the meadow of the birds? Consider the variegated body of the peacock, surpassing every dye, and the fowls of purple plumage. Contemplate with me the beauty of the sky, how it has been preserved so long without being dimmed and remains as bright and clear as if it had been fabricated today. Consider, moreover, the power of the earth, how its womb has not become effete [exhausted of vitality] by bringing forth over so long a time! Contemplate with me the fountains, how they burst forth and fail not, since the time they were begotten, to flow forth continually throughout the day and night!
>
> Contemplate with me the sea, receiving so many rivers, yet never exceeding its measure! But how long shall we pursue things unattainable! It is fit, indeed, that over every one of these which has been spoken of, we should say, "O Lord, how you have magnified your works; in wisdom you have made them all."

Nicene and Post-Nicene Fathers, vol. 9, 408

Reflection

In the beauty of creation, O God, we see your desire to reveal yourself and to make an abode for us, your creatures.

LEVITICUS 26:2 — AUGUST 11

Sabbath Spirituality

> *There is much more to a Sabbath spirituality than simply resting because one is tired from work. Sabbath spirituality invites us into a rest of celebrating God's goodness and of care for the neighbor, animals and the land.*

St. Aelred of Rievaulx, in his *Mirror of Love*, touches on some themes regarding Sabbath:

> Let us then listen to him who says: "If the Son sets you free, you will indeed be free." And I tell you that it is he whom we hear calling us, imploring us, bidding us who labour to the rest of his Sabbath. "Come," he says, "to me, all you who labour and are burdened down, and I shall refresh you."
>
> "Refresh," he says, offering us as it were a preparation for the Sabbath. And now let us hear him speak of the Sabbath itself: "Take upon you my yoke, and learn from me, for I am meek and humble of heart, and you will find rest for your souls." This is rest, this is tranquility, this is the Sabbath.
>
> "You will find rest for your souls, for my yoke is easy, and my burden is light." It is because this yoke is easy, this burden light, that you will find rest for your souls. This yoke does not bow you down to the earth, but lifts you up to him: this burden has wings, not weight. This yoke is divine love, this burden is brotherly and sisterly love. Here may rest be found, here may the Sabbath be kept, here is freedom from servile works. For "divine love is not perverse, and thinks no evil," and the love of one's neighbour cannot do evil.
>
> *The Mediaeval Mystics of England*, 118

Thought

Sabbath spirituality is drawing near to the restoring heart of God and is the inspiration for our small part in the restoration of others.

1 PETER 1:15–16   AUGUST 12

Holy

God is holy in perfection and beauty in himself. God's holiness is intrinsic to his being. We are made holy by grace and grow in holiness through the work of the Spirit.

The English Christian mystic St. Edmund Rich, in his *Mirror of Holy Church*, speaks of the way of holiness for all Christians:

> To live perfectly, as St. Bernard teaches us, is to live humbly, lovingly, and honourably. To live honourably towards God is to intend nothing except to do his will; and that means to do his will in everything, in the thoughts of your heart and the words of your mouth and the deeds of your hands, in each of your five senses.
>
> Seeing, hearing, tasting, smelling, touching, when you walk or stand, lie down or sit, always begin by asking yourself, is this his will or not?
>
> If it is God's will, do it with all your might: if not, die rather than do it.
>
> But now someone may be asking, what is the will of God? His will is for nothing else than our holiness: for as the apostle tells us, "This is God's will, that you be holy."
>
> There are two things, only two which make a person holy, knowledge and love: knowledge of truth and love of goodness. But the truth is the knowledge of God, and you can never come to that except through knowledge of yourselves: nor can you ever come to the love of God, which is goodness, except through love of your neighbour.

The Mediaeval Mystics of England, 125–26

Reflection

Holiness is not a legalistic piety but a passion and hunger
to know and do the will of God
in the whole gamut of one's personal and public life.

LUKE 6:37-38   AUGUST 13

Judge Not

The Christian community is often harsh on those who fail. The antidote to this is not to be naïve. Nor is it to close one's eyes to what is happening. Instead, we are invited to be compassionate and to commit ourselves to the work of restoration.

The unknown author of *The Cloud of Unknowing* cautions us against making hasty judgments of others and being judgmental:

> And who, we may ask, can judge the deeds of others? Surely those who have power over and care for others' souls may correct those who are under their authority. Someone may be given this authority through the decree and law of the holy church, or the Holy Spirit may privately inspire someone to assume this authority in perfect love.
>
> But everyone must be careful not to presume to claim for oneself the right to condemn or reprehend the faults of others, for such a one is liable to great error, unless he or she feels truly led in this work, interiorly, by the Holy Spirit. Otherwise, it is very easy to make errors in judgment.
>
> Therefore, judge yourself as you like, for this is a matter between you and God or between you and your spiritual counselor. But do not interfere in the lives of others.
>
> *The Cloud of Unknowing,* 178–79

Reflection

In the face of the other, including the other as sinner,
we can often most clearly see that part of ourselves that we hide so well.
So, rather than judge the other, let us reflect on ourselves,
and extend forgiveness to ourselves and healing to the other.

The Gift of Silence

We have become compulsive communicators in the modern world. We err, if we think we have to do this with God. This does not mean that God is not interested in the dynamics of our life. But it does mean that God invites us not only to speak, but also to be silent.

The early church father St. Ignatius, in *To the Ephesians XV*, speaks about the matter of silence:

> It is better to be silent and to be real, than to talk and to be unreal. Teaching is good, if the teacher does what he says. There is then one teacher who "spoke and it came to pass," and what he has done even in silence is worthy of the Father.
>
> Those who have the word of Jesus for a true possession can also hear his silence, that they may be perfect, that they may act through their speech, and be understood through their silence.
>
> Nothing is hidden from the Lord, but even our secret things are near to him.
>
> Let us therefore do all things as though he were dwelling in us, that we may be his temples, and that he may be our God in us.
>
> *The Apostolic Fathers*, vol. 1, 189

Reflection

God has spoken in the Word made flesh.
God has come to us in the silence of the Spirit.
We are invited to worship and witness.
We are called into the silence of contemplation.

GALATIANS 3:27–28 — AUGUST 15

Equality in Christ

> *The faith community is called to be an alternate society living the radical words of Jesus. But this radicality is so that society as a whole may experience something of God's shalom.*

St. Augustine writes about this equality in Christ:

> Come, Lord, work upon us: call us back, set us on fire and clasp us close; be fragrant to us and draw us to your loveliness; let us love you, let us run to you.
>
> Do not many people, who come from an even deeper pit of blindness than Victorinus, come back to you, illuminated by that light which gives power to those who receive it to become your children? But because they are not so well-known, there is less rejoicing over them, even by those who know them.
>
> For when many rejoice together, the joy of each one is richer, for they can warm one another and catch fire from one another. Furthermore, those who are widely known guide many to salvation and are followed by them, so that those who have gone before rejoice much on their account, because they do not rejoice for them alone.
>
> In your dwelling place, it would be shameful for the rich or nobly born to be welcomed before the poor, since "you have chosen the weak things of the world to confound the strong; and have chosen the base things of the world and things that are despised, and the things that are not, in order to bring to nothing the things that are." Indeed, through the tongue of "the least of the apostles," you uttered these words.
>
> *Confessions*, 128

Thought

In Christ a new humanity is formed
where the old social designations fall away.

JOHN 14:16–17

The Gift of the Holy Spirit

The work of the Spirit is all-pervasive, renewing the face of the earth, enlightening seekers, empowering the community of faith, and carrying the 'new world' towards its final fulfillment.

St. Basil, in his *De Spiritu Sancto*, speaks about the amazing work of the Holy Spirit:

> We are compelled to advance in our conceptions to the highest, and to think of an intelligent essence, in power infinite, in magnitude unlimited, unmeasured by times or ages, generous of its good gifts, to whom turn all things needing sanctification, after whom reach all things that live in virtue, as being watered by its inspiration and helped on towards their natural and proper end. Perfecting all things, but itself in nothing lacking, it lives not as needing restoration, but as supplier of life. Not growing by additions, but straightway full, established, omnipresent, origin of sanctification, it is light perceptible to the mind, supplying, as it were, through itself, illumination to every faculty in search for truth. By nature unapproachable, apprehended by reason of goodness, it fills all things with its power, but is communicated only to the worthy; not shared in one measure, but distributing its energy according to the "proportion of faith." In essence simple, in powers various, it is wholly present in each, and being wholly everywhere is impassively divided, shared without loss of ceasing to be entire, after the likeness of the sunbeam, whose kindly light falls on all who enjoy it as though it shone for that person alone, yet illumines land and sea and mingles with the air.
>
> So, too, is the Spirit to everyone who receives it, as though given to each one alone, and yet it sends forth grace sufficient and full for all humankind, and is enjoyed by all who share it, according to the capacity, not of its power, but of their nature.

Nicene and Post-Nicene Fathers, vol. 8, 15

Reflection

In and through all things
the Holy Spirit wings its way
to stave decay and bring to birth.

2 CORINTHIANS 9:6–8   AUGUST 17

Life in Balance

> *Jesus was an ascetic who went to weddings and parties. His example should remind us that dourness is not virtuous, rather simplicity, gratitude, and generosity are.*

Bonaventure, in writing about St. Francis has this to say about a way of life that knows joy and generosity:

> Although Francis fervently urged the brothers to lead an austere life, he was not pleased by rigid severity that did not have a heart of compassion and was not flavoured by the salt of discretion.
>
> One night, one of the brothers was tormented by hunger because of his excessive abstinence, and he could not rest. When the kindly shepherd perceived the danger that threatened his sheep, he called the brother and set bread before him. To take away his embarrassment, Francis began to eat first and then gently invited his brother to join him. The brother set aside his shame and took the food, rejoicing that through his wise and kindly shepherd, he had escaped bodily harm and received an edifying example. When morning came, Francis called the brothers together and told them what had happened during the night, adding this wise exhortation: "May the act of love, not the food, be an example to you, my brothers." Moreover, he taught them to follow discretion as the champion of the virtues, not discretion that is persuaded by the flesh, but the discretion that Christ taught, whose most holy life expressed for us the image of perfection.
>
> *The Little Flowers and the Life of St. Francis, with the Mirror of Perfection*, 333

Reflection

When Christ is the model, all false piety
and its practices are transcended.

LUKE 6:32-36   AUGUST 18

God's Common Grace

The created order and the human race are marked by the goodness of the God who sustains all things and whose Spirit permeates all that reflects the signs of kindness, justice and well-being.

The British lay monk Pelagius, whose teaching was virulently attacked by St. Augustine, made this observation about general human goodness:

> There are some who call themselves Christian, and who attend worship regularly, yet perform no Christian actions in their daily lives. There are others who do not call themselves Christian, and who never attend worship, yet perform many Christian actions in their daily lives.
>
> Which of these two groups are the better disciples of Christ? Some would say that believing in Christ and worshipping him is what matters for salvation. But this is not what Jesus himself said. His teaching was almost entirely concerned with action, and with the motives which inspire action.
>
> He affirmed goodness of behaviour in whomever he found it, whether the person was Jew or Roman, male or female. And he condemned those who kept all the religious requirements, yet were greedy and cruel.
>
> Jesus does not invite people to become his disciples for his own benefit, but to teach and guide them in the ways of goodness. And if someone can walk along that way without ever knowing the earthly Jesus, then we may say that this person is following the spirit of Christ in his or her heart.
>
> Quoted in *Listening for the Heartbeat of God: A Celtic Spirituality*, 17–18

Thought

All human love and goodness finds its ultimate source
in the hidden or overt love of God.

MATTHEW 1:22–23　　　　　　　　　　　　AUGUST 19

Immanuel: God with Us

The coming of Jesus is God's great gift to the world. He is the new being in whom we find our identity and destiny.

In the songs, prayers and blessings of the *Carmina Gadelica*, we hear the call to joy in the coming of the Christ child:

> God of the moon, God of the sun,
> God of the globe, God of the stars,
> God of the waters, the land, and the skies,
> Who ordained to us the King of promise.
>
> It was Mary fair who went upon her knee,
> It was the King of life who went upon her lap,
> Darkness and tears were set behind,
> And the star of guidance went up early.
>
> Illumed the land, illumed the world,
> Illumed doldrum and current,
> Grief was laid and joy was raised,
> Music was set with harp and pedal-harp.

The Celtic Vision, 225

Reflection

A new born child—so meek and mild.
The healing One
God's suffering Son.
In him is life—an end to strife.

JAMES 1:13-15 — AUGUST 20

Temptation

When we do not recognize the conflictual nature of the Christian life, we live in unreality. We are held in the grace and love of God, we have doubts and failures, and we are tempted by the Evil One. But in the midst of these struggles God is faithful in keeping us.

Richard of St. Victor, one of the great writers on Christian spirituality in the twelfth century, has this to say about temptation in his book, *The Mystical Ark*:

> Do you wish to know about chains of this sort, which are sometimes accustomed to ensnare severely the minds of worthy persons and even of high-ranking persons? Who does not know the irritations of voluptuous desires that arise at one time from outside, at another time from within; from outside, from delight; from inside, from suggestion; by means of delight, in the flesh; by means of suggestion, in the mind.
>
> At one time the flesh is inflamed by foul titillation, while at another time the soul is befouled by filthy thoughts. Therefore, we meet darkness like that of a prison when, after being ensnared in these entwinings of concupiscence, we wish to turn away from the blindness of our confusion, but we are not able to do it.
>
> But surely a showing of divine consolation is deserved by that mind which endures this darkness of its confusion, not so much because of personal listlessness of its sluggishness, but because of the wanton malice of another. Such a holy soul is set free by the coming of the divine ambassador, when the grace of divine inspiration and the light of a showing of it is relieved of the weight of its oppression.

The Twelve Patriarchs, The Mystical Ark, Book Three of the Trinity, 329-30

Reflection

Inwardly torn and conflicted,
seldom deeply convicted,
give me the grace of purgation
to be part of your holy nation.

GALATIANS 3:26–27   AUGUST 21

Living One's Baptismal Vows

In baptism we are linked by faith to Christ's death and resurrection in order to live a new life in the Spirit. Thus baptism calls us to faithfulness in following Christ and abandoning our old ways of being and doing.

The fifth-century ecclesiastical writer Salvian, in his *De Gubernatione Dei*, has this to say about baptismal faithfulness:

> The games [Roman circuses] involve a certain renunciation of the faith, a deadly deviation from the creed and the divine sacraments. For what is the first confession of faith made by Christians about the saving grace of baptism? What else than their vow to renounce the devil, his pomps and games and works? ... How, therefore, O Christians, can you frequent the games after baptism, the games which you confess to be the works of the devil?
>
> You have once renounced the devil and his games. You must know that when you return to the games, you are returning knowingly and deliberately to the devil. ... You say, "I renounce the devil, his pomps, and spectacles and works." What do you say next? You say, "I believe in God, the Father Almighty, and in Jesus Christ, his Son." The devil is renounced in order that we may believe in God, because if we do not renounce the devil, we do not believe in God. Therefore, anyone who goes back to the devil forsakes God.
>
> The devil is in his spectacles and in his pomps. Therefore, when we return to the spectacles of the devil, we forsake the faith of Christ. In this way, all the pledges of our faith are broken, and all that follows in the creed is shaken and overthrown. Nothing that follows is valid if the primary clause has fallen.
>
>   *The Writings of Salvian, the Presbyter*, 161–62

Thought

In the modern world, where God seems to be so absent,
the devil has also disappeared.
In times of renewal and revival, when God's presence becomes more evident,
the devil also reappears.

MATTHEW 6:33 — AUGUST 22

Seeking True Riches

We are by nature people who seek for more. So often, the more is simply material wealth. But we can never be fully satisfied with what we own.

The English Christian mystic St. Aelred of Rievaulx speaks about seeking riches that do not satisfy the longings of the human heart. He writes,

> It is madness to pursue the fleeting beauty of this world when the soul's beauty never ages and when sickness and death cannot mar it nor destroy it. No, happiness is not to be found in this direction, for it is to be found only where there is nothing left to wish for. Nor is there any use looking for physical health to provide peace and satisfaction, since great effort must be devoted to the curing of sickness, and even then a cruel death may be brought about by devastating disease.
>
> When healthy, we give much time and care to the preservation of our body's good condition in order to ward off plague and sickness, forgetting that death is inevitable.
>
> Some people think that perhaps peace and security are to be found in wealth. But they have to toil to amass a fortune. Then they worry about keeping it, for fear that they may lose it, and they are plummeted to the depths of sorrow when it melts away. The more money they have, the more they have grounds for fear: fear of the rich man who may swindle, fear of the robber who may steal, fear of the servant who may mismanage.

The Mirror of Charity, 25–26

Reflection

What are true riches?
They have to do with all of life, body, and spirit, lived in the embrace of God, the grace of Christ, the presence of the Spirit and in the blessing of relationships and the challenge of service.

COLOSSIANS 1:15–20	AUGUST 23

A Song to Christ the Lord

Christ is the Savior. In him we rejoice. In him we live. In him we are grateful. In him we serve. He is the purpose of our lives. We celebrate his coming to us.

The twelfth-century Welsh poet Cynddelw Brydydd Mawr, in his "Deathbed Song," rejoices in God's gift of his Son, Jesus Christ:

> Greatest Lord, when you were born
> Love came to us, there came salvation,
> Adam's children took leave of the party of paganism,
> Of vile lawlessness and of captivity.
> There came the object of our keen desire,
> Courage came and great plenty.
> Christ entered the flesh, his the primary,
> He came to Mary's womb, the desired Son.
>
> The world's five ages emerged from the pain of perdition,
> From deceit, from the darkness of a false home,
> Of grievous captivity, from harsh grief,
> From the enemy's prison, when they were freed.
> He is our leader and our perfect protection,
> Who will judge our achievement by our labour.
> He is the Lord of Heaven, destiny of peace,
> Who led us from destruction when he was pierced,
> He rises for us and offers his merits.
> He is the Lord who shall impede our welfare,
> And as a gift has been given,
> Entirely mortal, infinite his rights.

Celtic Spirituality, 282

LUKE 9:1-6   AUGUST 24

The Sent Ones

> *Christianity is no inward, narrow, and cultic religion. Rather, it is a missionary faith, and we are all called to be the servants of Christ to neighbor and stranger.*

St. Francis was more than a lover of birds. He was a lover of Christ and a lover of humanity. In his *Earlier Rule*, he speaks of missionising others, including Muslims. This is what he wrote:

> The Lord says: "Listen, I send you as sheep in the midst of wolves. Therefore, be wise as serpents and simple as doves" (Matt 10:16). Any brother who wishes, by divine inspiration, to go among the Saracens and other nonbelievers, let them go with the permission of their minister and servant. Let the minister permit them and not refuse them if he sees that they are fit to be sent; for he will be bound to give an account to the Lord (cf. Luke 16:2) if he acts without discretion in this or in other matters. The brothers who are sent may conduct themselves among the nonbelievers in two ways. First, they are not to engage in contentious disputes, but rather be "subject to every human creature for God's sake" (1 Pet 2:13) while confessing themselves to be Christians. Second, they are to announce the word of God when they sense that it would be pleasing to God, so that all may believe in the Almighty God—Father, Son, and Holy Spirit—the Creator of all, our Lord the Redeemer and Saviour, so that they can be baptized and become Christians. For "whoever has not been born again of water and the Holy Spirit cannot enter into the kingdom of God" (cf. John 3:5) . . .
>
> And let all the brothers, wherever they may be, remember that they have given themselves and have relinquished their bodies to our Lord Jesus Christ; and for love of him, they must become vulnerable to their enemies, both the visible as well as the invisible.
>
> *The Writings of Saint Francis of Assisi*, 29

Prayer

Lord, you know all about my self-preoccupations and my being locked within my comfort zones. Move me by your Spirit to follow the suffering Christ into the world.

2 CORINTHIANS 4:16–18　　　　　　　　AUGUST 25

Weight of Glory

> *In our present-day consumer Christianity, we see structures, programs, and projects, but we don't see the glory of God hovering over our corporate worship and our daily lives. Yet quite possibly, this is what we most need.*

One of the Desert Fathers had this to say about the presence of heavenly glory:

> This same Abbot Sisois sitting in his cell would ever have his door closed. But it was told of him how in the day of his sleeping, when the fathers were sitting round him, his face shone like the sun, and he said to them, "Look, the Abbot Antony comes."
>
> And after a little while, he said again to them, "Look, the company of the prophets comes." And again his face shone brighter, and he said, "Look, the company of the apostles comes." And his face shone with double glory, and he seemed as though he spoke with others.
>
> And the old men entreated him, saying, "With whom are you speaking, Father?" And he said to them, "Behold, the angels came to take me, and I asked that I might be left a little while to repent."
>
> The old men said to him, "You have no need of repentance, Father." But he said to them, "Truly, I know not if I have clutched at the very beginning of repentance." And they all knew that he was made perfect.
>
> *The Desert Fathers*, 132

Reflection

I thought I had already gained so much.
But in one moment all was stripped away.
And I was naked.
Yet you clothed me again in your glory.
It shines, but I know it not.

GALATIANS 6:10 — AUGUST 26

Good to All

In its long journey in history the Christian community has made the mistakes of compromise and the use of violence. But the greater story has been of Christians doing good, practicing charity and doing the work of justice.

The unknown author of the third-century *Constitutions of the Holy Apostles* has this to say about doing good to all:

> For it is our duty to do good to all people, not fondly preferring one or another, whoever they be. For the Lord says: "Give to everyone that asks of you." It is evident that it is meant of everyone that is really in want, whether friend or foe, whether a kinsman or a stranger, whether single or married.
>
> For in all the scripture the Lord gives us exhortations about the needy, saying first by Isaiah: "Give your bread to the hungry, and bring the poor which have no covering into your house. If you see the naked, then cover him; and you shall not overlook those who are of your own family and seed."
>
> And then by Daniel he says to the powerful: "Wherefore, O King, let my counsel please you, and purge your sins by acts of mercy, and your iniquities by opening your heart of compassion to the needy."
>
> And he says by Solomon: "By acts of mercy and of faith iniquities are purged." And he says again by David: "Blessed are those that have regard to the poor and needy; the Lord shall deliver them in the evil day."
>
> *The Ante-Nicene Fathers*, vol. 7, 427

Thought

Living with an open hand, rather than a grasping fist,
that generously gives,
is a sign that conversion is taking place.

PSALM 103:13–18   AUGUST 27

Held in the Goodness of God

The God of the Bible is the God who is for us. This means that we are not abandoned when we fail, for God holds us fast.

Julian of Norwich had a revelation of God's goodness and steadfastness. She writes,

> I understood that if we willingly choose God in this life for the sake of love, we can be certain that we are loved without end with an endless love that creates in us that grace. God wills that we should hold onto this with hope, as certain of the bliss of heaven while we are here as when we are there.
>
> I was shown that the more we delight and take joy in this certainty, with reverence and humility, the more it pleases him. The reverence I mean is a holy, gracious fear of our Lord, which is knit together with humility. That is, as creatures, we see the Lord as wondrously great, and we see ourselves as wondrously small.
>
> These virtues are possessed externally by the beloved of God, and this can be understood and experienced now in some measure when the presence of the Lord is felt. Recognizing his presence in everything is desirable, because it produces wonderful certainty when there is true faith, along with certain hope because of his great love, and an awe that is sweet and delightful.
>
> *A Lesson of Love*, 170–71

Meditation

Held in your grace we are forgiven.
Held in your love we are safe.
Held in your future we are whole.

EPHESIANS 5:8-9 — AUGUST 28

The Renewing Spirit

Our way of life is marked by the goodness of God and by the folly of our sinning. For God's way to captivate us, we need to be renewed by the heavenly man, Jesus Christ, in the power of the Spirit.

History attributed this writing to St. Macarius of Egypt (c. 300–c. 390). This is now doubted, but *The Fifty Spiritual Homilies* often attributed to him speak of our need for the renewing Spirit:

> As a certain strong wind blows in a dark and gloomy night and strikes all the plants and seeds, moving them this way and that in shaking agitation, so also have we fallen under the power of the might of the devil of darkness. . . . And we are moved, buffeted, and shaken by the stiff blowing wind of sin, and through all our nature . . . we are thoroughly affected. All the members of the body are shaken; not one part of the soul or the body is immune from the passions of sin dwelling in us.
>
> In a similar way, there is a day of light and the divine wind of the Holy Spirit, breathing through and refreshing souls who live in the day of divine light. It passes through the whole nature of the soul, the thoughts and the entire substance of the soul, and all the members of the body, as it recreates and refreshes them with a divine and ineffable tranquility . . .
>
> And just as in that other state of error the old self put on the whole, complete self and wore the garment of the kingdom of darkness . . . all who have put off the old and earthly self and from whom Jesus has removed the clothing of the kingdom of darkness have put on the new and heavenly self, Jesus Christ, so that once again the eyes are joined to new eyes, ears to ears, head to head, to be completely pure and bearing the heavenly image.

Pseudo-Macarius: The Fifty Spiritual Homilies and the Great Letter, 46

Reflection

Indeed, we are invited to believe.
But more importantly, Christ is to take shape in us.

EPHESIANS 1:18–23　　　　　　　　　　　AUGUST 29

Inner Contemplation

There is much to contemplate: God's word, God's creation, God's way with us, God's world and the neighbor and stranger. But we are also to contemplate the vast inner recesses of our own being.

Bonaventure, in his *Mind's Road to God*, speaks about this inner contemplation:

> The two previous stages,
> by leading us to God
> through his vestiges,
> through which he shines forth in all creatures,
> have led us to the point
> of entering into ourselves,
> that is, into our minds,
> where the divine image shines.
>
> Now, in the third stage,
> as we enter into ourselves,
> as if leaving the vestibule
> and coming into the holy sanctuary,
> we should strive to see God through a mirror.
> In this mirror, the light of truth is shining before our minds.
>
> *The Mind's Road to God*, 22

Reflection

In my inner being
you have sculpted your love.
In entering there
I see you, O my God!

Matthew 22:37-40   August 30

Take My Heart

The Christian life is lived in faith and trust in the God who has revealed himself in the face of Jesus Christ. As such, this life is one of ongoing surrender.

The English mystic Richard Rolle, in his poem on *A Meditation on Christ's Passion*, speaks about this surrender:

> Jesus, receive my heart, and to your love me bring;
> My desire to you will dart: I long for your coming.
> Make me now clean from sin, let love us ever join.
> You are my whole desire: I long to be with you:
> Kindle my fire within, that I, your love may win
> And see your face, Jesus: Now let the bliss begin.
>
> Jesus, my soul now mend, your love into me send,
> That I with you life spend in joy that has no end.
> In love now wound my thought, my heart lift up in glee;
> My soul you dearly bought: make it your lover be.

English Writings, 139

Prayer

You came so unexpected,
And turned my life around.
May I never wander,
In your love be found.
In faith I now surrender,
My all into your hand,
Help me, O God, ever to stand.

EPHESIANS 5:1–2 — AUGUST 31

Imitators of God

The invitation is not only to believe in God, but to become Christlike. This becoming is not a work of our own doing, but is the outcome of the forming and renewing work of the Spirit.

The early church father Origen of Alexandria, in his *Contra Celsus*, speaks of Christ being formed in us:

> Both Jesus and his disciples did not want Christ's followers to believe merely in his Godhead and miracles, as if he had not also been part of the human nature and had not assumed the human flesh that "lusts against the spirit." They saw that, along with these divine elements, Christ's power, which had descended into human nature, and into the midst of human miseries, and which had assumed a human soul and body, also contributed to faith and to the salvation of believers.
>
> They saw that from him, there began the union of the divine with the human nature, so that the human, by communion with the divine, might rise to become divine. This was possible not only in Jesus alone, but in all those who both believe and enter into the life that Jesus taught, which elevates everyone who lives according to the precepts of Jesus to friendship with God and communion with him.
>
> Origen: *Contra Celsus*, 3.28

Reflection

You forgive my sins.
You heal my inner being.
You draw me to your heart.
You sculpt in me your ways.
You call me to follow you,
All of my days.

September

ISAIAH 58:5–9 SEPTEMBER 1

Spirituality as a Way of Life

Contemporary Christianity in the Western world is not short on beliefs. But it is short on a way of life that reflects the gospel and the way of peacemaking, generosity, and justice.

John Cassian, the great fifth-century formator in monasticism, writes about a way of life that reflects God's passion for justice and our call to pray:

> The words of the gospels and the prophets teach us that there are different reasons for prayer being heard in accordance with the varied and changing conditions of the soul.
>
> You have the fruits of an answer whenever two people agree about something, as our Lord said: "If two of you on earth agree upon anything you ask for, it will be done for you by my Father who is in heaven" (Matt 18:19).
>
> You have another answer in the fullness of faith, which is compared to a grain of mustard seed; for, as he said, "if you have faith as a grain of mustard seed, you shall say to this mountain: be removed, and it shall be removed; and nothing shall be impossible to you" (Matt 17:19).
>
> You have another answer in persistent prayer, that unwearying perseverance in petitioning that the Lord called importunity: "For truly I say to you, he will rise up and give him as much as he needs, if not because of his friendship, yet because of his importunity" (Luke 11:8).
>
> You also have an answer in the fruits of almsgiving: "Shut up alms in the heart of a poor, and your alms shall pray for you in the time of tribulation."
>
> You have an answer as well in a purified life and in the works of mercy. As the prophet Isaiah said, "Break the chains of wickedness and loosen the bonds that oppress" (Isa 58:6). And after rebuking the barrenness of an unfruitful fast, the prophet continued, "Then you shall call and the Lord shall hear you; you will cry, and he shall say, here am I" (Isa 58:9).
>
> *The Conferences of John Cassian*, 9.34

Prayer

Lord, deepen my life with you so that I may all the more fully engage the world with its needs and injustices. Amen.

ACTS 7:54–60   SEPTEMBER 2

A Martyr's Prayer

> *The Christian church has a vast army of martyrs. These were women and men of faith who dared to believe that faithfulness is the way of God and forgiveness is the oil for the machinery of the world. They died in the hope of the resurrection.*

One of the early martyrs of the Christian church was Polycarp. Here is his prayer:

> So they did not nail him, but tied him instead. Then, having placed his hands behind himself and having been bound, like a splendid ram chosen from a great flock for sacrifice, a burnt offering prepared and acceptable to God, he looked up to heaven and said: "O Lord God Almighty, Father of your beloved and blessed Son Jesus Christ, through whom we received knowledge of you, the God of angels and powers of all creation, and of the whole race of the righteous who live in your presence, I bless you because you have considered me worthy of this day and hour, so that I might receive a place among the number of the martyrs in the cup of your Christ, to the resurrection to eternal life, both of soul and of body, in the incorruptibility of the Holy Spirit.
>
> May I be received among them in your presence today, as a rich and acceptable sacrifice, as you have prepared and revealed beforehand, and have now accomplished, you who are the undeceiving and true God. For this reason, indeed for all things, I praise you, I bless you, I glorify you, through the eternal and heavenly high priest, Jesus Christ, your beloved Son, through whom be glory to you, with him and the Holy Spirit, both now and for the ages to come. Amen."
>
> *The Apostolic Fathers in English*, 152

Reflection

> You are calling me, O my God,
> Through the fires.
> But it is only through the death of your Son
> That I am truly purged.

ISAIAH 42:6–7 — SEPTEMBER 3

Light in a Dark World

The people of God are called to be a light in world. They are a light of the gospel. They are a light in a life of prayer. They are light in and through good works.

Theonas, bishop of Alexandria, in a letter to Lucianas, chief chamberlain to the emperor (most likely Diocletian), writes as follows:

> I give thanks to Almighty God and our Lord Jesus Christ who has not given up the manifesting of the faith throughout the whole world, and the cause for our salvation. But extends it even in the course of persecution by despots.
>
> Yes, like gold purged in the furnace, this salvation has only been made to shine more clearly under the storms of persecution. Its truth and grandeur have only become more illustrious.
>
> And now that peace has been granted to the churches by our gracious ruler, the works of Christians are shining in the sight of the unbelieving. And God your Father in heaven is thereby glorified.
>
> If we desire to be Christians in deed rather than in word only we ought to seek and aspire after these works on account of our salvation and to the glory of God. For if we seek our own glory, we set our desire upon a vain and perishing object and one which leads us into death.
>
> But the glory of the Father and of the Son, who for our salvation was nailed to the cross, makes us safe for everlasting redemption. This is the greatest hope of Christians.
>
> *Ante-Nicene Fathers*, vol. 6, 158

Reflection

Times of difficulty and times of calm bring their own particular challenges.
In difficulty we can give up. In good times we can become lax.
Thus, there are particular temptations in all the circumstances of life.
May God keep us.
And may the light of Christ continue to shine through us.

John 16:12–15 — September 4

Life in the Spirit

We tend to live much of the Christian life by our own efforts. Little wonder that we become tired of trying to be good Christians. But we are called to live in a wholly different way: founded on Christ we are to live in the power of the enabling Spirit.

Hilary of Poitiers' famous work *De Trinitate* speaks of our need of the Spirit:

> Let us therefore make use of this great benefit, and seek for personal experience of this most needful Gift. For the Apostle says . . . "But we have not received the spirit of this world, but the Spirit which is of God, that we may know the things that are given unto us by God."
>
> We receive Him, then, that we may know. Faculties of the human body, if denied their exercise, will lie dormant. The eye without light, natural or artificial, cannot fulfil its office; the ear will be ignorant of its function unless some voice or sound is heard; the nostrils unconscious of their purpose unless some scent be breathed . . .
>
> So too, the soul of man [woman] unless through faith it has appropriated the gift of the Spirit, will have the innate faculty of apprehending God, but be destitute of the light of knowledge.
>
> That Gift, which in Christ is One yet offered . . . fully to all. . . . This gift is with us unto the end of this world, the solace of our waiting, the assurance . . . of the hope that shall be ours, the light of our minds, the sun of our souls.
>
> *Nicene and Post-Nicene Fathers*, vol. 9, 61

Reflection

O mysterious Spirit in your working
yet revealed as the Spirit of Christ,
enlighten us
and enable us to be like Christ.

LUKE 2:34-35 — SEPTEMBER 5

Falling into Grace

We need to fall out of our pride and our own ways of thinking and being. This is a huge fall, for these are the places where we like to dwell. And in falling we come to the surprise of being caught in God's embrace.

St. Basil, in a rather long letter to Bishop Optimus, has this to say about the art of falling:

> My view is, that the Lord is for falling and rising again, not because some fall and others rise again, but because in us the worst falls and the better is set up. The advent of the Lord is destructive of our bodily affections and it rouses the proper qualities of the soul.
>
> As when Paul says, "When I am weak, then I am strong," it is the same man that is both weak and strong, but he is weak in the flesh and strong in the spirit. Thus the Lord does not give to some occasions of falling and to others occasions of rising. Those who fall, fall from the station in which they once were, but it is plain that the faithless never stand, but are always dragged along the ground with the serpent whom they follow.
>
> These faithless have then nowhere to fall from, because they have already been cast down by their unbelief. Wherefore the first boon is, that those who stand in their sin should fall and die, and then should live in righteousness and rise, both of which graces our faith in Christ confer upon us.
>
> Let the worst fall that the better may have opportunity to rise. If fornication fall not, chastity does not rise. Unless our unreason be crushed, our reason will not come to perfection. In this sense Christ is for the fall and rising again of many.
>
> *Nicene and Post-Nicene Fathers*, vol. 8, 299

Thought

To let go of the old so that the new may arise is no easy journey.
The familiar old has a hold on us, even when it is destructive.
Thus we need to be disempowered by grace and the Spirit,
so that the new may spring into view.

JEREMIAH 32:38-39   SEPTEMBER 6

Single-Mindedness

We, in the modern world, are hardly single-minded. Instead, we are ever looking for the new and moving on to hoped-for better things. Thus we lack focus and commitment.

St. Clare of Assisi, in *The Second Letter to Agnes of Prague*, has this to say about being single-minded:

> What you hold, may you always hold,
> What you do, may you always do and never abandon.
> But with swift pace, light step,
> Unswerving feet,
> So that even your steps stir up no dust,
> May you go forward,
> Securely, joyfully, and swiftly,
> On the path of prudent happiness,
> Not believing anything,
> Not agreeing with anything,
> That would dissuade you from this resolution,
> Or that would place a stumbling block for you on the way,
> So that you may offer your vows to the Most High,
> In pursuit of that perfection,
> To which the Spirit of the Lord has called you.

Quoted in Franciscan Prayer, 53

Meditation

Reveal to me that restless inner self.
Help me to find true rest in your will and way for me.

1 SAMUEL 15:34–35 — SEPTEMBER 7

The Grief of Love

We usually associate love with joy and happiness. But love also has to bear the burden of grief. This takes place when love suffers the pain of rejection, abandonment or loss.

The Catalonian mystic, theologian, and missioner Ramon Lull, in his *Blanquerna*, writes about the suffering of love:

> The lover met the Beloved, and saw him to be very noble and powerful and worthy of all honour. And the lover cried, 'How strange a thing it is that so few know and love and honour you as you deserve!'
>
> And the Beloved answered and said: "Greatly have men and women grieved me; for I created them to know me, love me, and honour me, and yet, of every thousand, but a hundred fear and love me; and ninety of these hundred fear me lest I should condemn them to hell, and ten love me that I may grant them glory; hardly is there one who loves me for my goodness and nobility."
>
> When the lover heard these words, he wept bitterly for the dishonour paid to his Beloved; and he said: "Ah, Beloved, how much have you given to us and how greatly have you honoured us! Why, then, have we thus forgotten you."
>
> *Late Medieval Mysticism*, 161

Reflection

You came in love to win us.
With reluctance we responded.
We should have come in joy.
Hold us, though we are so recalcitrant.
Forgive us, when we are so ungrateful.
Love us in your disappointment.

ROMANS 14:17   SEPTEMBER 8

A Radiant Kingdom

The Kingdom of God is a kingdom of presence, where God's people rejoice in the presence, beauty and love of the King. In this rejoicing, the King is radiant.

In an old Irish homily of the ninth century, we find a reflection on the beauty of the reign of God:

> We should strive then for the Kingdom of heaven which is unlike the human dominion of the present world which earthly king's love. It blinds like mist, it slays like sleep, wounds like a point, destroys like a blade, burns like fire, drowns like a sea, swallows like a pit, devours like a monster.
>
> But not like that is the Kingdom which the saints and the righteous strive for.
>
> It is the bright flower in its great purity, it is an open sea in its great beauty, a heaven full of candles in its true brilliance, it is the eye's delight in its great loveliness and pleasantness, a flame in its fairness, a harp in its melodiousness, a feast in its abundance of wine, it is ... in its true radiance.

Celtic Christian Spirituality:
An Anthology of Medieval and Modern Sources, 79

Reflection

The Kingdom of God
is the presence of the King
whose nature it is
to draw his subjects
into his goodness and blessedness.
Having been welcomed home
his subjects then extend this goodness to others.
Such a Kingdom will never end.

GALATIANS 5:16–18   SEPTEMBER 9

In the Light of the Spirit

The Word and the Spirit work in unison. Knowledge of God and self-knowledge belong together. Gift and responsibility complement each other.

Bonaventure provided directives for the Poor Clare nuns regarding a life of prayer and reflection. These are relevant for all of us:

> Return to yourself;
> Enter into your heart;
> Ponder what you were, are, should have been, and are called to be;
> What you are by nature;
> What you are through sin;
> What you should have been through effort;
> What you can still be through grace.
> Meditate in your heart;
> Let your spirit brood (are you resentful, angry, jealous?);
> Plough this field, work on yourself;
> Strive for freedom within, the freedom that leads to relationship with God . . . ;
> Lack of self-knowledge and failure to appreciate one's own worth, make for faulty judgment in all other matters;
> If you are not able to understand (and accept) your own self, you will not be able to understand (or accept) what is beyond you.

Franciscan Prayer, 24

Thought

We are invited to see the grace of God
and the presence of the Spirit as gifts and as a project.
To receive these gifts means that we must
become defined and shaped by them.
But it also means that we must work with these gifts
to embrace humility and servanthood.

LUKE 6:36 — SEPTEMBER 10

Service to the Least

If we are truly honest with ourselves, we will acknowledge that we more readily give to those who will somehow benefit us than serve those who cannot give in return. Thus we need a deeper conversion and need to become more Christlike.

In *The Great Letter*, the author has this to say:

> Let them not be servants of the bodies and souls of others, but as servants of Christ and of us, let their work appear pure and sincere before God. Do not let servants of Christ believe that by zeal for good works they cannot do the things which will bring salvation to their souls.
>
> For God does not ask the impossible from his servants, but shows abundant and great love and divine goodness, so that of his own good will he rewards everyone by giving them some good work to do.
>
> Therefore, no one who seriously seeks salvation will lack the power to do good. The Lord says: "Whoever will give even a cup of cold water to someone simply in the name of a disciple, amen, I say to you, that one will not go unrewarded" (Matt 10:42).
>
> What can be more powerful than this commandment? Heavenly reward follows upon a cup of cold water. And look at the immense love for humankind! He says: "As long as you did it to one of these, you did to me" (Matt 25:40). Indeed, it is a small commandment, but when obeyed, it brings forth from God a great and abundant gain.

Pseudo-Macarius:
The Fifty Spiritual Homilies and *The Great Letter*, 271

Reflection

Brother, let me be your servant.
Sister, let me be as Christ to you.
Stranger, let me hold the Christ light for you.

JAMES 1:19   SEPTEMBER 11

A Deeper Listening

We are slow to listen because we are distracted and preoccupied.
But to listen well is to nurture the wounded places of the heart
and to water the dry wells within.

The fifteenth-century Irish poet Cormac Ruadh O'Huiginn invites us to a careful listening:

> Its words are but whispers;
> yet if I understand them aright it never ceases preaching.
> All things seen in the world and in Eve's race are a sermon;
> each generation passing, another takes its place.
> May we listen to the world's sermon, speed on the right road;
> not one, but all of us together have strayed . . .
>
> I must be humble by checking the glory of my pride;
> not in the evening of a life should folly be corrected . . .
> Merely as a loan has God given us life;
> this world is not our own land, we only have it on a lease.
>
> An invitation to heaven all have got;
> not some only of the race did you invite, but the assembly of us all . . .
> Enable me, O God, to pay you the tribute of penance due;
> a share in your crucifixion stands against me, help me to requite it.

Towards a History of Irish Spirituality, 145

Reflection

If the Word made flesh lies at the heart of the new world that God is
bringing into being,
then our most basic calling is, first of all, to listen.
Then it is to believe—and in believing we become like him.

Self-Judgment

In a corrective response to earlier strategies that were oppressive, we have now lapsed into a vapid tolerance, where everything is accepted as long as one is not emotionally traumatized. But one can't live well if one is not self-critical.

St. John Chrysostom, in one of his homilies on St. Matthew's Gospel, reminds us of the need for self-judgment:

> Would you however be a judge? You have a court of judgment which has great profit, and bears no blame. Make consideration, as judge, to sit down upon your conscience, and bring before it all your transgressions, search out the sins of your soul, and exact with strictness its account, and say, "where did you dare do this and that?"
>
> And if your soul shuns these, and begins searching into others' matters, say, "Not about these am I judging you, not for these did you come here to plead. For what, if this one be a wicked man and that one a wicked woman? You, soul, why did you commit this and that offence? Answer for yourself, not to accuse; look to your own matters, do not look to those of others" . . .
>
> And when you are searching out these things, let no one be present, let no one disturb you. But as the judges sit under curtains to judge, so do you, too, instead of curtains, seek a time and place of quiet. And when after your supper you are risen up, and are about to lie down, then hold this your judgment; this is the time convenient for you, and the place, your bed, and your chamber.
>
> *Nicene and Post-Nicene Fathers*, vol. 10, 271

Prayer

Lord, shine your light on me.
Let your word pierce my heart.
Comfort me in my distress.
Forgive my transgressions.
Heal my wounded places with the balm of your love.

1 CORINTHIANS 10:23–26   SEPTEMBER 13

A Gracious Attitude

Becoming a mature Christian has nothing to do with becoming more religiously narrow. The opposite is the case. One develops a more gracious spirit and attitude.

In the stories of the Desert Fathers, there is this account of St. Antony (251–356), the leader of the early hermits who went into the Egyptian desert:

> A hunter happened to come through the brush and saw Abba Antony talking gladly with the brothers, and he was displeased. Antony said to him: "Put an arrow in your bow, and draw it."
>
> He did so. And he said: "Draw it further." And he did so.
>
> He said again: "Draw it yet further." And he drew it.
>
> The hunter said to Antony: "If I draw it too far, the bow will snap."
>
> Abba Antony answered: "So it is with God's work. If we go to excessive extremes, the brothers quickly become exhausted. It is sometimes best not to be rigid."
>
> Quoted in *Christian Monasticism*, 16

Reflection

Hold it in faith.
Hold it with open hand.
Guard it with a gracious spirit.

PSALM 89:8 SEPTEMBER 14

The Greatness of God's Being

All the saints of old speak not only of the works of God, but also of the being of God. God's being is not fully disclosed in his actions. God is greater than the works of his hands.

Bonaventure, in his *Soul's Journey into God*, speaks of God's greatness:

> Once again reflecting upon these things,
> let us say that because the most pure and absolute being,
> which is being without qualification,
> is the first and the last,
> it is, therefore,
> the origin and consummating end of all things.
>
> Because it is eternal and most present,
> it therefore encompasses and enters all duration
> as if it were at one and the same time
> its centre and circumference.
>
> Because it is utterly simple and the greatest,
> it is, therefore,
> totally within all things and totally outside them
> and thus "is an intelligible sphere
> whose centre is everywhere
> and whose circumference is nowhere."

The Soul's Journey into God; The Tree of Life; The Life of St. Francis, 100

Prayer

Lord, before your mystery, I am silent.
In your greatness, I am humbled.
In your goodness, I rejoice.
Amen.

ISAIAH 6:1–7   SEPTEMBER 15

The Contemplative Vision

We are invited to love God with the whole of our being. This includes our imagination. Through the Spirit we can know God intellectually, but also through a revelatory power that always surprises us.

The English mystic Richard Rolle, the Hermit of Hampole, in his *Mending of Life*, speaks of the contemplative experience:

> To me it seems that contemplation is the joyful song of God's love taken into the mind, with the sweetness of angel's praise. This is the jubilation that is the end of perfect prayer and high devotion in this life. This is the spiritual mirth had in mind for the Everlasting Lover, with great voice outbreaking. This is the last and most perfect deed of all deeds in this life.
>
> Therefore the psalmist says: . . . "Blessed be the one that knows jubilation" in the contemplation of God. Truly none alien to God can joy in Jesus, nor taste the sweetness of his love. But if we desire to be ever kindled with the fire of everlasting love, in patience, meekness, and gentle manner, and to be made fair with all cleanness of body and soul and anointed with spiritual ointments, we are lifted up to contemplation.
>
> Let us unceasingly seek healthful virtues, by which in this life we are cleansed from the wretchedness of sins, and in another life, free from all pain, we joy endlessly in the blessed life. Yet in this exile, we thus shall be worthy to feel the joyful mirth of God's love.
>
> Therefore, be not slow to chastise yourself with prayer and waking, and use holy meditations; for doubtless with these spiritual labours, and with heaviness and weeping from inward repenting, the love of Christ is kindled in you, and all virtue and gifts of the Holy Spirit are shed into your heart.
>
> *The Mending of Life*, ch. 12

Reflection

I see you, O Lamb of God, with the eye of the Spirit.
I am cleansed and made whole.

PSALM 34:1–3　　　　　　　　　　　SEPTEMBER 16

The Greatest Good

All that is good is good. One kind of good is as good as another kind of good. But the greatest good is not simply what we do, it is what we are in the loving heart of God, in the shelter of God's embrace, and in being attentive to the God who calls us to love and service.

John Cassian, the great formator of Western monasticism, speaks about the counsel of Abbot Moses, who argued for the superiority of the contemplative life:

> The hope of our religious vocation is the Kingdom of God, but our immediate aim is purity of heart, without which it is impossible for anyone to attain that end.
>
> Anything therefore that can disturb the purity and tranquility of our mind, however useful and even necessary it may seem, must be avoided as harmful.
>
> Our principal endeavour . . . must be that our minds may cleave always to God. . . . The greatest good is not the active life, though it abounds in good and fruitful works, but the contemplation of God himself.
>
> Quoted in *Christian Monasticism*, 18–19

Reflection

Great love of neighbor
is born in the secret place
where selfishness is dissolved in the
burning love of God.
Love of God is the spring from which
the river of goodness flows.

GALATIANS 6:16 — SEPTEMBER 17

A Rule of Life

Monks and those in religious orders live by a rule. So should every Christian. A rule of life is not a set of constraints. It is a set of guideposts.

St. Isaac of Syria sets out a general rule that all could live by:

> The prayer of someone who harbours a grudge
> is like a seed upon a stone.
>
> An ascetic without compassion
> is a tree that bears no fruit.
>
> A rebuke springing from envy
> is a poisoned arrow.
>
> The praise of a crafty person
> is a hidden snare . . .
>
> Be persecuted, rather than be a persecutor.
> Be crucified, rather than be a crucifier.
> Be treated unjustly, rather than treat anyone unjustly.
> Be oppressed, rather than be an oppressor.
> Be gentle, rather than zealous.

The Joy of the Saints, 171

Task

Within the framework of prayer, reflection, contemplative listening, and life evaluation, map out a rule by which you seek to order your life as a follower of Christ.

2 TIMOTHY 1:8–10   SEPTEMBER 18

Suffering for the Sake of Church

In our age, where we are focused on receiving benefits, we need to recover the sense that we may also need to suffer for what is good for a community. The saints of old were willing to suffer for the sake of the church.

St. Basil, in a letter to Eusebius the bishop of Samosata, speaks about his willingness to suffer in order to bring disaffected churches together:

> Hitherto I have been unable to give any adequate and practical proof of my earnest desire to pacify the churches of the Lord. But in my heart I affirm that I have so great a longing, that I would gladly give up even my life, if thereby the flame of hatred, kindled by the evil one, could be put out.
>
> If it was not for the sake of this longing for peace that I consented to come to Colonia, may my life be unblessed by peace.
>
> The peace I seek is the true peace, left us by the Lord himself; and what I have asked that I may have for my assurance belongs to one who desires nothing but true peace . . .
>
> Not that I think it is absolutely our duty to cut ourselves off from those who do not receive the faith, but rather to have regard to them in accordance with the old law of love, and to write to them with one consent, giving them all exhortation with pity, and to propose to them the faith of the fathers, and invite them to union.
>
> If we succeed we should be united in communion with them; if we fail we must be content with one another and purge our conduct of this uncertain spirit, restoring the evangelical and simple conversation followed by those who accepted the Word from the beginning. "They," it is said, "were of one heart and of one soul."

Nicene and Post-Nicene Fathers, vol. 8, 196–97

Reflection

The wounded body of Christ is the divided community of faith.
Can I take that division into the pain of my heart
and into my prayers for healing?

MATTHEW 7:24 SEPTEMBER 19

Doing the Master's Bidding

Obedience is a difficult concept for us in the modern world. Self-determination is what we are all about. Yet, while our relationship with Christ can be one of deep friendship, Christ is Lord. We are therefore called to do Christ's bidding.

Julian of Norwich had a vision of the relationship between Christ and the disciple:

> And still I wondered as I examined the lord and his servant. I saw the lord sitting solemnly and the servant standing reverently before him. In the servant, there is a double meaning, one outward and one inward.
>
> Outwardly, he was dressed humbly, as a workman who was used to hard labor, and he stood very near the lord. His clothing was a white tunic, thin, old and all soiled, stained with sweat, tight fitting for him and short, coming just below the knee, undecorated, torn and worn out, almost ready to be turned to rags.
>
> I was greatly surprised at this, for I thought: "This is unfitting clothing for a servant who is so highly loved to stand before such a dignified lord." But inwardly, I saw in the servant the foundation of love that he had for the lord, which was equal to the love that the lord had for him.
>
> The wisdom of the servant saw inwardly that there was one thing he could do that would honor the lord. And the servant, for love, having no regard for himself nor for anything that might happen to him, hastily leaped up and ran at the bidding of his lord to do that thing which was the lord's will and his honor.
>
> *The Complete Julian of Norwich*, 239

Prayer

A love that loves your will, O Lord
is a love that needs to grow in me.
Breathe that love into my soul
with the breath of the life-giving Spirit, dear Lord.

ROMANS 12:9–11 — SEPTEMBER 20

A Virtuous Life

If it is true that at our deepest level we seek to be and do good, then it is equally true that most fundamentally we need to be empowered to live this way. Much can frustrate our best intentions. Therefore, we need the wind and wings of the Spirit to carry us forward.

The fourth-century bishop St. Hilary of Poitiers, in his *De Trinitate* (*On the Trinity*), writes about the virtuous life:

> When I began to search for the meaning of life, I was at first attracted by the pursuit of wealth and leisure. As most people discover there is little satisfaction in such things, and a life oriented to the gratification of greed or killing time is unworthy of our humanity.
>
> We have been given life in order to achieve something worthwhile, to make good use of our talents, for life itself points to eternity. How otherwise could one regard as a gift from God this life which is painful, fraught with anxiety, and which starts in infancy with a blank mind and ends in the rambling conversations of the old?
>
> It is my belief that human beings, prompted by our very nature, have always sought to raise our sights through the teaching and practice of the virtues such as patience, chastity, and forgiveness in the conviction that a good life is secured only through good deeds and good thoughts.

Celebrating the Saints, 36

Prayer

O God of life,
make my life whole in your love.
O Christ the giver of life,
may my life be patterned on yours.
O Spirit the renewer of life,
may my life be sustained by the breath of your power.

PSALM 105:4 — SEPTEMBER 21

The Seeking Heart

The One whom we have found, or more correctly who has found us, is the One we continue to seek. For at best we have merely entered the edges of his ways.

Gregory of Nyssa, in his *Commentary on the Song of Songs*, speaks about our ongoing longing for God:

> But as great and exalted as he was with such experiences, Moses still had an insatiable desire for more. He implored God to see him face to face, despite the fact that scripture already says that he had been allowed to speak with God face to face.
>
> But neither did his act of intimately speaking with God as a friend make him cease to desire more; rather, "If I have found favour before you, show me your face clearly" (Exod 33:11). And he who promised to grant this request said, "I have known you above others" (Exod 33:17).
>
> God passed Moses by at the divine place in the rock shadowed over by his hand. Moses could hardly see God's back even after he had passed by (Exod 33:22–23).
>
> I believe that we are taught that the person desiring to see God can behold the desired one by always following him. The contemplation of God's face is a never-ending journey toward him accomplished by following right behind the Word.
>
> *Commentary on the Song of Songs*, 219

Reflection

In desiring to see you, O God
I need to see your traces
in your creation,
in your hidden presence in human affairs,
in the symbols of the community of faith,
in pages of the gospel,
and in the signs of your Spirit.

ROMANS 6:15–18   SEPTEMBER 22

Grace and Obedience

We are saved in and through the grace of Christ. But grace transforms the willful heart into a heart of obedience to the gospel and the promptings of the Spirit.

Thomas à Kempis reminds us of the call to obedience. Here he pictures Jesus speaking to a disciple:

> My child, whoever attempts to escape from obedience withdraws from grace. Likewise, whoever seeks to benefit the self, will lose the graces that are shared by all. Those who do not submit freely and willingly to their superiors show that they are not yet perfectly obedient, but are rebellious and prone to complaint.
>
> Therefore, if you wish to conquer your own flesh, learn quickly to submit yourself to your superior. For the exterior enemy is more quickly overcome if the inner-self is not torn apart by struggles. You are your soul's most troublesome enemy, particularly when you are not in harmony with your spirit.
>
> Because you still love yourself too much, you are afraid to give yourself wholly to the will of others. Is it such a great matter for you, who are but dust and nothingness, to subject yourself to others for the sake of God, when I, the Almighty and Most High, who created all things out of nothing, humbly subjected myself to others for your sake? I became the most humble and the lowest of all humankind so that you might overcome your pride and follow the example of my humility.
>
> *The Imitation of Christ* (Croft and Bolton), ch. 13

Prayer

Lord, in the difficult challenges of life,
help me to be marked by humility and to entrust myself to you.
Amen.

ZECHARIAH 2:13 — SEPTEMBER 23

Solitude

We need to grow into the practice of coming to stillness and attentiveness. But solitude is never our achievement, rather it is a gift. In solitude our restlessness ceases, and we are still in the presence of God.

St. Basil, also known as Basil the Great, writes about the challenge and blessing of solitude:

> So in the end I have got very little out of my solitude. What I ought to have done, what would have helped me to walk securely in the footsteps of Jesus who has led me on the path of salvation, would have been to have heard long ago. Has not our Lord said: "If any would come after me, let them deny themselves, take up their cross and follow me?"
>
> We must strive for a quiet mind. The eye cannot appreciate an object set before it if it is perpetually restless, gazing here, there, and everywhere. No more can our mind's eye apprehend the truth with any clarity if it is distracted by a thousand worldly concerns.
>
> For just as it is impossible to write upon a wax tablet without first having erased the marks on it, so it is impossible to receive the impress of divine doctrine without unlearning our inherited preconceptions and habitual prejudices. Solitude offers an excellent opportunity in this process because it calms our passions, and creates space for our reason to remove their influence.
>
> *Celebrating the Saints*, 4–5

Thought

We are usually so full of ourselves and too preoccupied.
When we cease from our own concerns and open our lives to the Spirit,
we enter a place where we might be gifted
with things that we would not normally hear.

PSALM 70:1   SEPTEMBER 24

God as My Helper

We live the life of faith in the grace and goodness of God. But there are times when we are weak and vulnerable. Sometimes we are under threat. Thus we cry out to the Lord to help us.

John Cassian shares this wisdom from the desert monastic tradition:

> For the vigour of this courage to continue in me, by God's grace, I cry out with all my strength: "O God, hurry to rescue me: O Lord, hurry to help me." Whatever work you are doing, or office you are holding, or journey you are undertaking, you must ceaselessly and continuously pray this verse. When you are going to bed, or eating, or as you respond to the basic necessities of nature, do not cease to chant this verse.
>
> Meditating on this thought in your heart may become a saving formula for you, as it will protect you from attacks by devils and purify you from all faults and earthly stains. It may also lead you towards the contemplation of all that is heavenly and invisible, carrying you to that ineffable glow of prayer, which so few have experienced.
>
> Let sleep come upon you as you meditate on this verse so that you will become molded by its words, and you will begin to repeat it even as you sleep. . . . You will write this verse on the threshold and door of your mouth; you will place it on the walls of your house and in the recesses of your heart. And when you fall on your knees in prayer, this may be your chant, both as you kneel and as you rise up to tend all the necessary things of life.
>
> *The Conferences of John Cassian*, 10.10

Thought

This is what the ancients called "the Jesus prayer"
or "the prayer of the heart."
This is a prayer one is always praying.
You can choose your own words for such a prayer,
which you may wish to pray for a long time, even several years.

EXODUS 33:19   SEPTEMBER 25

The God of All Mercy

It is God's very nature to forgive, heal, and mend. This means that God is merciful towards all of his creatures. God gives us what we don't deserve.

Mygron, abbot of Iona (965–81), penned this prayer calling on God's mercy:

> Have mercy upon us, O God the Father Almighty,
> O God of the tempestuous sea and serene air,
> O God of the many languages 'round the circuit of the earth,
> O God of the waves from the bottomless house of the ocean,
> ... O Heavenly Father, who art in heaven.
>
> O Son twice born,
> O true knowledge,
> O true light of love that lightens every darkness,
> O intelligence of the mystical world,
> O mediator of all people
> O fountain of faith,
> O Redeemer of the human race.
>
> Have mercy on us, O God Almighty, O Holy Spirit,
> O finger of God,
> O imparter of true wisdom,
> O author of the Holy Scriptures,
> O septiform Spirit
> O Holy Spirit that rules all created things, visible and invisible.

Towards a History of Irish Spirituality, 80–81

ACTS 13:1–3　　　　　　　　　　SEPTEMBER 26

Fasting

Fasting is a spiritual discipline. But we can fast from much more than food. Anything that we do regularly becomes a domain in which we may fast—and doing this is a relinquishment for a spiritual purpose.

St. John Chrysostom, in one of his *Homilies*, provides this challenge in fasting:

> I have said these things, not that we may disparage fasting, but that we may honour fasting. For the honour of fasting consists not in abstinence from food, but in withdrawing from sinful practices; since the one who limits fasting only to an abstinence from meats, is one who especially disparages it.
>
> Do you fast? Give me proof of it by your works! If you see a poor man, take pity on him! If you see an enemy, be reconciled to her! If you see a friend gaining honour, envy him not! If you see a handsome woman, pass her by.
>
> For let not the mouth only fast, but also the eye, and the ear, and the feet, and the hands, and all the members of our bodies. Let the hands fast, by being pure from rapine and avarice. Let the feet fast, by ceasing from running to unlawful spectacles. Let the eyes fast, being taught never to fix themselves rudely upon handsome countenances, or to busy themselves with strange beauties.
>
> For looking is the food of the eyes, but if this be such as is unlawful or forbidden, it mars the fast; and upsets the safety of the soul; but if it is lawful and safe, it adorns fasting. For it would be among things the most absurd to abstain from lawful food because of the fast.
>
> *Nicene and Post-Nicene Fathers*, vol. 9, 359

Thought

We are called to fast from all that is not right in God's sight.
We may also fast, for a time, from all that is good
for the purpose of prayer and reflection.

2 CORINTHIANS 1:12 SEPTEMBER 27

The Matter of Conscience

We all have an inner voice, which we may call our conscience. Our conscience is not a pure unmediated guide, in that it is shaped by our beliefs and actions, but we should give attention to this inner voice. It may be a true guide.

The fourteenth-century Christian mystic Catherine of Siena has this to say about the conscience:

> The soul is either living in deadly sin, or imperfectly in grace, or she is perfect. Toward all I [God] am generous in my providence, but in different ways, very wisely, as I see people have need.
>
> Worldly people, who are dead in mortal sin, I wake up with the pricking or weariness they feel within their hearts in new and different ways—so many ways your tongue could never describe them. Sometimes, because of the insistence of the pains and pricking of conscience within their souls, they abandon the guilt of deadly sin. And sometimes their heart conceives love for deadly sin or for creatures apart from my will.
>
> But I always pluck the rose from the thorns. So I deprive them of places and times for fulfilling their own wishes until they are so tired of the interior suffering their sinfulness has brought them when they cannot fulfill their perverse wishes that they return to their senses. And the pricking of their conscience and heartfelt compunction lead them to throw away their madness.
>
> It can truly be called madness because, while they thought they had set their affection on something, when they begin to see they find nothing there. True, the creature they loved with such a wretched love was and is something, but what they got from it was nothing because sin is a nothing. But from this nothingness of sin, a thorn that pierces the soul, I pluck this rose to provide their salvation.
>
> *Catherine of Siena: The Dialogue*, 297

Reflection

God is at work in the midst of our stupidities and failures. And God's work is to turn us around and heal us.

PSALM 31:23　　　　　　　　　　　　SEPTEMBER 28

A Saint

A saint is not simply a person of virtue. A saint is also a person of conversion and transformation. And equally importantly, a saint is someone who sees the world with very different eyes.

G. K. Chesterton, in his famous *St. Francis of Assisi*, has this to say about this saint—and in general about all saints:

> The transition from the good person to the saint is a sort of revolution, by which one for whom all things illustrate and illuminate God becomes one for whom God illustrates and illuminates all things. It is rather like the reversal whereby a lover might say at first sight that a lady looked like a flower, and say afterwards that all flowers reminded him of his lady. A saint and a poet standing by the same flower might seem to say the same thing; but indeed though they would both be telling the truth, they would be telling different truths.
>
> For one the joy of life is a *cause* of faith, for the other rather a *result* of faith. But one effect of the difference is that the sense of divine dependence, which for the artist is like a brilliant Levin-blaze, for the saint is like the broad daylight.
>
> Being in some mystical sense on the other side of things, the saint sees things go forth from the divine as children going forth from a familiar and accepted home, instead of meeting them as they come out, as most of us do, upon the roads of the world. And it is the paradox that by this privilege the saint is more familiar, more free and fraternal, more carelessly hospitable than we. For us, the elements are like heralds who tell us with trumpet and tabard that we are drawing near the city of a great king; but the saint hails them with an old familiarity that is almost an old frivolity. The saint calls them Brother Fire and Sister Water.

St. Francis of Assisi, 76

Reflection

We so often only see with our eyes. The saint sees with eyes also, but is able to see *through*—to God who is on the other side.

ISAIAH 35:1–6 SEPTEMBER 29

Joy in the Lord

Joy is the heartbeat of the Christian life. It is joy in who God is and in all that God does to renew the earth and to bless humanity.

The early ninth-century Irish "Stowe Missal" celebrates God's goodness:

> My peace I give you, Alleluia,
> My peace I leave you, Alleluia.
> Those who love your law have great peace, Alleluia,
> They do not stumble, Alleluia.
>
> Bless the King of heaven who comes with peace, Alleluia.
> Full of the odour of life, Alleluia.
> O sing of him a new song, Alleluia . . .
>
> Come, eat of my bread, Alleluia,
> And drink of the wine I have mixed for you, Alleluia.
> All who eat my body, Alleluia,
> And drink my blood, Alleluia,
> Abide in me and I in them, Alleluia . . .
> The Lord fed them with bread from heaven, Alleluia,
> His children ate the bread of angels, Alleluia.

Celtic Theology: Humanity, World and God in Early Irish Writings, 143

Reflection

In the abundance of your love
and in the bounty of your gifts
let me rejoice
and give you thanks,
O my God and Redeemer.

PSALM 90:3–6 — SEPTEMBER 30

Mortality

We may be famous or insignificant, but we will all die. All of us are called to face our mortality and to live in the light that we only have the gift of a certain time here on earth.

St. Bernard of Clairvaux, in a letter to Bishop Alexander of Lincoln, has this to say about human mortality:

> And now a few words for you yourself. I thought I would add something, prompted by God and perhaps inspired by him, to presume to exhort you lovingly not to take the glory of the world seriously as something that will last and so lose that glory that will never pass away.
>
> Do not love your possessions more than yourself or for your own sake, and so lose both your possessions and yourself. Do not let the pleasure of your present prosperity hide your end from you, or endless adversity will follow.
>
> Do not let the joy of this world bring about while concealing from you, and conceal from you while bringing it about, the grief that is everlasting. Do not think death is a long way off, for it may catch you when you are not ready. And when you think life will go on and on, it may suddenly come to an end when you are in the wrong frame of mind, as it is written, "When they are saying, 'Peace and security,' then suddenly death will come, like the pains of a woman in labor, and they will not escape it" (1 Thess 5:3).
>
> *Bernard of Clairvaux: Selected Works*, 139

Reflection

The gift of life
a fragile treasure,
to guard, shepherd, and use—
and to live to the full,
to the glory of God and the love of neighbor.

October

JOHN 6:49–51   OCTOBER 1

The Bread of Life

The metaphor of Jesus as the bread of life is rich with meaning. But most basically, it means that Jesus is no luxury meal for an elite few. Jesus is the common source of life for every person.

Ephrem was a fourteenth-century master of Christian poetry. He writes about Jesus as the bread of life:

> O fairest ear of wheat
> which grew among the hateful tares
> and gave the Bread of Life
> without labour to the hungry!
>
> It undid the curse
> with which Adam was bound,
> who had eaten with sweat
> the bread of pain and thorns.
> Blessed is the one who eats
> of that Bread of blessing
> and makes the curse pass from him!

Quoted in *Christian Spirituality: Origins to the Twelfth Century*, 157–58

Reflection

Ordinary bread,
an ordinary carpenter in our midst.
The Bread of Life,
a beloved Son of the Father.
More than bread, more than an ordinary Man.

1 CORINTHIANS 7:1–7   OCTOBER 2

Modes of Life

Single or married. Priest or politician. Academic or motor mechanic. Farmer or scientist. Vocations in life and modes of life are myriad and varied.

In *City of God*, St. Augustine speaks about different ways of life:

> As to these three modes of life—the contemplative, the active, and the composite—one may choose any of them without harming eternal interests, so long as faith is preserved. Yet one must not overlook the claims of truth and duty.
>
> We do not have the right to lead a life of such rich contemplation that we forget in our ease the service due to our neighbor; nor do we have a right to be so immersed in active life that we neglect the contemplation of God.
>
> The charm of leisure must not foster lazy vacancy, but rather the investigation or discovery of truth, that we may make solid achievements without resenting others who do the same.
>
> And in active life, we should not covet the honors or power of this life, since all things under the sun are vanity, but we should seek to use our position and influence, as long as these have been honorably attained, for the welfare of those who are under us, as we have already explained.

Nicene and Post-Nicene Fathers, vol. 2, 413

Reflection

In my work, may I pray.
May my prayer guide my work.
In contemplation, may I be attentive
to God and the world.

PROVERBS 3:7–8   OCTOBER 3

Nourishment

Through Word and Spirit, through the gifts of creation and community, and in so many other ways, God seeks to nourish us in all goodness and grace.

St. Gregory of Nyssa speaks of the way in which God seeks to nourish us and fill our lives with good things:

> "We should talk to them like this," my teacher said. "Dear people, it is useless for you to grumble and complain at the necessary order and sequence of events. You do not know towards what goal each part in the universe is being directed, because everything must be united to the divine nature in a certain order and sequence according to the skilful wisdom of the Governor.
>
> Our rational nature came to birth for this purpose, so that the wealth of divine good things might not be idle. A kind of vessels and voluntary receptacles for souls were fashioned by the wisdom which constructed the universe, in order that there should be a container to receive good things, a container which would always become larger with the addition of what would be poured into it.
>
> For the participation in the divine good is such that it makes anyone into whom it enters greater and more receptive. As it is taken up it increases the power and magnitude of the recipient, so that the person who is nourished always grows and never ceases from growth. Since the fountain of good things flows unfailingly, the nature of the participants who use all the influx to add to their own magnitude . . . becomes at the same time both more capable of attracting the better and more able to contain it.

On the Soul and the Resurrection, 87

Prayer

O Lord, may my hands be idle so that they are ready for your bidding.
May my heart be empty so that it can receive all you wish to give.

JOHN 17:20–21 — OCTOBER 4

God's Self-Giving

God not only gives good gifts and sustains all of life. God also gives himself. This is most clearly seen in the gift of Christ, God's Son. In this giving, God most deeply identifies with us.

In one of Meister Eckhart's *Sermons*, he speaks about God's self-giving:

> When the Father gives birth to his Son, he gives him all he has in his being and nature. In this giving, the Holy Spirit bursts forth.
>
> God desires to give himself wholly to us. In the same way, when fire wants to draw wood into itself, and penetrate itself into the wood, it finds that the wood is unlike itself. Thus it needs time.
>
> First, fire makes the wood warm and hot. Then the wood smokes and cracks, because it is unlike the fire. As the wood grows hotter, it becomes quieter and calmer. The more the wood becomes like the fire, the more peaceful it is, until it becomes wholly fire itself. If the fire is to consume the wood, all dissimilarity must be expelled.
>
> By the truth that is God, if you are intent on anything other than God, or if you seek anything else than God, the work that you perform is not yours nor, indeed, God's.
>
> Your work is whatever you aim towards. Whatever is working in me is my Father, and I am dependent on him. There cannot be two Fathers in nature; there must always be one Father in nature. When the other things have been removed and "fulfilled," this birth will take place.

Master Eckhart and the Rhineland Mystics, 109

Reflection

God in me.
I in God.
The mystery of the true end and purpose of life.
The gift of the Spirit.

PSALM 40:11   OCTOBER 5

God My Protector

Christians are not magically kept safe from life's difficulties and challenges. But they are called to seek God's presence and protection and care in good and hard times.

In the *Carmina Gadelica* there is a prayer for protection:

> The Son of God be shielding me from harm,
> The Son of God be shielding me from ill,
> The Son of God be shielding me from mishap,
> The Son of God be shielding me this night.
> The Son of God be shielding me with might,
> The Son of God be shielding me with power;
> Each one who is dealing with me aright,
> So may God deal with each one's soul.
>
> May God free me from every wickedness,
> May God free me from every entrapment,
> May God free me from every gully,
> From every tortuous road, from every slough.
> May God open to me every pass,
> Christ open to me every narrow way,
> Each soul of holy man and woman in heaven
> Be preparing for me my pathway.

Carmina Gadelica, 99–101

Prayer

I can go alone,
but I won't travel well.
Be beside me, O God.
Be ahead of me so I may follow.

2 CORINTHIANS 1:20–22　　　　　　OCTOBER 6

God's Transforming Work

God's transforming work in us is one of infinite patience and persistence. We are hardly the most obedient of creatures. We move forward and slip back. Yet God continues to be with us. What grace is this?

Symeon the New Theologian spells out some of the contours of God's work in us:

> For this discourse teaches us of the total darkness and obscurity that at first rules in us, how benighted we are—that is to say, how remote we are from the divine light—when it clearly extends to ignorance of God. Then the reproaches on the part of the conscience, then the fear, then the desire for the remission of debts. Then we seek for both a mediator and helper for this purpose, for no one is able to journey alone without shame; all are overwhelmed and dishonored by their many sins. Then how, by the enlightenment of the Spirit, we see a mediator and a pastor and advocate. The Spirit also shows us the beginning of enlightenment, into which we had not been initiated previously.
>
> Then also how, having received this revelation, we fall into the darkness of many sins again when the contemplation of the Spirit goes from us and we are deprived of it. After this, our discourse shows us the second call made through the pastor and then our obedience, faith, humility, submission. And following these, little by little, in knowledge and contemplation, a very real transformation.
>
> The one who does not recognize this transformation happening, as this discourse has described, it is not possible that the Holy Spirit is dwelling within. But as this discourse has explained in detail, as I have said above, we cannot boast, but we tell of the wonders of God.
>
> *Catéchèses* 3, 327

Prayer

O Lord, may your gracious, gentle and yet focused work in me continue. May I be open to all you seek to do. Amen.

Isaiah 11:1–5   October 7

God's Righteous Judgment

Justice is a precious but precarious commodity in the modern world. The powerful seem to procure one form of justice. The poor are so often without any form of justice. God's justice has to do with what is right, particularly for the poor.

The early church father Irenaeus, in one of his writings toward the end of the second century, picks up the theme of God's judgment:

> But the words, "he shall not judge according to appearances, nor reprove according to report, but he shall give just judgement to the lowly and have pity on the lowly of the earth," show his divinity more strongly.
>
> For to judge without acceptance of persons or partiality, not favouring the noble, but rendering to the lowly what is right and equitable and fair, corresponds to the exaltation and sublimity of God's justice, for God is not subject to influence, and favours none but the just ones. And to have pity is especially proper to God, who can also save out of pity.
>
> And also, "he shall strike the earth with a word and slay the ungodly" by a word alone (Isa 11:4); this is proper to God, who works all things whatsoever by his word. But in saying "His loins shall be girded with justice, and his flanks clad in truth" (cf. Eph 6:14) he announces his outward human form, and his inward supreme justice.
>
> *Proof of the Apostolic Preaching*, 87

Prayer

O Lord, I am swayed so easily by appearances.
I am so biased in my preferences.
I am so open to making wrong compromises.
Help me to be grounded in your ways,
walking the path of justice and being an advocate for the poor.

2 CORINTHIANS 1:3–7   OCTOBER 8

The Precarious Nature of Friendships

In the area of friendships, we experience the joys of life as well as its vulnerabilities. In friendships, we find our greatest fulfillment and sustenance. But in the trials and loss of friendship, we often receive our deepest wounding.

St. Augustine of Hippo's monumental *City of God* touches on this important topic:

> In our present wretched condition, we frequently mistake a friend for an enemy, and an enemy for a friend. If we manage to escape this pitiful blindness, the genuine confidence and mutual love of true friendship is our one solace in human society, even though it is filled with misunderstandings and calamities.
>
> And yet the more friends we have, and the more widely they are scattered, the more we fear that one of the innumerable disasters of life may fall upon them.
>
> Not only are we anxious that they might suffer from famine, war, disease, captivity, or the inconceivable horrors of slavery, but we also painfully dread that their friendship may deteriorate into deceitfulness, malice, or injustice. When we realize that these circumstances have actually occurred—which happens more frequently as we have more friends who become more widely scattered—who but those who have experienced such suffering can describe the pangs that tear the heart?
>
> *Nicene and Post-Nicene Fathers*, vol. 2, 405

Reflection

Torn by love.
A wounded heart.
The greatest loss.
How can it heal?

1 CORINTHIANS 4:15–16   OCTOBER 9

Models

Whether we do this intentionally, or not, we are models for others, for good or for ill. Hopefully, we will do our best to be good models for others, all the while realizing our own foibles and weaknesses.

In *The Testament of Saint Clare*, we have an example of the call to be models to others as part of our Christian calling to be imitators of Christ:

> With what solicitude and fervour of mind and body, therefore, must we keep the commandments of our God and Father, so that, with the help of the Lord, we may return to him an increase of his talents (cf. Matt 25:15–23). For the Lord himself not only has set us as an example and mirror for others, but also for our own sisters, whom the Lord has called to our way of life, so that they in turn will be a mirror and example to those living in the world.
>
> Since, therefore, the Lord has called us to such great things, that those who are to be models and mirrors for others may behold themselves in us, we are truly bound to bless and praise the Lord and to be strengthened constantly in him to do good.
>
> Therefore, if we have lived according to the form of life given us, we shall, by very little effort, leave others a noble example, and gain the prize of eternal happiness.
>
> *Francis and Clare: The Complete Works*, 227–28

Reflection

Most happily I would be
your child in faith and love.
As such, may my life
reflect your Light.
And may it always be your light!

1 THESSALONIANS 5:23   OCTOBER 10

Lost in the Mystery of God

God may be apprehended by our mind and our inner being. This apprehension is in faith and by the Holy Spirit. The saints of old have tried to find ways to describe this. We hear them in the limitations of all language.

The medieval Christian mystic Marguerite Porete shares this song:

>Love has made me find my nobility in
>These verses of a song.
>It speaks of the deity pure,
>About whom reason does not know how to speak,
>And of a lover,
>Which I have without a mother,
>Who is the offspring
>Of God the Father
>And also of God the Son.
>His name is Holy Spirit,
>From whom I possess such a union in the heart,
>That He causes joy to remain in me.
>It is the peace of the nourishment
>Which the lover gives in loving.
>I wish to ask nothing of him,
>To do so would be too wretched of me.
>
>Instead, I owe him total faith
>In loving such a lover.

Marguerite Porete: The Mirror of Simple Souls, 199

ACTS 4:32–35   OCTOBER 11

A Monastic Vision

Throughout most of church history, some Christians have sought to live a monastic way of life or a variation of some form of intentional Christian community. Such a way of life seeks to be an icon of the Trinity.

The fourth-century monk St. Martin of Tours lived in a monastic community. In *Vita Martini*, we have Sulpicius Severus' biographical account of St. Martin of Tours:

> And now, having entered on the episcopal office, Martin distinguished himself in the discharge of its duties. With the unwavering constancy, he remained the same as he had been before. There was the same humility in his heart and the same plainness in his clothes. Filled with both dignity and courtesy, he maintained the position of a bishop properly, yet without laying aside the objects and virtues of a monk. For some time, he used the cell connected with the church, but when he could no longer tolerate the disturbance caused by the numbers of those who visited him there, he established a monastery for himself about two miles outside the city. This spot was so secret and remote that he enjoyed in it the solitude of a hermit. On one side, it was surrounded by the precipice of a lofty mountain, and the place could only be approached by one very narrow passage.
>
> His cell was constructed of wood. Many of the brothers had fashioned hermitages for themselves out of the rock, hollowed into caves. There were eighty disciples there, who were being trained after the example of their saintly master. No one possessed anything of his own; all things were shared in common. They were forbidden to buy or sell anything. No art was practiced there, except for the transcribers, and this was assigned to the younger brothers, while the elders spent their time in prayer. The brothers rarely left their cells, except when they assembled at the place of prayer. After the hour of fasting was past, they all ate together. Many of the brothers were of noble rank, and though they had been brought up far differently, they had forced themselves down to this degree of humility and patient endurance.
>
> *Sulpicius Severus on the Life of St. Martin*, ch. 10

PSALM 84:5   OCTOBER 12

On Pilgrimage

The Christian is a person on pilgrimage, who embarks on the journey from sin to holiness, from self-will to obedience, from earth to new heavens and a new earth.

St. Augustine speaks about the pilgrim status of the people of God:

> As for myself, I will enter into my closet and there sing to you the songs of love, groaning with groanings that are unutterable now in my pilgrimage, and remembering Jerusalem with my heart uplifted to Jerusalem my country, Jerusalem my mother, and to you yourself, the ruler of the source of light, its father, guardian, husband, its chaste and strong delight, its solid joy and all its goods ineffable—and all of this at the same time, since you are the one supreme and true Good!
>
> And I will not be turned away until you have brought back together all that I am from this dispersion and deformity to the peace of that dearest mother, where the first fruits of my spirit are to be found, and from which all these things are promised me which you do conform and confirm forever, O my God, my mercy.

The Confessions of St. Augustine, 252

Reflection

I am home in you, O triune God.
Yet, I am still on pilgrimage.
I have wandered far.
You have found me and brought me home.

But I am still coming home.
Close to your heart.
Immersed in your ways.
Longing for fulfilment.

PSALM 45:2   OCTOBER 13

A Gracious God; God's Gracious People

Grace is God's unmerited kindness towards us. This grace is to permeate the whole of our lives. This means we are to be gracious, grateful, and generous towards others.

From the *Carmina Gadelica*, we have a song celebrating grace:

> Grace of form,
> Grace of voice be yours;
> Grace of charity,
> Grace of wisdom be yours;
> Grace of beauty,
> Grace of health be yours;
> Grace of sea,
> Grace of land be yours;
> Grace of music,
> Grace of guidance be yours;
> Grace of battle-triumph,
> Grace of victory be yours;
> Grace of life,
> Grace of praise be yours;
> Grace of love,
> Grace of dancing be yours;
> Grace of lyre, Grace of harp be yours;
> Grace of sense,
> Grace of reason be yours;
> Grace of speech, Grace of story be yours;
> Grace of peace,
> Grace of God be yours.
>
> *Celtic Christian Spirituality:*
> *An Anthology of Medieval and Modern Sources*, 134–35

ACTS 20:1–2   OCTOBER 14

Words of Encouragement

The Christian life is not just a picnic. It is wonderful but also challenging, life-giving but also life-demanding. Therefore, we all need encouragement on the way.

Hildegard of Bingen was a spiritual advisor to many, including those from the nobility, the clergy and from monastic communities. She exercised a ministry of encouragement. Here is an excerpt from a letter to Eberhard, Archbishop of Salzburg:

> But Obedience also says to you: I remain with you, through the laws and the commandments of God. Therefore, hold me earnestly with all your strength, not as your overseer, but as your dearest friend. For you received me at your baptism, and you held me as you advanced in the discipline of obedience, and you embraced me when you were obedient to the commands of God. Divine love is my mother, for I was born from her.
>   O father, Wisdom says to you: be like the head of a household, who patiently hears the foolishness of his children, yet does not abandon his discretion. In the same way, I unite what is heavenly and the earthly for the benefit of the people. Therefore, touch and cleanse wounds and embrace simple, good-living people. In this way, as God assists you, you will have joy in both facets of your life.
>   Now, father, I am a poor little woman. I see that your will is longing for the door of virtue, which will come to you, so that in those virtues, as your body is ground down, you will complete the cycle of earthly life. May the One who is and who searches out all things keep your soul and body in his salvation.

The Letters of Hildegard of Bingen, vol. 1, 86

Prayer

Lord, may I build up, not pull down.
May my words be life-giving,
not death-dealing.

ECCLESIASTES 11:5 — OCTOBER 15

Not Knowing

Christians can sometimes claim that they know a lot about God and about God's ways. But our understanding is fragmentary, and we frequently have to bow before the mystery of who God is and of God's way with us.

In the long history of Christianity there is an emphasis on mystery and not knowing. The Desert Fathers also understood this:

> Once some brothers came to visit Antony, and Joseph was with them. Antony, wanting to test them, began to speak about scripture.
>
> He asked the younger monks first the meaning of text after text, and each of them answered as well as he could. To each he said, "You have not found the right answer."
>
> Then he said to Joseph, "What do you think is the meaning of this word?" Joseph replied, "I don't know."
>
> Antony said, "Indeed, Joseph alone has found the true way, for he said he did not know."
>
> *The Desert Fathers: Sayings of the Early Christian Monks*, 148

Reflection

I hear,
but I don't fully understand.
I know,
but I don't know all that I should.
I see,
but often ever so dimly.
I believe,
but Lord, help my unbelief.

LUKE 12:15 — OCTOBER 16

Overcoming Greed

The longing for something more seems to be an inbuilt human desire. The challenge is to direct this desire in a good way. So often this is merely directed towards much-having. Instead, it should be directed towards the flourishing of goodness.

St. Columbanus, in his *Monks' Rules*, has this to say about overcoming greed:

> For monks, to whom for Christ's sake "the world is crucified, just as they are crucified to the world," greed must be avoided, for it is wrong for them to have, or even to want, more than they need.
>
> Monks do not need possessions, but will. Leaving everything and following the Lord Christ with the cross of fear each day, they will store up treasure in heaven. Therefore, because they will have much in heaven, they should be satisfied with a few possessions of basic necessity on earth. For monks, greed is a leprosy, for they imitate the sons of the prophets. For the disciple of Christ, greed is betrayal and ruin, and for the uncertain followers of the apostles, it is death.
>
> Thus nakedness and disdain of riches are the first perfection of monks. The second, is the purging of vices. The third, is the most perfect and perpetual love of God and unceasing devotion for divine things, which flows from the relinquishment of earthly things.
>
> Because this is true, we have need of few things, or only one, according to the Word of the Lord. For few things are true necessities without which life cannot be led, or even one thing, such as food. . . . But we require purity of feeling by the grace of God, that we may understand spiritually the few gifts of love that are offered to Martha by the Lord.
>
> *Monks' Rules,* 6

Prayer

Help me, O Lord, to love spontaneously,
to live simply, to share generously,
to pray ceaselessly, to live fully.

MATTHEW 16:17–19   OCTOBER 17

Release from Sin

While we may come directly to God confessing our sins, there are also times where our confession should be made in the presence of another—priest or pastor, friend or spiritual director.

St. Augustine speaks of the importance of penitence and for our sins to be remitted:

> But even crimes themselves, however great, may be remitted in the holy church; and the mercy of God is never to be despaired of by anyone who truly repents, each according the measure of his or her sin.
>
> And in the act of repentance, where a crime has been committed of such a nature as to cut off the sinner from the body of Christ, we are not to take account so much of the measure of time as of the measure of sorrow; for a broken and a contrite heart God does not despise.
>
> But as the grief of one heart is frequently hid from another, and is not made known to others by words or other signs when it is manifest to him of whom it is said, "My groaning is not hidden from you," those who govern the church have rightly appointed times of penitence, that the church in which the sins are remitted may be satisfied. And outside the church sins are not remitted. For the church alone has received the pledge of the Holy Spirit, without which there is no remission of sins—such, at least, as brings the pardoned to eternal life.
>
> *Enchiridion on Faith, Hope, and Love,* 76–77

Prayer

My sin is a burden that is too heavy for me.
What grace it is that I may lay that burden at your feet, O God.

Exodus 23:20 — October 18

A Guardian Angel

In the modern world, not only is God doubted, but belief in the presence of angels has been relegated to the dustbin of superstition. But it's possible that our scientific worldview is too limited. In a re-enchanted world, such creatures may well be a gift.

The *Carmina Gadelica*, which has captured the deep sources of Celtic spirituality, speaks of the blessing of angels:

> You, angel of God, who has charge of me,
> From the dear Father of mercifulness,
> The shepherding king of the fold of the saints,
> To make 'round about me this night.
>
> Drive from me every temptation and danger,
> Surround me on the sea of unrighteousness,
> And in the narrows, crooks and straights,
> Keep my coracle, keep it always.
>
> Be a bright flame before me,
> Be a guiding star above me,
> Be a smooth path below me,
> And be a kindly shepherd behind me,
> Today, tonight, and forever.
>
> I am tired and I am a stranger,
> Lead me to the land of the angels;
> For me, it is time to go home,
> To the court of Christ, to the peace of heaven.

Celtic Christian Spirituality:
An Anthology of Medieval and Modern Sources, 96

ISAIAH 19:22 — OCTOBER 19

God's Heavy Hand

God is no Father Christmas. God is a God of mercy and judgment. And there are times when we experience God's heavy hand rather than the whispers of his Spirit, when all seems dark rather than light.

St. John Chrysostom, in *Letter to a Young Widow,* gives these words of encouragement:

> Under any circumstances, indeed, the female sex is . . . apt to be sensitive to suffering; but when in addition there is youth, and untimely widowhood, and inexperience in business, and a great crowd of cares—while the whole life previously has been nurtured in the midst of luxury, and cheerfulness, and wealth—the evil is increased many fold, and if she who is subjected to it does not obtain help from on high, even an accidental thought will be able to unhinge her.
>
> Now I hold this to be the foremost and greatest evidence of God's care concerning you: you have not been overwhelmed by grief, nor driven out of your natural condition of mind, when such great troubles suddenly concurred to afflict you. And this was not due to any human assistance, but to the almighty hand—the understanding of which there is no measure, the wisdom which is past finding out—of the "Father of mercies and the God of all comfort" (2 Cor 1:3).
>
> "For he himself," it is said, "has smitten us, and he will heal us; he will strike, and he will dress the wound and make us whole" (Hos 6:2).

Nicene and Post-Nicene Fathers, vol. 9, 159

Reflection

I may have expected, O God,
that you would have prevented my distress.
But may I find you
in the midst of all my difficulties.

EXODUS 33:19   OCTOBER 20

The God of Compassion

God's love encircles the Trinity. God's compassion encircles humanity. And it is God's great love that issues forth in God's compassion towards all he has made, including recalcitrant humanity.

St. Anselm seeks to understand God's great compassion. He writes,

> If you are entirely and supremely just, how can you spare the wicked? For how does the entirely and supremely just one do something that is unjust? What kind of justice is it to give everlasting life to one who deserves eternal death?
>
> O God of goodness, who is good to both good and wicked, how can you save the wicked, if doing so is not just, and you do not do anything that is not just?
>
> Since your goodness is beyond comprehension, is the answer hidden in the inaccessible light where you dwell? Truly, in the deepest and most secret place of your goodness, there is a hidden source from which the stream of your mercy flows.
>
> For because you are entirely and supremely just, you extend mercy to the wicked. Far better is the one who is good to both good and wicked than the one who is good only to the good.
>
> *Anselm of Canterbury: The Major Works*, 91

Reflection

You love, O Lord,
with a purpose,
to welcome home all your wandering daughters and sons,
in order to make them well,
in order to make them whole.

Ephesians 6:10–13 — October 21

The Christian Struggle

The saying "there is no rest for the wicked" is only half-true. For there is also no rest for the righteous, at least not in this life. The Christian life is one of struggle.

The unknown author of *The Book of Privy Counseling* concludes as follows:

> Yet you may say: "Rest? What can he possibly be talking about? All I feel is toil and pain, not rest. When I try to follow his advice, suffering and struggle beset me on every side. On the one hand, my faculties hound me to give up this work, and I will not; on the other, I long to lose the experience of myself and experience only God, and I cannot. Battle and pain assail me everywhere. How can he talk of rest? If this is rest, I think it is a rather odd kind of rest."
>
> My answer is simple. You find this work painful because you are not yet accustomed to it. Were you accustomed to it, and did you realize its value, you would not willingly give it up for all the material joys and rest in the world. Yes, I know, it is painful and toilsome. Still, I call it rest because your spirit does rest in a freedom from doubt and anxiety about what it must do; and because during the actual time of prayer, it is secure in the knowledge that it will not greatly err.
>
> And so persevere in prayer with humility and great desire, for it is a work that begins here on earth but will go on without end into eternity. I pray that the all-powerful Jesus may bring you and all those he has redeemed by his precious blood to this glory. Amen.
>
> *The Cloud of Unknowing and The Book of Privy Counseling*, 188

Thought

No part of the Christian life is just a breeze. It is also not just of our own making.
Instead, it is the triumph of grace moving an often reluctant obedience.
It is the Spirit softening hard hearts. It is learning to yield to the ways of God.
It is all about surrender.

2 CORINTHIANS 10:3–4   OCTOBER 22

The Christian's Warfare

The Christian life is lived in the midst of conflict. Such conflict should not be of our making. Rather, it is the conflict between flesh and spirit, renewal and tradition, the work of God and the forces of the Evil One.

Bonaventure, in his reflections on the life of St. Francis, calls all Christians into the fray to see God's Reign more fully come amongst us:

> Come now, knight of Christ,
> vigorously bear the arms of your
> unconquerable leader!
> Visibly shielded with these,
> you will overcome all adversaries.
>
> Carry the standard of the most high King,
> and at its sight,
> let all who fight in God's army,
> be aroused to courage.
>
> Carry the seal of Christ, the High Priest,
> by which your words and deeds,
> will be rightly accepted by all,
> as authentic and beyond reproach.
>
> For now because of the brand-marks of the Lord Jesus,
> which you carry in your body,
> no one should trouble you;
> rather every servant of Christ
> should show them deep devotion.

The Life of St. Francis, 147

PSALM 141:2   OCTOBER 23

The Pathway of Prayer

For the contemporary person, prayer is a difficult pathway, for we so often think that we have to do things ourselves or that God is not interested in our issues. But we are invited to walk the path of prayer, no matter how difficult it may be.

St. Isaac of Syria gives these helpful reminders regarding the way of prayer:

> If God is slow to grant your request and you do not receive what you ask for promptly, do not be grieved, for you are not wiser than God.
>
> When this happens to you, it is either because your way of life does not accord with your request, or because the pathways of your heart are at odds with the intention of your prayer. Or it may be because your inner state is too childish by comparison with the magnitude of the thing you have asked for.
>
> It is not appropriate that great things should fall easily into our hands—otherwise God's gift will be held in dishonour, because of the ease with which we obtain it. For anything that is readily obtained is also easily lost, whereas everything which is found with toil is preserved with care.

The Joy of the Saints, 12

Reflection

I ask, but may I demand?
I come in humility, but should I come in great boldness?
I say, "if it is thy will," but should I insist?
I come in hope, but should I come in faith?

Help me, O God, to find my way with you,
in the challenging pathways of prayer.

PSALM 69:29   OCTOBER 24

God's Protection

God's protection is no automatic right of the children of God. God's protection is always a prayer. It is always trust. And often it is about God keeping us in the midst of life's difficulties.

In the long tradition of the Celtic prayers captured in the *Carmina Gadelica*, we read of the cry of the people of God for God's protection:

> The sacred Three
> To save,
> To shield.
>
> To surround
> The hearth,
> The house,
> The household.
>
> This eve,
> This night.
> Oh! This eve.
> This night.
>
> And every single night,
> Each single night. Amen.

*Celtic Christian Spirituality:
An Anthology of Medieval and Modern Sources*, 123

Thought

Our prayers to God may be uttered in the greatest simplicity, but they must be prayers of the heart, prayers of childlike trust.

1 TIMOTHY 1:15–16   OCTOBER 25

Brutal Honesty

> *While we need to be discerning about the way in which we bare our souls—and to whom we bare them—there are times when we need to be brutally honest about the way things really are. We can always be like this in relation to God—and with a few trusted people.*

In *The Second Letter from Heloise to Abelard*, Heloise writes as follows:

> St. Gregory comments on this, saying, "There are some who confess their faults aloud, yet in that confession, they do not know how to be sorry. They speak cheerfully of what should be lamented." Thus, "whoever despises their sins and declares them, must declare them in bitterness of heart. It is this bitterness of heart that punishes for the deeds the mind has prompted the tongue to tell."
>
> The sorrow that belongs to true repentance is rare, as St. Ambrose remarks: "I have found those who have preserved their innocence more frequently than I have found those who have truly repented."
>
> Indeed, the delights that we enjoyed together as lovers were so sweet that I can neither hate them nor forget them except with the greatest difficulty. They are present to me, and so is my longing for them wherever I turn. I am not even spared their illusions when I sleep.
>
> Their unclean visions take such complete possession of my unhappy soul, even during the solemn moments of the Mass when prayer should be most fervent. Yet even then, my thoughts are fixed on vileness rather than prayer. When I ought to be deeply sorrowful for what I have done, I am lamenting what I have lost.
>
> *Mystics, Visionaries, and Prophets:*
> *An Anthology of Women's Spiritual Writings*, 123

Explanation

Heloise and Peter were lovers. They then married. They then separated to live a chaste life. Heloise became the Abbess of the Monastery of the Paraclete. Peter ended his days as a solitary in the diocese of Troyes. In this letter, we hear Heloise's utter honesty.

PROVERBS 8:10-12 OCTOBER 26

Wisdom

One can know a lot and not be wise. Wisdom is knowledge that has been forged on the anvil of life and has known both suffering and care. Rather than having only people of technological prowess, our world also needs wise women and men.

The early church father Origen speaks of the value of wisdom:

> Those who devote themselves to the pursuit of wisdom and knowledge have no end to their labours. How could there be an end, a limit, where the wisdom of God is concerned?
>
> The nearer we come to that wisdom, the deeper we find it to be. And the more we probe into its depths, the more we see that we will never be able to understand it or express it in words...
>
> Travellers, then, on the road to God's wisdom find that the further they go, the more the road opens out, until it stretches to infinity.

Quoted in *Christian Spirituality:
Origins to the Twelfth Century*, 402

Reflection

I wanted knowledge.
I wanted power.
I wanted influence and regard.

I needed wisdom.
I lacked humility.
I began to search for a servant heart.

Christ showed the way,
the wise One whom wise men worshipped.
In his wisdom is a suffering that brings life.

ACTS 26:19–20 OCTOBER 27

The Deeds of Repentance

It is one thing to be sorry for the wrong one has done to another person. It is quite another thing to go to that person and to admit one's fault and to ask for forgiveness. But it is even another thing altogether to seek to make restitution.

St. John Chrysostom, in one of his *Homilies*, speaks about the deeds of repentance:

> See, we have shown five ways of repentance: first the condemnation of sins, second the forgiveness of our neighbour's sins, third that which comes of prayer, fourth that which comes of almsgiving, fifth that which comes of humility.
>
> Do not be lazy then, but walk in all these day by day. For the ways are easy, nor can you plead poverty. For even if you live poorer than all, you are able to leave your anger, and be humble, and pray fervently, and condemn sins, and your poverty is in no way a hindrance.
>
> And why do I speak this way, when not even in that way of repentance in which it is possible to spend money (I speak of almsgiving), not even there is poverty any hindrance to us from obeying the command? The widow who spent the two mites is a proof.
>
> Having learned, then, the healing of our wounds, let us constantly apply these medicines, in order that we may return to health and enjoy the sacred table with assurance. And with much glory, may we reach Christ, the king of glory, and attain to everlasting good by the grace, compassion, and loving kindness of our Lord Jesus Christ, by whom and with whom be glory, power, honour, to the Father, together with the holy, good and quickening Spirit, now and always and forever and ever. Amen.
>
> *Nicene and Post-Nicene Fathers*, vol. 9, 190

Thought

Acts of repentance are a form of healing
for both the victim and the perpetrator.

GALATIANS 2:11–13 — OCTOBER 28

A Word of Challenge

> *The right thing to do is not to leave people to their own stupidities. The right thing is to love them enough in order to pray on their behalf and, where necessary, to have the courage to challenge them.*

St. Ambrose, in his letter to the Roman emperor Theodosius, issues this challenge:

> I have not written this to put you to shame, but to induce you, by royal examples, to put this sin away from your kingdom. That you will do by humbling your soul before God.
>
> You are a man, and temptation has come to you. Conquer it. Sin is only put away by tears and penitence. No angel can do it, no archangel. If we sin, the Lord himself, who alone can say: "I am with you," gives remission only to those who offer penitence.
>
> I advise, I entreat, I exhort, I admonish. I am grieved that you, who were an example of unheard-of piety, who exercised consummate clemency, who would not suffer individual offenders to be placed in jeopardy, that you, I say, should feel no pain at the destruction of so many innocent persons.
>
> You have been most successful in war, and in other ways you deserve praise; yet piety has ever been the crown of your achievements. The devil grudged you your chief excellence. Conquer him, while you still have the means to conquer. Do not add sin to sin by following a course which has injured many.
>
> *Early Latin Theology*, 256

Reflection

My words may seem harsh.
They are spoken in love,
and in anguish of heart.
Hear my words not,
but in them, may you hear the whispers of the Spirit.

1 TIMOTHY 3:16   OCTOBER 29

Jesus, the God-Man

Jesus is both Son of God and Son of Man. He is truly one of us, yet he is also fully one with the Father and the Spirit. He is both our brother and our Lord.

Hippolytus, the great third-century church writer, speaks of Jesus as the God-Man:

> When he came into the world, he was manifest as God and man. And it is easy to perceive the man in him when he hungers and shows exhaustion, and is weary and thirsts, and withdraws in fear, and is in prayer and in grief, and sleeps on a boat's pillow, and entreats the removal of the cup of suffering, and sweats in an agony, and is strengthened by an angel, and betrayed by a Judas, and mocked by Caiaphas, and set at nought by Herod, and scourged by Pilate, and derided by the soldiers, and nailed to the tree by the Jews. And with a cry commits his spirit to his Father, and drops his head and gives up the ghost, and has his side pierced with a spear, and is wrapped in linen and laid in a tomb, and is raised by the Father on the third day.
>
> The divine in him, on the other hand, is equally manifest when he is worshipped by angels, and seen by shepherds, and waited for by Simeon, and testified of by Anna, and inquired after by wise men, and pointed out by a star, and at a marriage makes wine of water, and chides the sea when tossed by the violence of winds, and walks upon the deep, and makes one see who was blind from birth, and raises Lazarus when dead for four days, and works many wonders, and forgives sins, and grants power to his disciples.
>
> *The Ante-Nicene Fathers*, vol. 5, 170

Reflection

In the God-Man,
we can see what God is really like.
In the God-Man,
we can see what we may become.

ISAIAH 35:5-7　　　　　　　　　　　　OCTOBER 30

The Desert Place

Clearly in our primal beginnings we lost the garden. We long to return to the garden of hope and innocence, but we must travel through the desert, the place of purgation.

In St. Basil's *Letter XLII*, he speaks about this:

> For I am living... in the wilderness, where the Lord dwelled. Here is the oak of Mambre; here is the ladder which leads to heaven, and the encampment of the angels that Jacob saw; here is the wilderness where the people, who had been purified, received the law...
>
> Here is Mount Carmel, where Elias lived and pleased God. ... Here is the wilderness where the blessed John ate locusts and preached repentance...
>
> Here is the Mount of Olives, which Christ ascended and where he prayed, teaching us how to pray. Here is the Christ who loved solitude.... Here is the narrow and straight way that leads to life.
>
> Here are the teachers and prophets, "wandering in deserts" ... Here are the apostles and evangelists and the lives of monks, citizens of the desert.
>
> *Saint Basil: The Letters*, vol. 1, 261

Reflection

The desert: invitation to solitude.
The desert: place of vulnerability.
The desert: place of the dark night of the soul.
The desert: place of God's provision.

Perfection

The quest for spiritual growth lies at the heart of the Christian story. While some think that this quest can come to completion in one's lifetime, most believe that we will always be on a journey towards fullness of life.

John Cassian provides us with some reflections on Christian perfection:

> We also ought forthwith to hasten on that by means of the indissoluble grace of love, we may mount to the third stage of sonship, which believes that all the father has is its own. So we may be counted worthy to receive the image and likeness of our heavenly Father, and be able to say after the likeness of the true Son, "All that the Father has is mine" (John 16:15). Which also the blessed apostle declares of us saying: "All things are yours, whether Paul or Apollos or Cephas, or the world, or life, or death, or things present, or things to come: all are yours" (1 Cor 3:22). And to this likeness the commands of our Saviour also summon us when he says: "Be perfect, even as your Father in heaven is perfect" (Matt 5:48) . . .
>
> We can only ascent to that true perfection when, as he first loved us for the grace of nothing but our salvation, we also have loved him for the sake of nothing but his own love alone. Wherefore, we must do our best to mount with perfect ardour of mind from this fear to hope, from hope to the love of God and the love of the virtues themselves. That as we steadily pass on to the love of goodness itself, we may as far as it possible for human nature, keep firm hold of what is good.
>
> *The Conferences of John Cassian*, 11.7

Prayer

O God of all grace,
O Blessed Son our great life-giver,
O empowering Spirit,
may we ever live in you and grow into your likeness,
until we see you face to face.

November

TITUS 3:4–7   NOVEMBER 1

God's Humiliation, Our Redemption

In Christ, the God of the heavens and earth stooped to embrace humanity with the intention of healing. God's humiliation brought hope to the world. The God who became a man is the God who makes humans godlike.

Gregory of Nazianzus, one of the Cappadocian Fathers, speaks of this:

> And God who gives riches becomes poor, for he assumes the poverty of my flesh, that I may assume the riches of his godhead.
>
> He that is full empties himself, for he empties himself of his glory for a short while, that I may have a share of his fullness . . .
>
> What is the mystery that is around me? I had a share in the image of God: I did not keep it. He partakes of my flesh, that he may both save the image and make the flesh immortal.
>
> He communicates a second communion far more marvelous than the first, inasmuch as then he imparted the better nature, whereas now he himself partakes of the worse.
>
> Quoted in *Christian Spirituality: Origins to the Twelfth Century*, 272

Reflection

You did not turn away from us, O God.
Your disappointment did not move you to abandon us.
Instead, you came close.
So very close.
In Christ, you became one of us.
We now can become one with you, Father, Son and Holy Spirit.

1 CHRONICLES 21:13 — NOVEMBER 2

The Works of Mercy

Mercy is not merely an idea, but an action. Mercy is the movement in love, kindness, and generosity towards another who is not deserving, but upon whom we wish to lavish goodness.

St. Augustine writes about the generosity of mercy:

> Two works of mercy set us free: forgive and you will be forgiven, and give and you will receive.
>
> When we pray we are all beggars before God: we stand before the great householder bowed down and weeping, hoping to be given something—and that something is God himself.
>
> What does a poor person beg from you? Bread. What do you beg from God? Christ, who said, "I am the living bread which came down from heaven."
>
> Do you really want to be forgiven? Then forgive. Do you hope to receive something? Then give to another. And if you want your prayer to fly up to God, give it two wings: fasting and almsgiving.

The Joy of the Saints, 37

Thought

There is a circular movement in the action of God.
God impacts us in particular ways,
and we in turn seek to extend what we have received to others.
Thus God's presence in our lives is not simply a protecting presence, but an empowering one. God graces us, and we then seek to extend that grace and goodness to others.

1 CHRONICLES 21:13 — NOVEMBER 3

The Purgative, Illuminative, and Unitive

Many ancient writers conceived the Christian journey as involving three stages or three interactive dimensions: the purgative, illuminative, and unitive. While it may be helpful to think in such stages, the more basic reality is our journey of growth as we live the gospel with an ever greater fidelity.

Bonaventure is one author who speaks of this threefold way:

> As far as possible, it is necessary that the church militant be conformed to the church triumphant, and our merits to our rewards, and those still in this life to the blessed in heaven.
>
> In glory there is a threefold gift that is the perfection of the reward: an eternal grasp of the highest peace, an open vision of the highest truth, and the full enjoyment of the highest goodness and charity.
>
> According to this there is a triple order in the supreme celestial hierarchy of Thrones, Cherubim, and Seraphim. For someone who wishes by merit to come to that state of blessedness, it is necessary to gain for oneself in this life a likeness to those three orders as far as possible. That is, the person should have the sleep of peace, the splendour of truth, and the sweetness of charity. God himself rests in these three things, dwelling in them as in his proper throne.
>
> Therefore, it is also necessary to ascend to each of these three through three steps according to the threefold way: through the purgative, which consists in getting rid of sin; through the illuminative, which consists in the imitation of Christ; and through the unitive, which consists in receiving the Bridegroom.
>
> *The Essential Writings of Christian Mysticism*, 154

Reflection

Whether in a life of prayer,
a life of virtue, worship, and service,
God is to be praised,
we are to grow, and the neighbor blessed.

JOHN 16:12-15 — NOVEMBER 4

The Illumination of the Spirit

The Spirit is the servant of Christ in that the Spirit is the Spirit of Christ. And the Spirit is the servant of the Word in that the Spirit accompanies the Word to bring it to light and life in the community of faith and in one's personal life.

Symeon the New Theologian speaks of the illuminating work of the Spirit:

> On the other hand just as the illiterate cannot read books like those who know how to read, neither can those who have refused to practice the commandments of Christ, have the authority to be worthy judges of the Holy Spirit's revelation. Not like those who have devoted themselves to them, lived them and shed their blood for them.
>
> In the same way, indeed, the one who takes a closed and sealed book cannot see what is written, nor understand what it is about, even if he had all the wisdom of the world, as long as the book remains sealed.
>
> Similarly even she who, as we have said, can recite all the divine Scriptures will never know and apprehend the mystical and divine glory and virtue hidden in them without living all God's commandments and receiving the help of the Paraclete. The Paraclete will open the words like a book and mystically show her the glory locked inside. Much more, eternal life will spring forth, and the Paraclete will reveal the blessings of God hidden in the words, blessings that stay veiled and absolutely invisible to those who despise them and continue to sin through negligence. This is normal, since they have nailed their all to the vanity of the world, and are passionate for life's charms and the body's splendors. But since the eye of their souls is darkened, they are unable to see and consider the intellectual beauties of God's unutterable blessings.
>
> *Catéchèses*, 45–47

Prayer

O God, open my heart to love,
open my understanding to know,
and open my hands to give and serve a needy world,
in the power of your Spirit.

JOHN 10:7–10   NOVEMBER 5

Jesus the Good Shepherd

Under the image of the Good Shepherd, we acknowledge Jesus as our protector, and we further recognize that he seeks the straying ones. But most importantly, we understand that he gives his life for his flock.

In the Celtic devotional texts of Moucan, we have this emphasis:

> I wandered on the mountains, Good Shepherd,
> Place me upon your shoulders.
> As the heart desires a spring of living water, so my soul thirsts for you.
> And may you rest, O Holy One, between my breasts.
>
> You who feed and lie down at midday,
> Guard me as the pupil of your eye,
> And bring me into the house of wine
> With the bunches of grapes in the vineyards of Eingedi . . .
>
> May my heart burn with the fire of your love and fear,
> Your love and holy fear which knows not how to yield.
> Give me, Jesus, water springing up into eternal life,
> I have sought only my soul from the Lord, this I require,
> That I shall never thirst in eternity.

Celtic Spirituality, 305

Reflection

In the midst of life's journey,
including its dark and desert places,
may I know your presence
and your guiding and sustaining hand.

JOHN 4:34 — NOVEMBER 6

To Will the Good

> *Our human will is a powerful dimension in who we are. We are often proud in our willing, and our willing is often about us. Yet our wills need to be reoriented to the ways of the gospel.*

The English theologian Pelagius writes about our wills:

> The ability for anyone to will and to do good comes from God alone.... For this will is in us, even if we wished it not to be; nor does nature ever take her rest in this will. Some examples may make my meaning clear.
>
> Our ability to see with our eyes does not depend on us; but whether we use our eyes to see good or ill does depend on us. So that I may encompass all things with a general statement, the fact that we *can* do, say, or think any good thing comes from God, who gave us this ability and helps us in it. But whether we actually do, speak, or think *rightly* is dependent on us, because we can turn all these abilities to evil.
>
> Therefore, and this point must be repeated often, ... when we say that we can live without sin, we praise God by confessing the possibility of this power, which he alone has given to us. There is no occasion for praising human capacity in this possibility, because it is God's matter alone that we are considering. For the discussion does not concern the will, nor the action, but only the thing that might be possible.
>
> *An Historical Presentation of Augustinianism and Pelagianism*, 106–7

Thought

I can see myself as self-sufficient and independent.
Or I can more truly see myself as sustained by the God of grace.
Whatever our viewpoint may be, there are huge consequences.

1 CORINTHIANS 4:10–13   NOVEMBER 7

In This Vale of Tears

The Christian life is not a special existence, but rather ordinary life lived amidst the beauty, stresses and failures of life. Yet it is also a life lived in hope that with God all things will finally be well and whole.

Julian Norwich, in one of her *Showings*, has this to say about Christian hope and struggle:

> God shall never enjoy his full joy in us until we enjoy our full joy in him, truly seeing his beautiful and blessed face. For we were created to enjoy him in this way, and we live into this joy through grace. Through this, I saw how sin is mortal only for a short time in those who are blessed with eternal life.
>
> The more clearly that the soul sees this blessed face by grace and love, the more it yearns to see it in fullness. Even though our Lord dwells in us and is here with us, nevertheless he calls us and enfolds us in his tender love so that he is never apart from us. We will never cease moaning nor weeping nor yearning until the time when we clearly see his blessed face, for in that precious, blessed sight, there can be no grief nor any lack of well-being.
>
> *A Lesson of Love*, 185–86

Reflection

It is not only what you will be to us
at the end of the ages
that sustains me now.
It is your often hidden presence
that holds me now
in places where sustenance is scarce
and the wells have run dry.

PSALM 27:14   NOVEMBER 8

Waiting

Because we are future-oriented creatures, we are always waiting for what lies ahead. Waiting is also key to the Christian life. We wait for God to act. We wait for a move of the Spirit. We wait for the kingdom of God to come more fully amongst us.

Thomas à Kempis also touches on the theme of waiting:

> Do not ask, therefore, for what is pleasing and helpful to yourself, but ask for what is acceptable to me and gives me honor. For if you judge rightly, you should prefer to follow my will rather than your own desire or whatever things you wish.
>
> I know your longings and I have heard your frequent sighs. Already you wish to be in the glorious liberty of the children of God. Already you desire to delight in your eternal home, the heavenly land that is full of joy. But that hour has not yet come. There still remains another hour, a time of war, of labor, and of trial. You long to be filled with the highest good, but you cannot attain it now. I am that sovereign good. Wait for me until the kingdom of God comes.
>
>   *The Imitation of Christ* (Croft and Bolton), ch. 49

Waiting

When I first met you, O God,
I thought my waiting was over,
I thought I had come home.
But the life of faith has called me to wander
and enter unfamiliar places.
I am now tired, my Lord,
may the waiting soon be over.

Pride

It takes no great feat of insight to see the sin of arrogance in ourselves and others. But pride is our most fundamental sin, in that we go our way rather than to listen and obey the voice of God.

St. Augustine identified pride as humanity's most basic folly:

> Pride is the great sin, the head and cause of all sins, and its beginning lies in turning away from God. Beloved, do not make light of this vice, for the proud who disdain the yoke of Christ are constrained by the harsher yoke of sin: such people do not wish to serve but have to, because if they will not be love's servant, they will inevitably be sin's slaves.
>
> From pride arises apostasy: the soul goes into darkness and, misusing its free will, it falls into other sins, wasting its substance with harlots, and the one who was created a fellow of the angels becomes a keeper of the swine.
>
> Because of this great sin of pride, God humbled himself, taking the nature of a servant, bearing insults, and hanging on a cross. To heal us, he became humble. Shall we not be ashamed to be proud?

The Joy of the Saints, 70

Prayer

When I pray, "Lord, make me humble,"
what will you do to me?
When I ask, "Bend my will to yours,"
what will that mean for me?
Am I safe in your humility?
Will you care for me in the doing of your will?

LEVITICUS 16:29–31   NOVEMBER 10

Rest from Day's Toil

What is an honest day's work? This is a hard question, and to answer it, we have to decide what we mean by good work. But work well done brings its own reward.

St. John Chrysostom, in one of his *Homilies*, addresses the issue of work and rest:

> But at the same time, so powerful and persuasive is labour, that . . . servants are able to sleep. For since throughout the whole day, they are running about everywhere, ministering to their masters, being knocked about and hard pressed, and having but little time to take a breath, they receive a sufficient recompense for their toils and labour in the pleasure of sleeping.
>
> And thus it has happened through the goodness of God toward us, that these pleasures are not to be purchased with gold and silver, but with labour, with hard toil, with necessity, and every kind of discipline.
>
> Not so the rich. On the contrary, while lying on their beds, they are frequently without sleep through the whole night; and though they devise many schemes, they do not obtain such pleasure.
>
> But the poor, when released from their daily labours, having their limbs completely tired, fall almost before they can lie down into a slumber that is sound, and sweet, and genuine, enjoying this reward, which is not a small one, of their fair day's toils.

Nicene and Post-Nicene Fathers, vol. 9, 352

Prayer

Lord, may I do good work,
and may I be fair in all I do.
May my reward be just and fair.
And may I know how to rest well
in the grace of your smile.

ISAIAH 40:1–5   NOVEMBER 11

Prophetic Spirituality

Spirituality is not just about nurture and comfort. It is also about the cry of pain for a wounded world, an often impotent church and a broken self. And it is also about the cry for freedom and justice.

Bonaventure, in recounting the story of St. Francis, speaks of his prophetic life:

> The power of the prophetic spirit
> in the man of God
> was certainly extraordinary,
> which restored vigour to dried-up limbs
> and impressed piety on hardened hearts.
> The lucidity of his spirit
> was no less an object of wonder;
> for he could foresee future events
> and even probe the secrets of conscience,
> as if he were another Elisha,
> who had acquired the two-fold spirit of Elijah.
>
> *The Life of St. Francis*, 118

Reflection

In this spiritual wilderness and wasteland
I cry to you,
O God of hope and restoration.
May justice be done,
may peace flourish,
may people be reconciled,
may the earth flourish,
may your kingdom come.

JOHN 17:5 — NOVEMBER 12

The Blessedness of the Trinity

Jesus came to do the Father's will in the power of the Holy Spirit and in the unity, love and purpose of the Trinity. Each fully there for the other, each sustained in the other—blessed, indeed, is the Holy Trinity.

The famous fourteenth-century Dutch mystic John Ruusbroec, in *The Little Book of Enlightenment,* celebrates the blessedness of the Trinity:

> Here the persons give way and lose themselves in the whirlpool of essential love, which is joyful unity. Nevertheless, they remain active as persons in the work of the Trinity. You can therefore see that the divine nature is forever active according to the mode of the persons while at the same time being eternally at rest and without mode according to the simplicity of its essence.
>
> Thus everything that God has chosen and embraced with eternally personal love, he has also possessed essentially, in joyful unity with essential love. The divine persons embrace one another mutually in eternal contentment through infinite and active love in unity. This activity is constantly renewed in the living life of the Trinity. Here there occurs a perpetually new birth in new knowledge, together with a new sense of contentment and a new breathing forth of the Spirit in a new embrace accompanied by a new flood of eternal love.
>
> All the elect, angels and humans, from the last to the first, are embraced in this contentment. On this contentment depend heaven and earth and the being, life, activity and preservation of all creatures, with the single exception of any turning away from God through sin, which arises from creatures' own blind perversity. From God's contentment flows grace, glory and all the gifts in heaven and on earth, with each person receiving according to his or her own need and ability . . .
>
> *John Ruusbroec: The Spiritual Espousals and Other Works,* 262

Reflection

Blessed, and Holy Trinity!
May the love and unity of your life together
spill over into the broken and wounded spaces of our lives and world.

PSALM 23:4 — NOVEMBER 13

A Prayer in the Shadow of Death

In the goodness and grace of God, we are invited to approach the end of life without fear. We trust God to carry us over the abyss into the fullness of eternal life.

Here is a Celtic prayer, from the eleventh century, for the end of life:

> God shall not refuse or reject whoever strives
> To praise God at the beginning and end of the day,
> Mary's only Son, the Lord of Kings.
> Like the sun he shall come from east and north,
> Mary, Christ's mother, chief of the maidens,
> Call for the sake of your great mercy
> Upon your Son to chase away our sin.
>
> God above us, God before us.
> May the God who rules,
> Heaven's King, grant us a share of his mercy.
>
> Royal-hearted one, peace between us
> Without rejection, may I make amends
> For the wrong I have done before going
> To my tomb, my green grave,
> My place of rest, in the dark without candle,
> My burial place, my recess, my repose.

Celtic Christian Spirituality:
An Anthology of Medieval and Modern Sources, 32

Meditation

At the end of life celebrate what was good,
confess what was wrong,
and entrust oneself to the grace and goodness of God.

DEUTERONOMY 10:21　　　　　　　　　NOVEMBER 14

Praise to Our God

Our relationship with God is often cast in terms of intercession and thanksgiving, but we are also invited to praise God. When we praise, we speak extravagantly well of others and extol their blessedness and virtues. Praise is a celebration of God for who God is.

St. Francis, in the *Earlier Rule*, has a segment where God is glorified:

> Let us therefore desire nothing else
> wish for nothing else
> and let nothing else please
> and delight us
> except our Creator and Redeemer, and Saviour,
> the only true God,
> who is full of the good
> all good, entire good, the true and supreme good,
> who alone is good,
> merciful and kind,
> gentle and sweet,
> who alone is holy
> just, true, and upright,
> who alone is benign,
> pure, and clean
> from whom, and through whom, and in whom is
> all mercy,
> all grace,
> all glory
> of all penitents and of the just,
> and of all the blessed rejoicing in heaven.

The Writings of Saint Francis, 34

EZEKIEL 1:1 — NOVEMBER 15

Visionary Power

We can plan things. We can work things out. We can live by the inspiration of our thinking. But we can also live by the power of a vision.

The unknown author of *The Shepherd of Hermas* speaks of this visionary power:

> Now, in the second vision, you saw her standing with a youthful and more joyful face than before, but she still had the skin and hair of an aged woman. "Listen," he said, "to this parable as well. When a man becomes somewhat old, he despairs of himself on account of his weakness and poverty, and he looks forward to nothing but the last day of his life.
>
> Then suddenly he receives an inheritance, and hearing of this, he rises up and in his joy, he becomes much stronger. Now, he no longer lies down, but stands up; and his spirit, which had been destroyed by his previous circumstances, is renewed, and he no longer sits, but acts with vigour."
>
> So it happened with you, when you heard the revelation that God gave you. For the Lord had compassion on you and renewed your spirit, and you laid aside your weaknesses. Vigour arose within you, and you grew strong in faith, and when the Lord saw your strength, he rejoiced. On this account, he showed you the building of the tower, and he will show you other things if you continue to be at peace with each other with all your heart.
>
> *The Shepherd of Hermas*, Vision 3

Reflection

In one moment in time,
a flash of your light,
spawned by the Spirit,
can make everything new.

GENESIS 28:10–12   NOVEMBER 16

Guardian Angels

In Celtic Christian spirituality, the veil between heaven and earth is thin. For most modern people, these two spheres are radically separated. Somehow our world needs to be re-enchanted, and the whispers and care of angels may well be a part of that.

In the *Carmina Gadelica*, we have frequent references to the protection and care of angels:

> O Angel guardian of my right hand,
> Attend to me this night,
> Rescue me in the battling floods,
> Array me in your linen, for I am naked,
> Succour me, for I am feeble and forlorn.
> Steer my coracle in the crooked eddies,
> Guide my step in gap and in pit,
> Guard me in treacherous turnings,
> And save me from the harm of the wicked,
> Save me from harm this night.
> Drive from me the taint of pollution,
> Encompass me till doom from evil,
> O kindly Angel of my right hand,
> Deliver me from the wicked this night,
> Deliver me this night.

Carmina Gadelica, 151

Reflection

So this day, this night,
I commit myself
into the care of Christ
and his holy angels.

GALATIANS 4:7   NOVEMBER 17

Refashioned in Christ

The work of Christ is not to add something new to our old existence. Rather, Christ has come to refashion us, re-shape us, and transform us into something new: his image and likeness.

The great church father St. Gregory of Nazianzus, in his *On the Nativity of Christ*, speaks of this transformative work of Christ:

> So shortly you will also see the purification of Jesus in the Jordan for my purification; or rather he is cleansed for the purification of the waters, for he indeed did not need purification, who takes away the sin of the world.
>
> The heavens are parted and he receives the testimony of the Spirit, who is akin to him. He is tempted and conquers the tempter and is served by angels. He heals every sickness and every infirmity, and gives life to the dead. Would that he would give life to you who are dead through your false doctrine! He drives out demons, some by himself and others through his disciples. With a few loaves he feeds tens of thousands, and he walks on the sea.
>
> He is betrayed and crucified and crucifies my sin with himself. He is offered as a lamb and offers as a priest, he is buried as a human being, raised by God, then also ascends, and he will return with his own glory.
>
> How many celebrations there are for me corresponding to each of the mysteries of Christ! Yet all have one completion, my perfection and refashioning and restoration to the state of the first Adam.
>
> *Festal Orations*, 74–75

Thought

This church father is right that the work of Christ is all about restoration.
But Christ's salvation does not simply
bring us back to the innocence of Adam,
for our full restoration comes as gift from the Christ
who suffered and gave his life for us.
Restoration on the other side of suffering is different
from a continuation of innocence.

PSALM 27:1　　　　　　　　　　　　　　　　NOVEMBER 18

Light

Natural light is a source of life. Spiritual light is the light of the Word and the inspiration of the Holy Spirit. While light can be gently sustaining, light can also suddenly break forth.

The German Christian mystic Meister Eckhart speaks of the light in the soul:

> Sometimes I have spoken of a light in the soul that is uncreated, a light that is not able to be created. I mention this light frequently in my sermons. This same light reveals God undisguised and uncovered, naked as he is in himself. This light conveys the divine act of creating and giving birth.
>
> This light has more unity with God than it has with the powers of the soul, even though it is one in being.
>
> For you should know that this light is not nobler in my soul than the feeblest or crudest power, such as hearing or sight or anything else that can be affected by hunger or thirst, frost or heat. This is because of the simplicity of my being. Because of this, if we take the powers as they are in our being, they are all equally noble, but if we take them as they work, one is much nobler and higher than another.
>
> That is why I say that if a person will turn away from himself or herself and all created things, by so much will you be made one and blessed in the spark in the soul, which has never touched either time or place . . .
>
> In the innermost part, where no one dwells, there is contentment for that light, and there it is more inward than it can be to itself, for this ground is a simple silence, in itself immovable.

Meister Eckhart, the Essential Sermons, Commentaries, Treatises and Defense, 198

Prayer

Lord, by your Word and Spirit,
may I enter into the nurture, care and wisdom of who you are
and who I may become in you. Amen.

JOB 42:4–6   NOVEMBER 19

A Call to Repentance

In the community of faith we do need others to challenge us, even to call us to repentance. The reason for this is all too obvious, as we are often blind to our own faults and wrongdoings.

The third-century church father St. Cyprian, in his *Epistles of Cyprian*, issues such a call to the clergy of his day:

> Cyprian to the presbyters and deacons, his brethren, greeting.
>
> Although I know, brethren beloved, that from the fear which we all of us owe to God, you also are instantly urgent in continual petitions and earnest prayers to him, still I myself remind your religious anxiety, that in order to appease and entreat the Lord, we must lament not only in words, but also with fastings and with tears, and with every kind of urgency.
>
> For we must perceive and confess that the so disordered ruin arising from that affliction, which has in a great measure laid waste, and is even still laying waste, our flock, has visited us according to our sins, in that we do not keep the way of the Lord, nor observe the heavenly commandments given to us for our salvation.
>
> Our Lord did the will of his Father, and we do not do the will of our Lord; eager about our patrimony and our gain, seeking to satisfy our pride, yielding ourselves wholly to emulation and strife, careless of simplicity and faith, renouncing the world in words only, and not in deeds, all of us pleasing ourselves and displeasing others.

The Ante-Nicene Fathers, vol. 5, 285

Reflection

Let your light shine upon me, O God—
not the light that warms, but the light that liberates.
And having repented, may your light warm and guide me.

JOHN 1:1–5   NOVEMBER 20

Christ the Light

Christ as the light bearer has come amongst us. But Christ is the light from all eternity.

The great Celtic theologian John Scotus Eriugena, in his *Homily on the Prologue to the Gospel of St. John*, speaks of Christ the light:

> Thus the light
> shines in the darkness,
> for the Word of God—
> the light and life of human beings—
> does not cease
> to shine into our nature which,
> investigated and considered in itself,
> is found to be without form and dark.
>
> Nor, despite its fall,
> does the Word wish to forsake human nature
> nor will he ever forsake it.
> For he forms it,
> since he contains it by nature,
> and he reforms it
> by deifying grace.

The Voice of the Eagle: The Heart of Celtic Christianity, 93

Reflection

We are not only found in you through grace, O God.
We are also your created handiwork.
But do remake us
into the fullness of your Son.

Ephesians 4:25–27 — November 21

The Virtuous Life

The heartbeat of the Christian life is that the salvation that Christ gives us ushers in a new way of life. And this new way of life is patterned on the life of Christ. He is our savior and example.

St. Athanasius, in his famous *Life of Antony*, tells of some of Antony's teaching:

> After a few days Antony returned once more to the mountain. Afterwards, many visited him, and some who suffered were bold enough to approach him. For all the monks who came to him, he had the same message: to have faith in the Lord and to love him; to guard themselves from crude thoughts and pleasures of the flesh, and, as it is written in Proverbs, not to be "deceived by feeding the belly"; to flee pride, and to pray constantly; to sing holy songs before and after sleep, and to take to heart the commands in the Scriptures; to keep in mind the actions of the saints, so that the soul, being mindful of the commandments, might be educated by devotion to them.
>
> But even more, he urged them to practice constantly the word of the Apostle, "do not let the sun go down on your anger," and to consider that this had been spoken with every commandment in mind, so that the sun would not set on our anger or on any other sins.
>
> He continued: "For it is good, even urgent, that the sun should not condemn us for an evil of the day, nor the moon for a sin, nor even for an inclination of the night. In order for this to be preserved in us, we must hear and obey the Apostle when he says, 'Examine yourselves and test yourselves.'"

Life of Antony and The Letter to Marcellinus, 72

Reflection

I wait for the revealing Word.
I need the purging Spirit.
I long for the grace of forgiveness.

1 CORINTHIANS 11:1 — NOVEMBER 22

Followers of the Way of Christ

> *It is one thing to believe that Jesus Christ died to bring us new life. It is quite another thing to be willing to emulate Christ, to live his words and deeds—and still another to have the life and death of Christ repeated in our lives.*

The unknown author of the fourth-century *Constitutions of the Holy Apostles* writes about following Christ:

> Everyone, therefore, who learns any art, when they see their master by diligence and skill perfecting his or her art, do themselves earnestly endeavour to make what they take in hand [and become] like to it. If they are not able, they are not perfected in their work.
>
> We, therefore, who have a master, our Lord Jesus Christ, why do we not follow his doctrine? Since he renounced repose, pleasure, glory, riches, pride, the power of revenge, his mother and brethren, and moreover his own life, on account of his piety towards his Father, and his love to us the race of humankind—and suffered not only persecution and stripes, reproach and mockery, but also crucifixion, that he might save the penitent, both Jews and Gentiles.
>
> If therefore, he for our sakes renounced his repose, was not ashamed of the cross, and did not esteem death inglorious, why do not we imitate his sufferings, and renounce on his account even our own lives, with that patience which he gives us?
>
> For he did all for our sakes, but we do it for our own sakes: for he does not stand in need of us, but we stand in need of his mercy. He only requires the sincerity and readiness of our faith, as the scripture says: "If you are righteous, what do you give to him, or what does he receive from your hand? Your wickedness affects only someone like yourself, and your righteousness only the children of humankind" (Job 35:7–8).
>
> *The Ante-Nicene Fathers*, vol. 7, 438–39

Reflection

O, to be a small light of the great light, Jesus Christ, Son of God!
O, to be but a tiny repetition of the suffering servant,
Jesus Christ, Son of Man!

EPHESIANS 5:3–5 NOVEMBER 23

Attachments

We are religious creatures. When we neglect the worship of God, we all too readily worship something else, creating our own gods.

In *The Fifty Spiritual Homilies*, we have a reflection on the topic of our tendency to create idols:

> As an example, one person sets his heart on possessions, while another sets her heart on gold and silver. One pursues the persuasive wisdom of the world to gain glory, while another passionately seeks power. Some crave the praise and honor of others, while others live by anger and violence.
>
> When we yield readily to such passions, we reveal our love and preference for the objects we desire through inappropriate actions. One might be consumed by her jealousy, while another full of pride amuses himself all day long. One deceives himself with meaningless thoughts, while another parades as a know-it-all just to impress people. Some take satisfaction in laziness and carelessness, while others are absorbed by dress and clothing. Someone else might be devoted to earthly pursuits, while another overindulges in sleep, trivial gossip, or rude conversation.
>
> But regardless of how we are bound to the world, either by small or great chains, we become possessed by our attachments and cannot liberate ourselves from them. For if we do not resolutely fight against our passions, they will become the objects of our love. These attachments will dominate and impede us, becoming chains that prevent us from directing our minds to God and seeking to please him. Bound up in this way, we cannot serve God alone, nor obtain the kingdom and reach eternal life.

Pseudo-Macarius: The Fifty Spiritual Homilies and The Great Letter, 68

Reflection

We need to turn away from our idolatries and turn to God.
His deliverance is our freedom.
His healing power makes us whole.

Practical Proverbs

Growing up in a Dutch Christian family, we were the daily recipients of certain practical proverbs. While out of fashion today, we may well need to recover some of them to give shape to a lifestyle that reflects something of God's wisdom.

The seventh-century Celtic *De Duodecim Abusivis Saeculi* contains some of this practical wisdom, but casts it in terms of a sadness in what may be lacking:

> A wise woman without good works,
> An old man without religion,
> A young woman without obedience,
> A rich man without alms,
> A woman without modesty,
> A master without virtue,
> A grumbler of a Christian,
> A poor man who is proud,
> An evil king, a negligent bishop,
> A crowd without discipline,
> A people without law.

Towards a History of Irish Spirituality, 31–32

Prayer

O Lord, grant me a loving heart,
a clear mind, a willing spirit,
and serving hands.
O Lord, grant me insight and discernment,
a listening heart, a willing spirit,
and serving hands.

SONG OF SOLOMON 2:16–17   NOVEMBER 25

Love's Longing for Union

The nature of love is not simply to know something about the beloved. Love wants to know everything. Love wants to possess. Love seeks to merge. Love longs for union.

The great medieval theologian Thomas Aquinas speaks of the movement of love:

> It belongs to love to seek union, as Dionysius says. For since, on account of likeness or compatibility between lover and the beloved, the affection of the lover is somehow united to the beloved, the tendency inclines to the completion of the union: namely, that the union that was begun in the affections may be completed in actions.
>
> Wherefore, it belongs to friends to rejoice in mutual companionship, living together, and in common pursuits.
>
> Now God moves all other things to union, for inasmuch as he gives them being and other perfections, he unites them to himself as far as possible. Therefore, God loves both himself and other things.

An Aquinas Reader, 274

Prayer

Lord, may your knowing me,
and my feeble understanding of who you are
and of your ways with us
lead me to seek after you
with the whole of my being.
May I lose myself in your grace
and love.

EXODUS 3:1-6   NOVEMBER 26

A Flame for God

Glory belongs to God. Sometimes this glory is revealed, and sometimes God's glory radiates out of a person touched by the presence of God. This is only and always a gift.

Here is a story from one of the Desert Fathers pointing us to become the recipients and bearers of the presence of God:

> Abba Lot went to see Abba Joseph, and he said to him, "Abba, as far as I can, I say my little office, I fast a little, I pray and meditate, I live in peace and as far as I can I purify my thoughts. What else can I do?"
>
> Then the old man stood up and stretched his hands toward heaven; his fingers became like ten lamps of fire and he said to him, "If you will, you can become all flame."
>
> *Paradise of Desert Fathers*

Reflection

Lord, I am but a most ordinary servant of yours.
In my daily life I seek to be faithful,
to live the gospel,
to listen to your voice of direction,
to participate in my faith community,
and to serve my neighbor.
But Lord, do set me on fire for your kingdom.

REVELATION 5:9–10 · NOVEMBER 27

Generativity

There are people who are life-giving. There are others who are death-dealing. But God is the great life-giver who in Christ seeks to bring forth the new humanity.

Methodius, bishop of the See of Tyre in Phoenicia, in his *Banquet of the Ten Virgins*, writes about Christ as the great life-giver:

> Thus it was that the Apostle [Paul] directly applied to Christ the words which had been spoken to Adam. For it will most certainly be agreed that the church is formed out of Christ's bones and flesh.
>
> And it was for this cause that the Word, leaving his Father in heaven, came down to be "joined to his wife" and slept in the trance of his passion and willingly suffered death for her.
>
> He did this so that he might present the church to himself glorious and blameless, having cleansed her by the laver for the receiving of the spiritual and blessed seed.
>
> This is sown by him who with whispers implants it in the depths of the mind. It is conceived and formed by the church, as by a woman, so as to give birth and nourishment to virtue.
>
> In this way too, the command "Increase and multiply" is duly fulfilled. The church increases daily in greatness, beauty and multitude by the union and communion of the Word, who still [continues] to come down to us.

The Ante-Nicene Fathers, vol. 6, 319

Reflection

You birthed us, O Christ.
Your death gave us life.
Your gospel turned us around.
Your Spirit renews us.
Your life sustains us.

JOB 1:20 — NOVEMBER 28

The Lord Takes Away

In the majority world, Christians know something about the reality of suffering. In the minority world [the West], we only know the quest of much-having—so much so that we have even cast God into a benign Father Christmas. But God not only gives; God also takes away.

St. John Chrysostom, in one of his *Homilies*, addresses this topic:

> Let this speech be our utterance also over each event which befalls us—whether it be loss of property, or infirmity of body, or insult, or false accusation or any other form of evil incident to humankind—let us say these words: "The Lord gave, the Lord has taken away; as it seemed good to the Lord so has it come to pass; blessed be the name of the Lord forever."
>
> If we practice this spiritual wisdom, we shall never experience any evil, even if we undergo countless sufferings. But the gain will be the greater than the loss, the good will exceed the evil: by these words you will cause God to be merciful unto you, and will defend yourself against the tyranny of Satan.
>
> For as soon as your tongue has uttered these words, the Devil will hasten from you. And when he has hastened away, the cloud of dejection also is dispelled, and the thoughts which afflict us take flight, hurrying off in company with him. And in addition to all this, you will win all manner of blessings both here and in Heaven.
>
> And you have a convincing example in the case of Job, and of the Apostle, who having for God's sake despised the troubles of this world, obtained the everlasting blessings.

Nicene and Post-Nicene Fathers, vol. 9, 220

Reflection

When things are taken from us, there is the invitation to reflect and to live our lives with open hands and greater surrender than before.

LUKE 6:43-45   NOVEMBER 29

Fruitfulness

> *To become fruitful in one's spiritual life is often a mysterious unfolding. But there are dimensions to this which are discernible, including the characteristics of openness and receptivity. Fruitfulness may also include purgation and suffering.*

Meister Eckhart, in one of his *Sermons*, speaks about fruitfulness:

> Married couples hardly produce more than a single child each year, but I am referring to a different kind of "married couple." I am speaking of those who are married to prayer, fasting, vigils, external disciplines and ascetic practices.
>
> By a "year" I mean every kind of self-attachment to work, which removes our freedom to be at God's disposal in each present moment and to follow him alone into the light. By this light, he prompts us to do certain things and to refrain from doing other things, so that we cannot do anything else, nor do we wish to do anything else.
>
> By a "year" I mean any form of self-attachment or any regimented work that takes from us this freedom, which is new every moment. Our souls will not produce fruit unless we have first completed the work we have committed to do. We will lack trust both in ourselves and in God unless we have first completed this work, and thus we will not have peace. For we cannot become fruitful until we have finished our work.
>
> *Meister Eckhart: Selected Writings*, 159–60

Reflection

In doing your work, O God,
I want so often to be in control.
But to be fruitful, I need to surrender myself
to the promptings of your Spirit and to your strange ways with me.
Help me to trust you
and to walk the way you have set before me.

Meditate

Ours is an immediately connected way of life, and time for stillness and reflection are scarce commodities. Our ancient forebears challenge us to ways of prayers and meditation.

Bonaventure, in his *Tree of Life*, invites us to become contemplatives:

> Come now, disciple of Christ,
> search into the secrets of solitude
> with your loving teacher,
> so that having become a companion of wild beasts,
> you may become a companion and sharer of
> the hidden silence, the devout prayer, the daylong fasting
> and the three encounters with the clever enemy.
>
> And so you will learn
> to have recourse to him
> in every crisis of temptation
> because "we do not have a high priest
> who cannot have compassion on our infirmities,
> but one tried
> in all things as we are,
> except sin."

The Soul's Journey into God; The Tree of Life; The Life of St. Francis, 134

Prayer

Lord, draw me beyond the false values
of thinking that my significance lies in achievement
and draw me to your heart of love.
Help me to live and serve out of that blessed welcome.

December

2 KINGS 6:15–19 — DECEMBER 1

Open Our Eyes

We see what we see—and most often that means that we see what we want to see. Inner spiritual renewal can give us "new" eyes with which to see.

Bonaventure, in his *Soul's Journey into God*, speaks of having eyes to see the presence of God:

> Whoever, therefore, is not enlightened
> by such splendour of created things
> is blind;
> Whoever is not awakened by such outcries
> is deaf;
> Whoever does not praise God
> because of all these effects
> is dumb;
> Whoever does not discover
> the first principle from such clear signs
> is a fool.
>
> Therefore, open your eyes,
> alert the ears of your spirit,
> open your lips,
> and apply your heart
> so that in all creatures you may see,
> hear,
> praise,
> love and worship,
> glorify and honour your God.

Quoted in *Franciscan Prayer*, 139

LUKE 11:20-22 — DECEMBER 2

Jesus: The Strong One

Christ came to set us free from our sins and our bondage. He is the Strong One who disables all that we have done to harm ourselves and all that the Evil one would do against us. Jesus is the true liberator.

Methodius, in his *Oration on the Psalms*, lauds this powerful Savior:

> Blessed is he who comes in the name of the Lord: God against the devil; not manifested in his might, which can't be looked upon, but in the weakness of the flesh, to bind the strong man who is against us.
>
> Blessed is he who comes in the name of the Lord: the King against the tyrant; not with omnipotent power and wisdom, but with that which is accounted as the foolishness of the cross, which has taken the spoils from the serpent who is wise in wickedness.
>
> Blessed is he who comes in the name of the Lord: the True One against the liar; the Saviour against the destroyer; the Prince of Peace against him who stirs up wars; the Lover of humankind against the hater of humanity.
>
> Blessed is he who comes in the name of the Lord: the Lord to have mercy upon the creatures of his hand.
>
> Blessed is he who comes in the name of the Lord: the Lord to save humans who have wandered in error; to put away error; to give light to those who are in darkness; to abolish the imposture of idols; in its place to bring the saving knowledge of God; to sanctify the world; to drive away the abomination and misery of the worship of false gods.
>
> Blessed is he who comes in the name of the Lord: the one for the many; to deliver the poor out of the hands of those who oppress them . . . from those who bring the poor to spoil.
>
> Blessed is he who comes in the name of the Lord: to pour wine and oil upon those who have fallen among thieves and have been passed by.

The Ante-Nicene Fathers, vol. 6, 397

Reflection

The Redeemer has come.
Nothing need remain the same.
All things can be made new.

1 THESSALONIANS 4:18 — DECEMBER 3

Encouragement

To be encouraged by someone we trust and respect is a great blessing. Encouragement helps us through the rough places in life's journey. It also helps us to see the goodness to which we are so often blind.

St. Basil had the gift of encouragement. Here, in a letter to Ambrose the bishop of Milan, we see evidence of this:

> I have given glory to God, who in every generation selects those who are well-pleasing to him; who of old indeed chose from the sheepfold a prince for his people; who through the Spirit gifted Amos the herdsman with power and raised him up to be a prophet; who now has drawn forth for the care of Christ's flock a man from the imperial city, entrusted with the government of a whole nation, exalted in character, in lineage, in position, in eloquence, in all that this world admires.
>
> This man has flung away all the advantages of this world, counting them all loss that he may gain Christ, and has taken in his hand the helm of the ship, great and famous for its faith in God, the church of Christ.
>
> Come, then, O man of God—not from people have you received or been taught the Gospel of Christ; it is the Lord himself who has transferred you from the judges of the earth to the throne of the Apostles. Fight the good fight; heal the infirmity of the people, if any are infected by the disease of Arian madness; renew the ancient footprints of the fathers and mothers.
>
> You have laid the foundation of affection towards me; strive to build upon it by the frequency of your salutations. Thus shall we able to be near one another in spirit, although our earthly homes are far apart.
>
> *Nicene and Post-Nicene Fathers*, vol. 8, 235

Prayer

Lord, give me a heart that seeks to bless and encourage others.
Amen.

ISAIAH 38:4–6   DECEMBER 4

The Gift of Tears

There are many forms of prayer. One is to pray without words, so that our prayers are the very longings of the heart. But prayer can also be expressed in tears of sadness or joy.

St. Catherine of Siena records a vision in which God spoke to her:

> O dearest daughter whom I so love, you have asked me for the will to know the reasons for tears and their fruits, and I have not scorned your desire. Open your mind's eye wide, and I will show you, through the spiritual stages I have described for you, those imperfect tears whose source is fear.
>
> First of all, there are the tears of damnation, the tears of this world's evil ones.
>
> Second are the tears of fear, of those who weep for fear because they have risen up from sin out of fear of punishment.
>
> Third are those who have risen up from sin and are beginning to taste me. These weep tenderly and begin to serve me. But because their love is imperfect, so is their weeping.
>
> The fourth stage is that of souls who have attained perfection in loving their neighbours and love me without any self-interest. These weep and their weeping is perfect.
>
> The fifth stage (which is joined to the fourth) is that of sweet tears shed with great tenderness.
>
> I will tell you, too, about tears of fire, shed without physical weeping, which often satisfy those who want to weep but cannot. And I want you to know that a soul can experience all these different stages as she rises from fear and imperfect love to attain perfect love and the state of union.

Catherine of Siena: The Dialogue, 4.4.13

Reflection

The life of faith is never simply and only an intellectual pursuit,
for it involves all of who we are—
including our feelings, will and service, as well as our sensitivities.

MATTHEW 6:13 — DECEMBER 5

Trials

The Christian is not guaranteed a sacred cocoon sheltered from life's difficulties. Rather, the Christian, like all others, has to live life in the full cacophony of everyday existence.

The unknown author of the fourteenth-century *Theologia Germanica* speaks about these matters:

> There is always something to be suffered here, consider it as you will. And as soon you are free of one adversity, perhaps two others will come in its place.
>
> Therefore yield yourself willingly to them, and seek only that true peace of the heart which none can take away from you, that you may overcome all adversity: the peace that breaks through all adversities and crosses, all oppression, suffering, misery, humiliation, and what more there may be of the like, so that you may be joyful and patient therein, as were the beloved disciples and followers of Christ.
>
> Now if you were lovingly to give your whole diligence and might to this, you would very soon come to know that true eternal peace which is God himself, as far as it is possible to a creature. So much so that what was bitter to you before would become sweet, and your heart would remain ever unmoved among all things, and after this you would attain everlasting peace.
>
> *Theologia Germanica*, ch. 12

Reflection

When things come my way
do I not ask, why me?
But may I learn
to yield my all
into the purging fire
and the healing hand of God
who wounds and heals me.

PROVERBS 18:10   DECEMBER 6

Encircle Me, O God

This is not a prayer born out of fear, but rather a prayer seeking and longing for God's all-encompassing presence.

A Celtic prayer from the Northumbria Community:

> Circle me, Lord.
> Keep comfort near,
> and discouragement afar.
> Keep peace within,
> and turmoil out. Amen.
>
> Circle me, Lord.
> Keep protection near,
> and danger afar.
>
> Circle me, Lord.
> Keep hope within,
> keep despair out.
>
> Circle me, Lord.
> Keep light near,
> and darkness afar.
>
> Circle me, Lord.
> Keep peace within,
> and anxiety without.

Celtic Daily Prayer: From the Northumbria Community, 297–98

ACTS 1:8 — DECEMBER 7

Mission to the Ends of the Earth

> *The Christian faith is about prayer and piety as well as witness and service. Sometimes, this service takes us to the ends of the earth.*

Gregory the Great, in a letter of AD 598 to Eulogius, the patriarch of Alexandria, speaks about the mission to England:

> Since your good deeds bear fruit in which you rejoice as well as others, I am making you a return for benefits received by sending news of the same kind.
>
> And this is that while the people of the English, placed in a corner of the world, still remained without faith, worshipping stocks and stones, I resolved, aided in this by your prayers, that I ought with God's assistance to send to this people a monk from my monastery to preach.
>
> He, by licence given from me, was made bishop by the bishops of the Germanies, and with their encouragement was brought on his way to the people aforesaid in the ends of the world. And already letters have reached us telling of his safety and his work, that both he and they who were sent with him are radiant with such great miracles amongst this people, that they seem to reproduce the powers of the apostles in the signs that they display.
>
> Indeed, on the solemn feast of the Lord's Nativity now past, more than ten thousand Angles, according to our information, were baptized by the same our brother and fellow-bishop.
>
> I have told you this that you may know not only what you do among the people of Alexandria by speaking, but also what you accomplish in the ends of the world by prayer. For your prayers are in that place where you are not, while your holy deeds are exhibited in that place where you are.
>
> *Documents of the Christian Church*, 151–52

Prayer

Lord, may your Spirit ever move me beyond my own narrow concerns. Move me into the wide spaces of your love for all humanity. Amen.

ACTS 17:22-23 — DECEMBER 8

The Traces of God

We see the traces of the action and presence of God in his work of creation and in our being made in his image and likeness. But with eyes to see, we may see the signs of God everywhere in our daily lives and in human affairs.

When asked why people are often so reluctant to seek God in earnest, Meister Eckhart has this to say in his *Fragments*:

> When one is looking for a thing and finds no trace of its existence, one hunts half-heartedly and in distress. But if one comes across some trace of the thing being sought, the chase grows lively, light-hearted and earnest. Whoever seeks after fire is cheered when heat is felt and then joyfully looks for the source of the blaze. So it is with those who quest after God: if they do not taste divine sweetness, they grow listless; but once they taste divine sweetness, they cheerfully seek after God.

The Best of Meister Eckhart, 137

Reflection

I have looked hard and long.
Why is it so hard to find you, O God?
Did I look in the wrong places?
Was I not desperate enough?
Was my heart not ready?

And yet you came,
unexpectedly,
when I was not looking.
You surprised me and I am glad you came.

1 CORINTHIANS 15:42–49   DECEMBER 9

The Resurrection

Christians believe in the resurrection of the dead. This is not because we are inherently immortal, for only God has immortality. The resurrection lies solely in the power of God and in the purposes of Christ for us.

St. Gregory of Nyssa writes about the resurrection:

> But I think that the apostolic word agrees with our idea of the resurrection and shows what our definition means when it says that the resurrection is nothing other than the restoration of our nature to its original state.
>
> In the beginning of the creation, we have learned from the scripture that first the earth sprouted the plant of the grass, as the story tells, and then seed came from the plant. When this fell on the earth, the same species as that which grew originally sprang up again. The divine apostle says that this happens also at the resurrection.
>
> We learn from him not only that humankind changes to greater magnificence, but also that what we hope for is nothing other than what was at first.
>
> Since in the beginning the ear did not come from the seed, but the seed from the ear, and after this the ear grew around the seed, the order of the symbolic narrative clearly shows that all the blessedness which will spring up for us through the resurrection will bring us back to the grace of the beginning.
>
> *On the Soul and the Resurrection*, 118–19

Prayer

Lord, I commit myself into your hands.
Hold me in death.
Carry me through all its dark places
and bring me into the light
of your presence.

PSALM 17:8 — DECEMBER 10

Hidden in the Wounds of Christ

> *To use this kind of language is to think metaphorically, but there is a deep truth here. Not only are we healed through the death of Christ, but his death shelters us, in the sense that his death is the gateway of new life for us. And in this new life in Christ, we are safe.*

St. Aelred of Rievaulx, in his *Mirror of Charity*, writes movingly about our being in Christ:

> Can there be perfect knowledge when we live under the shadow of death? What true delight can be found in this howling waste and boundless desert? Is there any greatness in this world that fear does not totter and cast down? Does anyone have knowledge who truly knows himself or herself? Even the horse and the mule, who have no intellect, delight in flesh.
>
> If you find pleasure in riches, can you take your wealth with you when you die? If you seek after worldly glory, will your glory have power in the grave?
>
> We will not find true excellence until our ambition yearns for nothing higher. We will not obtain true knowledge until nothing remains beyond our grasp. We will not experience true delight until there is nothing that diminishes our pleasure. We will never have true riches until they can never be exhausted . . .
>
> "If only I had a dove's wings, I would fly to you and find my rest!" Meanwhile, O Lord Jesus, I beg you to let my soul grow wings in the nest of your teaching. May my soul embrace you, who was crucified for me, and drink the life-giving draught of your most sweet blood.
>
> The Mirror of Charity, 8–9

Reflection

By faith I am in you, my Lord Jesus—
you who have travelled the darkness of death
will carry me into your resurrection and my new life.

2 CHRONICLES 6:36–40   DECEMBER 11

The Call to Repent

The movement to repentance is a grace-filled event. While the journey may seem onerous, it is the gift of joy and freedom.

The unknown author of the early writing of 2 *Clement* has this to say about the call to repentance:

> Wherefore, brothers and sisters, since we have received no small opportunity for repentance, let us, while we have time, turn unto the God who has called us, while we still have one who will receive us.
>
> For if we bid farewell to the luxuries of this world, and conquer our soul so that we do not fulfill evil lusts, we shall partake of the mercy of Jesus.
>
> But know that the day of judgment is already coming as a burning furnace, and certain of the heavens shall be melted, and the whole earth shall be as lead melting on the fire; and then shall both the secret and open deeds of all be made manifest.
>
> Good, therefore, is almsgiving, as showing repentance from sin; better is fasting than prayer, and almsgiving than both; for love covers a multitude of sins, and prayer that goes forth from a good conscience saves from death. Happy is everyone who is found full of these things, for almsgiving becomes a lightening of sin.
>
> 2 *Clement*, ch. 16

Reflection

Repentance is not the fruit of the fear of judgment,
but the gift of righteousness,
the desire to live
to the glory of God and for the well-being of others.

GALATIANS 5:22–26   DECEMBER 12

In Praise of Virtue

In a world full of words and promises, a life of goodness and virtue is the most complete word that can be spoken.

St. Francis, in his "The Salutation of the Virtues," paints us this picture:

> Hail, queen wisdom!
> May the Lord save you with your sister, holy pure simplicity!
> O Lady, holy poverty,
> may the Lord save you with your sister, holy humility!
> O Lady, holy charity,
> may the Lord save you with your sister, holy obedience!
> O most holy virtues, may the Lord save you,
> from whom you come and proceed!
> There are none in the whole world
> who can possess any one of you unless they first die.
> Whoever possesses one of you and does not offend the others
> possesses all.
> And whoever offends one of you
> possesses none and offends all.
>
> *The Writings of Saint Francis of Assisi,* 19

Reflection

Virtues are formed in the crucible of life
through grace and much suffering.

MATTHEW 5:43–45   DECEMBER 13

God's Providential Care

In the light of the biblical narrative, it is clear that the world lies in God's care. God sustains all that is and fans with life-giving breath all that is good.

Lactantius, in his *On the Workmanship of God*, had this to say about God's providential care:

> Everything beyond this is the work of God—namely, the conception of itself, and the moulding of the body, and the breathing in of life, and the bringing forth in safety, and whatever afterwards contributes to the preservation of humankind; it is his gift that we breathe, that we live, and are vigorous.
>
> For, besides that we owe it to his bounty that we are safe in body, and that he supplies us with nourishment from the various sources, he also gives us wisdom, which no earthly father or mother can by any means give. And therefore it often happens that foolish sons are born from wise parents, and wise sons from foolish parents, which some people attribute to fate and the stars.
>
> But this is not now the time to discuss the subject of fate. It is sufficient to say this, that even if the stars hold together the efficacy of all things, it is nevertheless certain that all things are done by God, who both made and set in order the stars themselves. They are therefore senseless who detract this power from God, and assign it to the work of humankind.

The Ante-Nicene Fathers, vol. 7, 299

Reflection

God's providence
is not blazed in human affairs
with self-evident certainty.
It is always shrouded in mystery
and held in faith.

2 PETER 2:21–25   DECEMBER 14

The Winsome Christ

All sorts of things have been perpetrated in the name of Christ. But Christ does not fit into our schemes. He is radically other. And if we would only follow him in his otherness, the world would be renewed.

The church father Arnobius, in his *Against the Heathen*, speaks about the winsome Christ:

> Explain to us and say what is the cause, what is the reason, that you pursue Christ with such bitter hostility? Or what offenses [do] you remember which he did, that at the mention of his name you are so roused to bursts of mad and savage fury?
>
> Did he ever, in claiming power for himself as king, fill the world with bands of the fiercest soldiers; and at nations at peace at the beginning, did he destroy and put an end to some, and compel others to submit to his yoke and serve him?
>
> Did he ever, excited by grasping avarice, claim as his own by right all that wealth and have it in abundance which humans strive after so eagerly?
>
> Did he ever, transported by lustful passions break down by force the barriers of purity or stealthily lie in wait for other men's wives?
>
> Did he ever, puffed up with haughty arrogance, inflict at random injuries or insults . . . ?
>
> [Yet] he showed you things concerning salvation. He prepared for you a path to heaven and the immortality for which you long. . . . Is he then . . . the destroyer of religion and promoter of impiety . . . [or should you] prefer the friendship of Christ to all that is in the world?
>
> *The Ante-Nicene Fathers*, vol. 6, 433–35

Reflection

What the church has done in the name of Christ, is one thing.
But who Christ is, is quite another matter.
While the church has a stained reputation, the sinless Christ calls the church and all women and men to repentance and to follow him.

PSALM 51:3–6 DECEMBER 15

Examination of Conscience

In Ignatian spirituality, there is the invitation to identify what was life-giving and death-dealing at the end of each day. This is a helpful practice in keeping short accounts with ourselves, others, and God.

From Thomas à Kempis, who belonged to the Brethren of the Common Life, we have a list that may help us in our end-of-day reflections:

> Lament and grieve
>
> because you are still so worldly and carnal,
>
> so passionate and shameless, so full of wandering lust,
>
> so careless in guarding your external senses, so often occupied with vain fantasies,
>
> so drawn towards worldly things but so indifferent to the interior life,
>
> so prone to laughter and squandering but so averse to sorrow and tears,
>
> so inclined to comfort and bodily pleasure but so aloof to austerity and godly devotion . . .
>
> so greedy for abundance and so tenacious in keeping but so stingy in giving,
>
> so inconsiderate in your speech and so reluctant to keep silence,
>
> so undisciplined in character and so disordered in action,
>
> so greedy at meals but so deaf to the Word of God . . .
>
> so quickly distracted and so rarely recollected . . .
>
> so happy in prosperity and so weak in adversity,
>
> so often making resolutions, yet so unwilling to keep them.
>
> *The Imitation of Christ* (Croft and Bolton), ch. 7

Prayer

Lord, as I descend into my foolish heart, may you lift me up into the goodness of your grace.
Amen.

ROMANS 14:8 — DECEMBER 16

I Am Ready to Be with Christ

There comes a point in the journey of faith when we begin to move to a different way of being. Rather than wanting to do more for Christ by serving him in our world, we want to be with him in the world to come.

St. Ignatius, in *To the Romans*, speaks about this:

> The ruler of this world wishes to carry me off and to deflect my purpose, which is set on God. Let none of you who are on my side aid him. Rather, become God's champions, through being mine. Do not have Jesus Christ on your lips and the world in your hearts. Let envy have no place in you.
>
> If, when I am with you, I should call for your help, do not believe me. Believe rather what I now write to you. I am writing to you as one living but longing to die. My earthly affections are crucified, and there is in me no fire of fleshly passion. But I have a fountain of living water which speaks within me saying, "Come to the Father." I take no pleasure in perishable food, nor in the pleasures of this life. My desire is for God's Bread, the flesh of Christ, born in former time of David's seed: and for drink I desire his Blood, a love-feast undefiled.
>
> I desire to live no longer, as one thinks of living; and my desire will be fulfilled, if only you would wish it also. Do wish it, so that your wishes and mine might be accomplished. I entreat you in these few words. Believe me, Jesus Christ will make it clear to you that I speak truly, he, the unerring mouth of God, through whom the Father has spoken truly. Pray for me, that I may attain my end through the Holy Spirit.

To Any Christian: Letters from the Saints, 68

Prayer

O Lord, I commit into your care
not what I am and have done,
but what I hope to be
through your grace. Amen.

EPHESIANS 1:11–12 DECEMBER 17

The Inner Movement of the Spirit

The Spirit lifts the heart to God and moves us to serve others. The Spirit also helps us to discern the inner movements in our own being.

Julian of Norwich, in her various visions, which she called "showings," speaks about these inner movements of the Spirit:

> I perceived within myself the following five activities: rejoicing, mourning, longing, fearing and confident hoping.
>
> I rejoiced because God gave me the understanding and knowledge that I was seeing him. I mourned because of my failings. I longed to see him more and more, while acknowledging that we will never fully rest until we see him truly and clearly in heaven. I feared because the whole time I worried that my vision would fail and I would be left to myself. I hoped with confidence in his endless love, which I knew would protect me under his mercy and bring me to eternal blessedness. My joy and confident hope in his merciful protection gave me such comfort that mourning and fear were not too painful. Yet at the same time, I saw in this showing of God that this way of seeing him would not be constant in this life—both for his own honour and for the increase of our eternal joy.
>
> *The Complete Julian of Norwich*, 216–17

Thought

My spirituality is not isolated
from my daily struggles,
my volatile feelings,
my role in life,
my triumphs and insecurities.
It is woven into the very fabric of my being.

PSALM 36:7–9   DECEMBER 18

The Fount of Life

God is the creator of all that is and sustains all that is. God is the life-giver and the great nurturer. We may drink at God's fountains of life.

Columbanus, in one of his *Sermons*, speaks of God as the fount of life:

> Merciful God, righteous Lord, please stoop to admit me to that fountain, so that I might drink from the living stream of the living fount of living water along with your thirsty ones and be gladdened by his overflowing loveliness and hold to him and say: "How lovely is the fountain of living water, whose water does not fail, but springs up to eternal life."
>
> O Lord, you are that fountain, always desired, even as we consume you over and over again. Give us this water, Lord Christ, that it may be in us a ceaseless fountain of water that lives and springs up to eternal life.
>
> I ask for great gifts, indeed, as anyone knows, but you, King of Glory, know how to give greatly, and you have promised great things. Nothing is greater than yourself, and you have given yourself to us, and you gave yourself for us. Therefore, we ask that we may know what we love, since we pray for nothing other than that you should be given to us; for you are our all, our life, our light, our salvation, our food, our drink, our God.
>
> *Sermons*, 13.3

Prayer

O Lord, may we ever stop long enough
to recognize our hunger and thirst.
May we ever know
to run to you.
May we ever stoop low enough
to drink.

ACTS 10:38–41   DECEMBER 19

A Shining Witness

We do want our lives—and not only our words—to reflect the light of God. But this light can only come from the Spirit of God renewing, endowing, and empowering us.

Hildegard of Bingen, in a letter to Nun Gertrud, has these encouraging words:

> Daughter of God, in the pure knowledge of faith, hear these words spoken to you: "the voice of the turtledove is heard in our land." This is the Son of God, who—against the laws of the flesh—was born from the wholeness of the earth, the flesh of the Virgin Mary. And the flowers of all the virtues came forth and the beauties of all the fragrances. For the garden of these virtues arose in the prodigal son, who, when he came to himself, ran to confess his sins to the father, that is, to the omnipotent Father. And his Father received him with the kiss of his Son's humanity.
>
> When with our own will we give up the world for the love of God, then the voice of the turtledove is heard, for above all other birds the turtledove remains alone when she loses her mate. Dearest daughter, you also did this when you gave up the pomp of this world. How beautiful your shoes were, daughter of the king, when for the love of God you entered upon the strait and narrow path of the spiritual life!
>
> Therefore rejoice, daughter of Zion, for the Holy Spirit dwells in the middle of your heart. Consider that your comforter created you "as a lily among thorns." . . . You also shone red like a rose of Jericho in the passion of your conversion to the spiritual life.

Hildegard of Bingen: Selected Writings, 83

Reflection

Whether married or celibate,
famous or unknown,
introvert or extrovert,
priest, banker, or farmer,
we all are to be a sweet fragrance
of the life of Christ within us.

ISAIAH 1:11 — DECEMBER 20

Useless Piety

We are very strange, indeed, when we try to impress God and others with our piety. And we are acting in even stranger ways when we add our own practices of piety to our repertoire of supposed spirituality. No one is impressed and no one is edified.

One of the stories from the Desert Fathers picks up this theme:

> One of the Fathers told how a certain old man was ever diligently toiling in his cell, and clothed himself in a mat. And when he sought out the abbot Ammon, the abbot Ammon saw him wearing his mat, and said to him, "This profits you nothing."
>
> And the old man said to him, "Three thoughts harry me: one, that would compel me to withdraw myself elsewhere in the desert; another, that I should seek a strange land where no one knows me; and a third, that I should shut myself up in my cell so as to see no man, and eat only every third day."
>
> And the abbot Ammon said to him, "None of these three things would profit you to do: but do sit in your cell, and eat a little every day, and have ever in your heart the saying of the publican that is read in the Gospel, and so you shall be saved."
>
> *The Desert Fathers, 104–5*

Reflection

A renewed heart,
a willing spirit,
a listening demeanour,
a loving attitude,
a sustained humility,
a prayerful life,
a servant hand—
these things, O Lord,
you will not despise.

1 Kings 19:11-13 — December 21

Whispers from the Edge of Eternity

God makes himself known in many ways, most clearly revealing himself in word and deed. But there are also hints of God's presence, whispers that we can only see and hear if we are attentive.

Meister Eckhart, in his *Sermons*, touches on this theme:

> Concerning this, the wise man said: "In the middle of the night when all things were in a quiet silence, there was spoken to me a hidden word." It came like a thief, by stealth. What does he mean by a word that was hidden? The nature of a word is to reveal what is hidden.
>
> It appeared and shone before me, declaring its intent to reveal the knowledge of God to me. Thus it is called a word. But ... it remained hidden from me. That was its stealthy coming "in a whispering stillness to reveal itself."
>
> Because it is hidden, one must always pursue it. It appears and disappears: we are meant to yearn and sigh for it. St. Paul says we ought to pursue this until we catch sight of it and not to stop until we grasp it.
>
> After he had been caught up into the third heaven, where God was made known to him and he beheld all things, he returned, and he had forgotten nothing, but it was so deep down in the ground of his being that his intellect could not reach it, for it was veiled from him. Therefore he had to pursue it and search for it within himself, not outside himself.
>
> It is not outside, but inside: wholly within. And being convinced of this, he said: "I am sure that neither death nor any affliction can separate me from what I find within me."
>
> *Meister Eckhart: Sermons*, 1

Reflection

God's revelation to us is not simply one of words.
When God reveals himself,
his Word and Spirit can well up like fresh springs of water
within the very depths of our being.

COLOSSIANS 3:13–14   DECEMBER 22

Clothed in Christ

> *One core biblical notion is that sin leaves us naked and exposed. But God's redemptive work in Christ clothes us in his righteousness, and in this way, he cares for us, shelters us and keeps us safe.*

St. Ammonas the Hermit writes about this:

> To my dearly beloved in the Lord: If anyone has been stripped of the heavenly garment of the new life, which is the Spirit of truth and the power which comes from him, he must go on pleading tearfully with the Lord until he clothes his or her soul in the power which comes from above, in place of the shame and confusion with which it is now covered. For just as bodily nakedness is a source of confusion and dishonour for humankind, so, too, do God and his saints turn their faces away from those who are not clothed in the Holy Spirit. If Adam and Eve felt shame when they saw that they were naked, how much more shame is going to be felt by the soul stripped of its Lord! So all who have been stripped of the clothing of the Spirit must be ashamed; let them realize their disgrace and blush for their nakedness. Let their spirits cry out loudly to God, and let them carry on the struggle within their hearts until the heavenly glory, appearing visibly above them, comes to clothe them. Glory be to the immeasurable mercy!
>
> When the woman suffering from a flow of blood truly believed and touched the hem of the Lord's clothing, her flow of blood dried up. In the same way, every soul which is wounded by sin and punished by a flood of evil thoughts, will be saved if it draws near to the Lord in faith, and the stream of its evil thoughts will be dried up through the power of Jesus Christ, the Lord of the world.

To Any Christian: Letters from the Saints, 207–8

Reflection

The new "clothes" that Christ gives us
are forgiveness, adoption, homecoming,
and the empowerment of the Holy Spirit.

ROMANS 5:18–21 — DECEMBER 23

Grace Abounds in Christ

In this Christmas season, the focus is on the incarnation: the gift of Christ to the world. He is the gateway to salvation. In Christ, grace, forgiveness, and new life are to be found.

Gregory of Nazianzus, in his *On the Nativity of Christ*, speaks of celebrating the gift of Christ to the world:

> This is our festival, this is the feast we celebrate ... in which God comes to live with human beings, that we may journey toward God. Or return—for to speak thus is more correct—that laying aside the old human being, we may be clothed with the new, and that as in Adam we have died, so we may live in Christ, born with Christ and crucified with him, buried with him and rising with him.
>
> For it is necessary for me to undergo the good turn-around, and as painful things came from more pleasant things, so out of painful things more pleasant things must return. "For where sin abounded, grace superabounded," and if the taste of forbidden fruit condemned, how much more does the passion of Christ justify?
>
> Therefore we celebrate the feast not like a pagan festival but in a godly manner, not in a worldly way but in a manner above the world. We celebrate not our own concerns but the one who is ours, or rather what concerns our Master, things pertaining not to sickness but to healing, not to the first moulding but to the remoulding.
>
> *Festal Orations*, 63

Prayer

Thanks be to God
for this unimaginable gift!
Thanks be to the Son
for his faithful life and service and self-giving!
Thanks be to the Spirit
for bringing all the blessings of Christ home to us!

MARK 1:1–3   DECEMBER 24

The Coming of the Promised One

Longed for over the ages, the promised one comes. He does not come as expected, but in his own way—and his coming opens the fountains of new life.

St. Bernard of Clairvaux speaks of the coming Messiah:

> Here are sweet promises full of consolation: "Behold the Lord will appear; and he will not lie. If he seems slow, wait for him, for he will come, and that soon" (Heb 2:3).
>
> Again, "The time of his coming is near, and his days will not be prolonged" (Isa 13:22), and, from the person of him who promised, "Behold," he says, "I am running toward you like a river of peace, and like a stream in flood with the glory of the nations" (Isa 66:12).
>
> In these words, both the urgency of the preachers and the lack of faith of the people are clear enough. And so the people murmured and faith wavered and, as Isaiah puts it, "The messengers of peace weep bitterly" (Isa 33:7). Therefore, because Christ delayed his coming lest the whole human race should perish in desperation while they thought their weak mortality condemned them, and they did not trust that God would bring them the so often promised reconciliation, those holy men and women who were made sure by the Spirit looked for the certainty that his presence could bring. . . . O Root of Jesse, who stands as a sign to the peoples, how many kings and prophets wanted to see you and did not? Simeon is the happiest of them all because by God's mercy, he was still bearing fruit in old age. For he rejoiced to think that he would see the sign so long desired. He saw it and was glad.
>
> *Bernard of Clairvaux: Selected Works*, 102–3

Reflection

So long desired, so humbly he comes,
that only the eyes of faith can see
that the Messiah has come,
the hope for a new world.

LUKE 2:8–14 DECEMBER 25

Songs of Joy

The coming of Christ into the world is a sign of hope. We see forgiveness trump hatred, welcome defeat rejection, grace made stronger than the law, and God's love healing all our stupidities and wrongdoing.

A Christmas carol from the *Carmina Gadelica*:

> Hail king! Hail king! Blessed is he! Blessed is he! . . .
> Hail king! Hail king! Blessed is he, the King of whom we sing,
> All hail! Let there be joy . . .
>
> Born is the Son of Mary the Virgin,
> The soles of his feet have reached the earth,
> The Son of glory down from on high,
> Heaven and earth glowed to him,
> All Hail! Let there be joy!
> The peace of earth to him, the joy of heaven to him,
> Behold his feet have reached the world;
> The homage of a King be his, the welcome of a Lamb be his,
> King all victorious, Lamb all glorious,
> Earth and ocean illumed by him,
> All hail! Let there be joy! . . .
> Shone to him the earth and sphere together,
> God the Lord has opened a door;
> Son of Mary, Virgin, hasten to help me,
> Christ of hope, door of joy,
> Golden Sun of hill and mountain,
> All hail! Let there be joy!

Carmina Gadelica, 133

LUKE 7:6-7 — DECEMBER 26

A Prayer to Christ

Christ has come amongst us—not as a mighty lord, but as the suffering servant. We are touched by his love, and we are made whole in his life-giving presence.

St. Anselm offers this prayer to Jesus. We can join him in this prayer:

> Most merciful Lord,
> turn my lukewarmness into a fervent love for you.
> Most gentle Lord,
> my prayer tends towards this—
> that by remembering and meditating
> on the good things you have done
> I may be enkindled with your love.
>
> Your goodness, Lord, created me;
> your mercy cleansed what you created
> from original sin;
> your patience has hitherto borne with me,
> fed me, waited for me,
> when after I had lost the grace of my baptism
> I wallowed in many sordid sins.
>
> You wait, good Lord, for my amendment;
> my soul waits
> for the inbreathing of your grace
> in order to be sufficiently penitent
> to lead a better life.

The Prayer and Meditations of Saint Anselm with the Proslogion, 94

PSALM 145:3   DECEMBER 27

God's Beauty and Greatness

God's greatness gives and God's power empowers. Both are expressed in a beauty that cares and fructifies. Therefore God is not be feared, and we can bask in God's love.

Hilary of Poitiers (c. 300–c. 367) became bishop of Poitiers in 350. His main writing is on the Trinity, where he touches on the above themes.

> But if the mind can estimate this beauty of the universe by natural instinct . . . must not the Lord of this universal beauty be recognized as himself most beautiful amidst all the beauty that surrounds him? For though the splendour of his eternal glory overtaxes the mind's best powers, it cannot fail to see that he is beautiful . . .
>
> Thus my mind, filled with the fruits of its own reflection upon the teaching of Scripture, rested with assurance, as on some peaceful watchtower . . . in the conviction that his greatness is too vast for our comprehension, but not for our faith.

Nicene and Post-Nicene Fathers, vol. 9, 42

Reflection

God's greatness and power
spoke a world into being.
God's power and beauty
became the Man of Nazareth.
God's beauty
is the unbounded Spirit.

COLOSSIANS 4:12　　　　　　　　　　DECEMBER 28

Prayers for All

Our prayers should never be parochial. Since God has bathed the world in love, we may bathe the world in our prayers. Such prayers are never ones of judgment, but only of blessing.

The medieval Christian mystic, Margery Kempe, invites us to pray:

> Good Lord Jesus, I ask for your mercy on all who are in our church, the order of priesthood, of religious men and women, for those too busy to save and defend the faith of your holy church. For all that are in grace at this time, God send them perseverance until the end of their lives, and make me worthy to partake of their prayers as they do of mine, each of the others.
>
> I cry your mercy for the king of England, the lords and ladies, that they use authority well. I ask your mercy for the rich and powerful, that you would give them the grace to use these for your pleasure. I ask mercy for the Jews and Saracens, for unbelievers, for you have spread mercy to all on this earth. If there is anyone who is not drawn to you, I ask you to draw them to you now, for you have drawn me, and I did not deserve it.
>
> I ask mercy for all misbelievers, false tithe-payers, thieves, adulterers, common women, those who are tempted, the wicked. . . . I ask for mercy for all my spiritual and bodily children, for all people in this world, for my friends and enemies, for the sick, lepers, bedridden, prisoners, and all who have spoken well or ill of me until the world ends. Be as gracious to all of these as you have been to me.
>
> May the peace and rest that you have bequeathed to your blessed friends in heaven be mine and be to all who ask you for mercy.

The Book of Margery Kempe, 294

Reflection

Prayer can build a new world.

MATTHEW 22:37–40 DECEMBER 29

Love of God and Love of Neighbor

It matters little how much one claims to love God. If that love is not expressed in love of others, including the neighbor and the stranger, the friend and the enemy, it is hardly love of God.

The unknown author of *The Cloud of Unknowing* develops this theme:

> It is quite right that in contemplation God should be loved for himself alone above all created things, . . . this work is fundamentally a naked intent, none other than single-minded intention of our spirit directed to God himself alone.
>
> I call it "single-minded" because in this matter the perfect apprentice asks neither to be spared pain, nor to be generously rewarded, nor indeed for anything but God himself. So that he cares not whether he is grieved or glad, but only that the will of him whom he loves is fulfilled. And so it is that God is perfectly loved for himself, and above all his creation.
>
> For in this work a contemplative will not permit the least thought of the very holiest thing to share her attention. As she does this, she fulfills the second, the lower branch of charity (which is love to her fellow Christians) truly and perfectly, as you can prove. For the perfect contemplative has no special regard for any person, be he kinsman, sister, stranger, friend or foe. For all men alike are his brothers and sisters, and none strangers. He considers all persons his friends, and none his foes. To such an extent that even those who hurt and injure her she reckons to be real and special friends, and she is moved to wish for them as much good as she would wish for her dearest friend.
>
> *The Cloud of Unknowing and Other Works*, 92

Reflection

The God to whom I am drawn in prayer is the God
who loves my friends and my enemies.
Thus I am also drawn to them as I am drawn to God.

PSALM 23:5   DECEMBER 30

The Oil of Restoration

Christ is the healer and restorer. The Holy Spirit imparts that healing to us, and we, as the people of God, may be channels in the service of the master healer.

St. Ambrose has this to say on this matter:

> But the church has oil, with which she tends the wounds of her children, that the wound may not harden and spread deep. . . . With this oil, then, the church anoints the necks of her children, that they may take on the yoke of Christ. With this oil she anointed the martyrs, that she might wipe off from them the dust of this world. With this oil she anointed the confessors, that they might not give in to their labours or succumb to fatigue, that they might not be overcome by the heat of this world. She anointed them to refresh them with the oil of the Spirit . . .
>
> The church, then, washes Christ's feet and wipes them with her hair and anoints them with oil and pours ointment upon them, in that she not only cares for the wounded and tends the weary, but also sprinkles them with the sweet odour of grace. She pours the same grace not only on the rich and mighty, but also on those of low estate. She weighs them all in an equal balance, gathers them all into the same bosom, cherishes them in the same lap.
>
> Christ died once and was buried once, but he would have his feet anointed every day. What feet of Christ do we anoint? Those feet of which he said: "As much as you have done it unto one of these least, you have done it unto me" . . . These feet he kisses who loves the lowest of the holy people. These feet he anoints who confers the favours of his gentleness even upon the poor.

Letters of St. Ambrose, 41.20

Prayer

Lord, may I ever live in your blessing and healing grace.
And may I bless you in blessing others, especially the poor.
Amen.

1 CORINTHIANS 13:1–3 DECEMBER 31

Love's Way

To love and to be loved is the joy of life. But love has its own way with us, for it may lead us where we cannot always go, and it may ask what we cannot always give, and it often beckons us down unknown pathways.

The medieval mystic and poet Hadewijch, in her *Poems in Stanzas*, speaks about this:

> In the beginning Love always contents us.
> When Love first spoke to me of love,
> O how with all that I was I greeted all that she is!
> But then she made me resemble the hazelnut trees that bloom early in the dark season,
> And for whose fruit one must wait a long time.
>
> Fortunate is the one who can wait
> Until Love gives all in exchange for all.
> O God! What is patience to me?
> To wait, on the contrary, gives me greater joy, for I have abandoned myself wholly to Love.
> But woe has treated me all too harshly.
>
> This is all too hard for the lover:
> To stray after Love without knowing where,
> Be it in darkness or in daylight,
> In wrath or in lovingness: Were Love to give her true consolation unmistakably,
> This would satisfy the exiled soul.

Hadewijch: The Complete Works, 174

Reflection

Love's way will lead us to places where we never thought we could go.
For the pathway is not only strewn with flowers,
but also with the dark stains of suffering.

A Brief History of Authors and Writings Cited

Abelard, Peter: 1079–1142. Controversial philosopher and theologian. Alternate spelling: Peter Abailard.

Ailred, Saint: 1109–1167. Abbott of Rievaulx. Regarded as the English St. Bernard. Alternative spelling: Aelred.

Ambrose, Saint: c.339–397. Bishop of Milan. Former governor. Famous preacher.

Ammonas the Hermit, Saint: Fourth-century Christian ascetic. Founder of a famous monastery in Egypt.

Anselm, Saint: c.1033–1109. Archbishop of Canterbury. Theologian and writer on Christian spirituality.

Arnobius of Sicca: Died c. 330. Early Christian Apologist.

Athanasius, Saint: c.296–373. Bishop of Alexandria. Supporter of Nicaean orthodoxy and opponent of Arianism.

A BRIEF HISTORY OF AUTHORS AND WRITINGS CITED

Augustine, Saint: 354–430. Bishop of Hippo in Nth. Africa. One of the great church fathers of the Western Church. Famous for his *Confessions*.

Basil, Saint: c.330–379. Lived for many years as a hermit. Later became a church bishop. One of the Cappadocian Fathers.

Benedict, Saint: c.480–c.550. Father of Western Monasticism. Famous for *The Rule of St. Benedict*.

Bernard, Saint: 1090–1153. Abbot of Clairvaux. He made the Cistercian Order an influential movement in Europe.

Bonaventure, Giovanni di Fidanza, Saint: 1221–1274. Franciscan theologian. Minister General of the Franciscan Order and author of the famous *Life of St. Francis*.

Book of Privy Counseling: Presumed to be written by the same unknown author of *The Cloud of Unknowing*.

Bridget of Sweden, Saint: c.1303–1373. Married and later widowed. Founded the Brigittines. Visionary.

Carmina Gadelica: Prayers, blessings, hymns, songs and tales collected by Alexander Carmichael in the Outer Hebrides. Born in 1832, Carmichael collected this rich tradition over sixty years.

Cassian, John: c.360–435. Student of Egyptian monasticism. Key articulator of monastic practices and founder of several monasteries near Marseilles.

Catherine of Genoa, Saint: 1447–1510. Mystic and minister to the sick and dying.

Catherine of Siena, Saint: 1347–1380. Dominican tertiary. Visionary. Her sanctity impressed many, including the nobility.

Chalcedon, Council of: 451. Articulated the Orthodox Faith accepted by both Western and Eastern Churches.

Chrysostom, John, Saint: c.347–407. Bishop of Constantinople. Famous theologian.

Clare, Saint: 1194–1253. Foundress of the Poor Clares, a monastic community based on the teachings of St. Francis.

Clement of Rome, Saint: c.96. Bishop of Rome.

The Cloud of Unknowing: An English mystical treatise of the fourteenth century. Author is unknown.

Colombanus, Saint: c.550–615. Irish missionary to Gaul. Founder of Monastic communities.

A BRIEF HISTORY OF AUTHORS AND WRITINGS CITED

Constitutions of the Holy Apostles: Written by unknown author of the third century CE.

Cuthbert, Saint: Died 687. Bishop of Lindisfarne and later Abbot of the Monastery at Lindisfarne.

Cyprian, Saint: Died 258. Bishop of Carthage. Early Church Father.

Cyril of Jerusalem, Saint: c.315–386. Famous for his *Cathecheses* which prepared inquirers for baptism.

De Duodecim Abusivis Saeculi: Seventh-century Celtic wisdom.

Deogratias: Bishop of Carthage.

Desert Fathers and Mothers: Third and fourth century movement of Christians leaving the cities to live in deserts as hermits. Later they formed cenobitic communities.

Dhouda of Septimania: Wife of the Duke of Septimania. For her son William began *Liber Munualis* in 841.

Didache: Second century early church manual settings out ethics of the Christian life and church practices.

Divine Liturgy of James, the Holy Apostle and Brother of the Lord: Post-apostolic writing.

Eckhart, Meister: c.1260-1327. A German Dominican mystic. He attempted to set out an ontological understanding of God and the inexpressibility of our relationship with God.

Edmund Rich, Saint: c.1180–1240. Archbishop of Canterbury. Also known as Edmund of Abingdon.

Ephrem: Fourteenth-century poet.

Epistle of Barnabas: Author unknown. Possible origin in Alexandrian Christianity between AD 70–130.

Epistle of Diognetus: Written by author unknown between 150 and 225. This writing was an attempt to defend the Christian faith and therefore belongs to early Christian apologetic writing.

Erigena, John Scotus: c.810–c.877. Irishman. A deeply original thinker. Strong pantheistic flavor in his writings. Was head of palace school in Paris. Eriugena alternative spelling.

Francis of Assisi, Saint: 1181-1226. Founder of the Franciscan Order. Imitator of Christ. Servant to the poor. Lover of nature.

A BRIEF HISTORY OF AUTHORS AND WRITINGS CITED

Gertrude the Great, Saint: 1256–c.1302. German mystic and member of the monastery at Helfta. One of the first exponents of the devotion of the Sacred Heart.

Gregory the Great, Saint: c.540–604. Pope from 590. Prior to becoming Pope he sold his riches to help the poor, founded many monasteries and wrote extensively on pastoral and spiritual topics.

Gregory VII: c.1021–1085. Was elected Pope in 1073. Aim was to revitalize the church.

Gregory of Nazianzus, Saint: 329–389. Bishop of Nazianzus in Cappadocia and one of the famous Cappadocian Fathers known for their orthodoxy and Trinitarian theology.

Gregory of Nyssa, Saint: c.330–c.395. Bishop of Nyssa and one of the Cappadocian Fathers. An outstanding early theologian and orator.

Hadewijch: Lived as a Beguine in first half of thirteenth century. One of the greatest Dutch female poets of the Middle Ages.

Heloise: c.1098–1164. Lover and then wife of Peter Abelard. Both committed themselves to celibacy. She became the Abbess of the Monastery of the Paraclete.

Hilary of Poitiers: c.300–c.367. Bishop of Poitiers. Trinitarian theologian.

Hildegard of Bingen: 1098–1179. Abbess of Rupertsberg, mystic, author, playwright, musician and medico. She was an advisor to kings and popes.

Hilton, Walter: Died 1396. English mystic and Augustinian canon. He articulated that faith and feeling are separated by a dark night of the soul.

Hippolytus, Saint: c.170–c.236. One of the most important Catholic theologians of the third century.

Hugh of Saint Victor: c.1096–1141. Theologian and mystic.

Irenaeus, Saint: c.130–c.200. Bishop of Lyons. First great Catholic theologian.

Isaac the Syrian, Saint: Died c.700. Ascetic writer.

Jacopone da Todi: 1236–1306. Italian Franciscan friar. Poet.

Jacques de Vitry: 1180–1240. French theologian. Made cardinal in 1229. Biographer of *The Life of Mary of Oignies*.

Jerome, Saint: c.342–420. Ascetic, priest, secretary to the Pope, biblical scholar. Translator of the Bible into Latin, *The Vulgate*.

John of Damascus: c.675–c.749. Greek theologian. Doctor of the church.

A BRIEF HISTORY OF AUTHORS AND WRITINGS CITED

Julian of Norwich: c.1342–1413. English mystic. Her writings focused on visions of the Passion of Christ and on the Holy Trinity.

Justin Martyr, Saint: c.100–c.165. One of the early Christian apologists.

Kempe, Margery: Fifteenth-century English laywoman. Visionary.

Lactantius: c. 240–c.320. Christian apologist.

Lull, Ramon: c.1235–c.1315. Great writer of spiritual works in Catalan, Latin and Arabic. Missionary to Asia, Armenia and Africa. Was stoned to death by a mob of Arabs in Bougie, North Africa.

Macarius, Saint: c.300–c.390. From Alexandria and one of the Egyptian desert fathers. The Homilies ascribed to him came from elsewhere, possibly from early Syrian monasticism.

Martin of Tours, Saint: Died 397. Bishop of Tours. Encouraged the spread of monasticism in Gaul.

Mawr, Cynddelw Brydydd: Twelfth-century Welsh poet.

Mechthild of Magdeburg, Saint: c.1210–1280. A German Beguine, mystic and visionary.

Meilyr: Celtic poet.

Methodius: Bishop of the See of Tyre.

Moucan: Celtic devotional texts.

Mygron: Abbot of Iona from 965–981.

Nicholas of Cusa: c.1400–1464. German cardinal and philosopher.

O'Huiginn, Cormac Ruadh: Fifteenth-century Irish poet.

Origen: c.185–c.254. Biblical critic, exegete, theologian and writer on spirituality. He was an ascetic. In 250 he was imprisoned and tortured for his faith.

Patrick, Saint: c.389–c.461. Known as the apostle to the Irish. Founder of churches and religious communities.

Pelagius: 354–420. British lay monk. Acquired a reputation for learning and piety in Rome. Later worked in North Africa. Opposed by St. Augustine.

Polycarp: c.69–c.155. Bishop of Smyrna in Asia Minor. An important figure in the post-apostolic church. Was martyred aged 88.

Porete, Marguerite: A Beguine and mystical writer who was condemned by the church and burned at the stake in Paris some time after 1312.

Possidius, Saint: c.370–c.440. Biographer of St. Augustine.

A BRIEF HISTORY OF AUTHORS AND WRITINGS CITED

Prayers of Moucan: Eighth-century Celtic spiritual writing.

Pseudo-Macarius: *Fifty Spiritual Homilies and The Great Letter,* the work of an unknown fourth-century Syrian monk. Advocates a "heart" spirituality.

Richard of St. Victor: Died 1173. Native of Scotland. Prior of monastery of St. Victor. Author of *The Mystical Ark.*

Rolle, Richard: c.1295–1349. English hermit and mystic. His latter years were spent at Hampole where he gave spiritual guidance to Cistercian nuns.

Salvian: Fifth-century ecclesiastical writer.

Shepherd of Hermas: Treatise of early Christian writer, Hermas.

Symeon, the New Theologian, Saint: 949–1022. Abbot of the Monastery of St. Mamas in Constantinople and Byzantine medieval mystic.

Tertullian: c.160–c.220, significant African Church Father and apologist.

Theonas, Saint: Died 300. Bishop of Alexandria.

Thomas Aquinas, Saint: c.1225–1274. Possibly the greatest Dominican philosopher and theologian of the Middle Ages. Famous for his *Summa Theologica.*

Theologica Germanica: written around 1350 possibly from someone within the Friends of God renewal movement.

Thomas a Kempis: c.1380–1471. Belonged to the Brethren of the Common Life and a leading ascetical writer. Famous for his *The Imitation of Christ.*

van Ruysbroeck, Jan: 1293–1381. Flemish mystic. Founder of the *Devotio Moderna.* Alternative spelling Ruusbroec.

Voyage of Brendan: Author unknown. Saint Brendan 486–575 founded several monasteries including Clonfert. He is remembered for his sea voyages.

Bibliography

Aelred, of Rievaulx, Saint. *The Mirror of Charity*. Translated by Geoffrey Webb and Adrian Walker. London: Mowbray, 1962.

———. *Spiritual Friendship*. Translated by Lawrence C. Braceland. Edited by Marsha L. Dutton. Collegeville, MN: Liturgical, 2010.

Alexander, Francis, trans. *Legends of Saints and Martyrs*. London: David Nutt, 1905. http://archive.org/stream/MN5110ucmf_3/MN5110ucmf_3_djvu.txt.

Ambrose, Saint. *Letters of Saint Ambrose*. In vol. 10 of *Nicene and Post-Nicene Fathers*, Series 2. Translated by H. de Romestin. New York. 1896. http://www.fordham.edu/halsall/source/ambrose-let21.asp.

———. *Letters of Saint Ambrose*. http://www.orthodoxebooks.org/node/421.

Ancelet-Hustache, Jeanne. *Master Eckhart and the Rhineland Mystics*. Translated by Hilda Graef. London: Longmans, 1957.

Anselm of Canterbury, Saint. *The Devotions of Saint Anselm*. Edited by Clement C. J. Webb. London: Methuen, 1903. http://www.ccel.org/ccel/anselm/devotions.iii.vii.iv.html.

———. *The Major Works*. Edited by Brian Davies and G. R. Evans. Oxford: Oxford University Press, 1998.

———. *Meditation Concerning the Redemption of Mankind*. http://enlargingtheheart.wordpress.com/category/benedictine-cistercian/anselm-of-canterbury/.

———. *Monologion*. Translated by Sidney N. Deane. www.logoslibrary.org/anselm/monologion/77.html.

———. *The Prayers and Meditations of Saint Anselm with the Proslogion*. Translated by Benedicta Ward. London: Penguin, 1973.

———. *Oratio 52* (PL 158, 955–56). *Office of Readings for the Solemnity of the Immaculate Conception*. http://enlargingtheheart.wordpress.com/category/benedictine-cistercian/anselm-of-canterbury/.

The Apostolic Fathers. Translated by Kirsopp Lake. Vol. 1. Loeb Classical Library. London: Heinemann, 1977.

Athanasius, Saint. *Life of Antony and The Letter to Marcellinus*. Translated by R. C. Gregg. New York: Paulist, 1980.

Atwell, Robert, ed. *Celebrating the Saints*. London: SCM, 2004.

Augustine. *The Augustine Catechism: The Enchiridion on Faith, Hope and Love*. Translated by Bruce Harbert. Edited by Boniface Ramsey. New York: New City, 1999.

———. *City of God; Christian Doctrine*. In vol. 2 of *Nicene and Post-Nicene Fathers*, Series 1. Edited by Philip Schaff. Peabody, MA: Hendrickson, 1994.

———. *Confessions.* Translated by Frank J. Sheed. Edited by Michael Foley. 2nd ed. Indianapolis: Hackett, 2006.

———. *Confessions of Saint Augustine.* Translated by Tobie Matthew. London: Burns and Oates, 1954.

———. *The Confessions of Saint Augustine.* Translated by Edward Pusey. 1838. www.ccel.org/ccel/augustine/confess.i.html.

———. *The Confessions of Saint Augustine.* Translated by Albert C. Outler. 1955. Reprint. Mineola, NY: Dover, 2002.

———. *Enchiridion on Faith, Hope, and Love.* Translated by J. F. Shaw. Washington, DC: Regnery, 1996.

Backhouse, Halcyon. *The Best of Meister Eckhart.* New York: Crossroad, 1993.

Basil, Saint. *The Letters.* Translated by R. J. Deferrari. Vol. 1. Loeb Classical Library. London: Heinemann, 1972.

Benedict, Saint. *The Rule of Saint Benedict.* Edited by Timothy Fry. New York: Vintage, 1998.

Bernard of Clairvaux, Saint. *Bernard of Clairvaux: Selected Works.* Translated by G. R. Evans. New York: Paulist, 1997.

———. *On Loving God.* http://www.ccel.org/ccel/bernard/loving_god.txt.

———. *Song of Songs.* Edited by Darrell Wright. http://archive.org/stream/St.BernardOnTheSongOfSongs/StBernardOnTheSongOfSongsall_djvu.txt.

Bettenson, Henry, ed. *Documents of the Christian Church.* 2nd ed. London: Oxford University Press, 1963.

Bonaventure, Saint. *The Life of St. Francis.* Translated by Ewert Cousins. New York: HarperOne, 2005.

———. *The Life of Saint Francis of Assisi.* Translated by E. Gurney Salter. London: Catholic Way, 2013.

———. *The Mind's Road to God.* Translated by George Boas. New York: Liberal Arts, 1953.

———. *The Soul's Journey into God; The Tree of Life; The Life of St. Francis.* Translated by Ewert Cousins. London: SPCK, 1978.

Brendan, Saint. *The Voyage of St Brendan the Abbot.* Translated by Denis O'Donoghue. Dublin: Browne and Nolan, 1895. https://archive.org/stream/gbu0U49kFVbJcsC/gbu0U49kFVbJcsC_djvu.txt.

Burns, J. Patout, and Gerald M. Fagin. *The Holy Spirit.* Message of the Fathers of the Church 3. Wilmington, MA: M. Glazier, 1984.

Butcher, Carmen A., trans. *The Cloud of Unknowing with the Book of Privy Counsel.* Boston: Shambhala, 2009.

Carmichael, Alexander. *Carmina Gadelica: Hymns and incantations.* 1900. http://www.sacred-texts.com/neu/celt/cg.htm.

Cassian, John, Saint. *Conferences.* Translated by Colm Luibheid. New York: Paulist, 1985.

———. *The Conferences of John Cassian.* Translated by Edgar C. S. Gibson. In *Nicene and Post-Nicene Fathers of the Christian Church.* 1894. http://www.ccel.org/ccel/cassian/conferences.i.html.

Catherine of Genoa, Saint. *Purgation and Purgatory; The Spiritual Dialogue.* Translated by Serge Hughes. London: SPCK, 1979.

Catherine of Siena, Saint. *The Dialogue.* Translated by Suzanne Noffke. New York: Paulist, 1980.

BIBLIOGRAPHY

———. *Dialogue of Catherine of Siena*. Translated by A. Thorold. London: Kegan Paul, Trench, Trubner, 1904. www.ccel.org/ccel/catherine/dialog.ii.html.

Chesterton, G. K. *St Francis of Assisi*. Garden City, NY: Image, 1957.

Clément, Olivier. *The Roots of Christian Mysticism: Text and Commentary*. New York: New City, 1995.

Colledge, Edmund, ed. *The Mediaeval Mystics of England*. New York: Scribner's, 1961.

Columbanus Hibernus. *Monks' Rules*. Translated by G. S. M. Walker. www.ucc.ie/celt/online/T201052.html.

———. *Sermons*. Translated by G. S. M. Walker. www.ucc.ie/celt/online/T201053.html.

Cyprian, Saint. *The Letters of St. Cyprian of Carthage*. Translated by G. W. Clarke. Vol. 3. Ancient Christian Writers 46. New York: Newman, 1986.

———. *On the Church: Select Treatises by Saint Cyprian*. Translated by Allen Brent. Crestwood, NY: St Vladimir's Seminary Press, 2006.

Davies, Olivier, ed. and trans. *Celtic Spirituality*. New York: Paulist, 1999.

Davies, Olivier, and Fiona Bowie, eds. *Celtic Christian Spirituality: An Anthology of Medieval and Modern Sources*. London: SPCK, 1995.

"The Desert Fathers and Mothers on Solitude." *Hermitary*. www.hermitary.com/solitude/desert.html.

Didache. Translated by Alexander Roberts and James Donaldson. http://www.earlychristianwritings.com/text/didache-roberts.html.

Delio, Ilia. *Franciscan Prayer*. Cincinnati, OH: St. Anthony Messenger, 2004.

De Waal, Esther, ed. *The Celtic Vision: Prayers and Blessings from the Outer Hebrides*. Petersham: St. Bede's, 1990.

Eckhart, Meister. *The Essential Sermons, Commentaries, Treatises and Defense*. Translated by Edmund Colledge and Bernard McGinn. London: SPCK, 1981.

———. *Meister Eckhart, from Whom God Hid Nothing: Sermons, Writings, and Sayings*. Edited by David O'Neal. Boston: Shambhala, 1996.

———. *Meister Eckhart: A Modern Translation*. Translated by Raymond Bernard Blakney. New York: Harper, 1941.

———. *Meister Eckhart: Selected Treatises and Sermons*. Translated by James W. Clark and John V. Skinner. London: Fontana, 1963.

———. *Meister Eckhart: Selected Writings*. Translated by Oliver Davies. New York: Penguin, 1994.

———. *Meister Eckhart: Sermons*. www.eleggua.com/Objects/Eckhart_Sermons1.html.

Eriugena, John Scotus. *The Voice of the Eagle: The Heart of Celtic Christianity*. Translated by Christopher Bamford. Great Barrington, MA: Lindisfarne, 2000.

Fairweather, Eugene R., ed. and trans. *A Scholastic Miscellany: Anselm to Ockham*. London: SCM, 1956.

Ferrante, Joan, trans. *Epistolae: Medieval Women's Latin Letters*. New York: Columbia University, Center for New Media Teaching and Learning. epistolae.ccnmtl.columbia.edu/letter/125.html.

Francis, Saint. *The Admonitions of Saint Francis*. www.franciscanmissionaries.com/about-us/admonitions/.

———. *Francis and Clare: The Complete Works*. Translated by Regis J. Armstrong and Ignatius C. Brady. New York: Paulist, 1982.

———. *The Little Flowers and the Life of St Francis, with the Mirror of Perfection*. London: J. M. Dent, 1910. http://archive.org/stream/thelittleflowersoofrancuoft/thelittleflowersoofrancuoft_djvu.txt.

———. *The Rule of St Francis*. https://www.ewtn.com/padrepio/franciscan/rule.htm.

———. *The Writings of Saint Francis of Assisi*. Translated by Paschal Robinson. Philadelphia: Dolphin, 1906. http://www.sacred-texts.com/chr/wosf/wosf15.htm.

Gasper, Giles E. M. *Anselm of Canterbury and His Theological Inheritance*. Aldershot, UK: Ashgate, 2004.

Gertrude, Saint. *The Life and Revelations of Saint Gertrude*. London: Burns and Oates, 1870. http://archive.org/stream/thelifeandrevelaoogertuoft/thelifeandrevelaoogertuoft_djvu.txt.

Gregory I, Pope. *The Book of Morals of St Gregory the Pope, or an Exposition on the Book of Blessed Job*. London: Rivington and Rivington, 1844. www.lectionarycentral.com/Gregory/Moralia/Books05.html.

———. *Dialogues*. Translated by Odo John Zimmerman. Fathers of the Church 39. Washington, DC: Catholic University of America Press, 1959.

Gregory VII, Pope. *Letter of Gregory VII to Bishop Hermann of Metz, March 15, 1081*. http://avalon.law.yale.edu/medieval/inv14.asp.

Gregory Nazianzen. *Oration*. In *The Fathers of the Church*. http://www.newadvent.org/fathers/310243.htm.

Gregory of Nazianzus, Saint. *Festal Orations*. Translated by Nonna V. Harrison. Crestwood, NY: St. Vladimir's Seminary, 2008.

Gregory of Nyssa. *Commentary on the Song of Songs*. Translated by Casimir McCambley. Brookline, MA: Hellenic College Press, 1987.

———. *The Life of Moses*. Translated by Abraham Malherbe. New York: Paulist, 1978.

———. *On the Soul and the Resurrection*. Crestwood, NY: St. Vladimir's Seminary, 1993.

Hadewijch. *Hadewijch: The Complete Works*. Translated by Columba Hart. Classics of Western Spirituality. London: SPCK, 1981.

Hannay, James O. *The Wisdom of the Desert*. 1904. http://archive.org/stream/WisdomOfTheDesert/wd_djvu.txt.

Hilary of Poitiers. *De Trinate*. In vol. 9 of *Nicene and Post-Nicene Fathers*, Series 2. Edited by Philip Schaff and Henry Wace. Reprint. Peabody, MA: Hendrickson, 1994.

Hildegard, Saint. *The Letters of Hildegard of Bingen*. Translated by Joseph L. Baird and Radd K. Ehrman. 3 vols. Oxford: Oxford University Press, 1994.

———. *Mystical Writings*. Edited by Fiona Bowie and Oliver Davies. Translated by Robert Carver. New York: Crossroad, 1999.

———. *The Personal Correspondence of Hildegard of Bingen*. Selected by Joseph L. Baird. New York: Oxford University Press, 2006.

———. *Scivias*. Translated by Columba Hart and Jane Bishop. Mahwah, NJ: Paulist, 1990.

———. *Selected Writings*. Translated by Mark Atherton. London: Penguin, 2001.

———. *Symphonia*. Translated by Barbara Newman. 2nd ed. New York: Cornell University Press, 1998.

———. *The Ways of the Lord*. Edited by Emilie Griffin. Translated by Columba Hart and Jane Bishop. New York: HarperOne, 2005.

Hilton, Walter. *The Scale of Perfection*. Translated by John P. H. Clark and Rosemary Dorward. New York: Paulist, 1991.

———. *The Scale (or Ladder) of Perfection*. Translated by Serenus Cressey. 1870. www.ccel.org/ccel/hilton/ladder.i.html.

Holmes, Michael W., ed. *The Apostolic Fathers in English*. 3rd ed. Grand Rapids: Baker Academic, 2006.

Hoole, Charles H., trans. *The Epistle of Barnabas*. From *The Apostolic Fathers*. 1885. http://www.earlychristianwritings.com/text/barnabas-hoole.html.

———. *2 Clement*. From *The Apostolic Fathers*. 1885. http://www.earlychristianwritings.com/text/2clement-hoole.html.

Ignatius. *The Apostolic Fathers, Vol. 1*. Translated by K. Lake. The Loeb Classical Library. London: William Heinemann, 1977.

Irenaeus, Saint. *The Demonstration of the Apostolic Preaching*. Translated by J. Armitage Robinson. London: SPCK, 1920.

———. *Proof of the Apostolic Preaching*. Translated by Joseph P. Smith. New York: Paulist, 1952.

Jacob the Deacon. *The Life of St Pelagia the Harlot*. Translated by Eustochius. http://www.vitae-patrum.org.uk/page46.html.

Jacopone da Todi. *The Lauds*. Translated by Serge Hughes and Elizabeth Hughes. London: SPCK, 1982.

Jacques, de Vitry. *The Life of Marie d'Oignies*. Translated by Margot H. King. Toronto: Peregrina, 1987.

Jerome, Saint. *Letter XIV: To Heliodorus, Monk*. http://www.tertullian.org/fathers2/NPNF2-06/Npnf2-06-03.htm#P363_64884.

———. *Letter XXII: To Eustochium*. http://www.earlychurchtexts.com/public/jerome_in_the_desert.htm.

John of Damascus. In vol. 13 of *Nicene and Post-Nicene Fathers*, Series 2. Edited by Philip Schaff and Henry Wace. Reprint. Peabody, MA: Hendrickson, 1994.

Johnston, William, trans. *The Cloud of Unknowing and The Book of Privy Counseling*. Garden City, NY: Image, 1973.

Julian of Norwich. *The Complete Julian of Norwich*. Translated by John-Julian. Brewster, MA: Paraclete, 2009.

———. *A Lesson of Love: The Revelations of Julian of Norwich*. Edited and translated by John-Julian. London: Darton, Longman and Todd, 1988

———. *Revelations of Divine Love*. Translated by Grace Warrack. 1901. http://www.ccel.org/ccel/julian/revelations.i.html.

———. *Revelations of Divine Love*. Translated by Elizabeth Spearing. London: Penguin, 1966.

———. *Revelations of Divine Love Shewed to a Devout Ankress by Name of Julian of Norwich*. Edited by Roger Hudleston. London: Burns, Oates, and Washbourne, 1927.

———. *A Shewing of God's Love*. Translated by Anna Maria Reynolds. London: Longmans, Green, 1958.

———. *Showings*. Translated by Edmund Colledge and James Walsh. New York: Paulist, 1978.

Justin. *Apology*. In *The Apostolic Fathers with Justin Martyr and Irenaeus*. http://www.ccel.org/ccel/schaff/anf01.viii.ii.lxvii.html.

BIBLIOGRAPHY

Kempe, Margery. *The Book of Margery Kempe*. Translated by Barry Windeatt. London: Penguin, 1994.

King, Ursula. *Christian Mystics: Their Lives and Legacies throughout the Ages*. Mahwah, NJ: HiddenSpring, 2001.

Knowles, D. *Christian Monasticism*. New York: McGraw-Hill, 1969.

Llewelyn, Robert, ed. *The Joy of the Saints*. London: Darton, Longman and Todd, 1988.

Macarius of Egypt. *Pseudo-Macarius: The Fifty Spiritual Homilies and the Great Letter*. Edited by George A. Maloney. New York: Paulist, 1992.

Madigan, Shawn, ed. *Mystics, Visionaries, and Prophets: A Historical Anthology of Women's Spiritual Writings*. Minneapolis, MN: Fortress, 1998.

McCracken, G. E., ed. *Early Medieval Theology*. London: SCM, 1957.

McGinn, Bernard, ed. *The Essential Writings of Christian Mysticism*. New York: Modern Library, 2006.

McGinn, Bernard, et al., eds. *Christian Spirituality: Origins to the Twelfth Century*. London: SCM, 1989.

McGuire, Brian, P. *Friendship and Community: The Monastic Experience, 350–1250*. Ithaca: Cornell University Press, 2010.

Mechthild of Magdeburg. *The Flowing Light of the Godhead*. Translated by Frank Tobin. Mahwah, NJ: Paulist, 1997.

Mendes-Flohr, Paul, ed. *Ecstatic Confessions: The Heart of Mysticism*. Translated by Esther Cameron. New York: Harper and Row, 1985.

Morison, E. F. *St Basil and His Rule: A Study in Early Monasticism*. London: Oxford University Press, 1912. http://archive.org/stream/basilsruleoomoriuoft/basilsruleoomoriuoft_djvu.txt.

Murphy, Francis X. *The Christian Way of Life*. Message of the Fathers of the Church 18. Wilmington: M. Glazier, 1986.

Mursell, Gordon. *English Spirituality: From Earliest Times to 1700*. SPCK: London, 2001.

Newell, J. Philip. *Listening for the Heartbeat of God: A Celtic Spirituality*. London: SPCK, 1997.

Northumbria Community. *Celtic Daily Prayer*. New York: HarperOne, 2002.

O'Dwyer, Peter. *Towards a History of Irish Spirituality*. Dublin: Columba, 1995.

O'Loughlin, Thomas. *Celtic Theology: Humanity, World and God in Early Irish Writings*. London: Continuum, 2000.

Origen of Alexandria. *Contra Celsus*. http://www.newadvent.org/fathers/04163.htm.

Patrick, Saint. *Confession of St Patrick*. http://www.ccel.org/ccel/patrick/confession.i.html.

———. *The Confession of St. Patrick*. Translated by Thomas Olden. London: Eremitical, 2010.

Petry, Ray C., ed. *Late Medieval Mysticism*. Library of Christian Classics 13. London: SCM, 1958.

Polycarp. *The Epistle of Polycarp to the Philippians*. Translated by Alexander Roberts and James Donaldson. http://www.earlychristianwritings.com/text/polycarp-roberts.html.

Porete, Marguerite. *The Mirror of Simple Souls*. Edited by Clare Kirchberger. Vancouver: Soul Care, 2012.

———. *The Mirror of Simple Souls*. Classics of Western Spirituality. Translated by Ellen L. Babinsky. New York: Paulist, 1993.

BIBLIOGRAPHY

Possidius, Bishop. *The Life of St. Augustine*. Translated by Herbert T. Weiskotten. 1919. http://www.tertullian.org/fathers/possidius_life_of_augustine_02_text.htm.

Richard of St. Victor. *The Twelve Patriarchs, The Mystical Ark, Book Three of the Trinity*. Translated by Grover A. Zinn. New York: Paulist, 1979.

Roberts, Alexander, and James Donaldson, eds. *The Ante-Nicene Fathers: Translations of the Writings of the Fathers Down to AD 325*. 10 vols. Grand Rapids: Eerdmans, 1969–73.

Rolle, Richard. *The English Writings*. Translated and edited by Rosamund S. Allen. Mahwah, NJ: Paulist, 1988.

———. *The Mending of Life*. Translated by Richard Misyn. 2nd ed. London: Methuen, 1920. http://www.ccel.org/ccel/rolle/fire.ix.html.

Ruusbroec, Jan van. *The Sparkling Stone*. Translated by C. A. Wynschenk. 1916. http://www.sacred-texts.com/chr/asm/asm107.htm.

———. *The Spiritual Espousals and Other Works*. Translated by James A. Wiseman. New York: Paulist, 1985.

Salvian. *The Writings of Salvian, the Presbyter: Governance of God, Letters, Books to the Church*. Translated by Jeremiah F. O'Sullivan. Fathers of the Church. Berkshire, UK: Cima, 1947.

Schaff, Philip, and Henry Wace, eds. *A Select Library of Nicene and Post-Nicene Fathers of the Christian Church*. Second Series. 14 vols. Grand Rapids: Eerdmans, 1978–79.

Sheerin, Daniel J. *The Eucharist*. Message of the Fathers of the Church 7. Wilmington: M. Glazier, 1986.

The Shepherd of Hermas. *The Shepherd of Hermas*. Mandate 1–2. http://www.earlychristianwritings.com/text/shepherd-lightfoot.html.

———. *The Shepherd of Hermas*, 3.1. http://www.earlychristianwritings.com/text/shepherd.html.

Spearing, Elizabeth, ed. *Medieval Writings on Female Spirituality*. New York: Penguin, 2002.

Stevenson, James, ed. *Creeds, Councils, and Controversies: Documents Illustrative of the History of the Church, AD 337–46*. London: SPCK, 1972.

Symeon the New Theologian. *Catéchèses*. Translated by Joseph Paramelle. Sources Chrétiennes. Paris: Cerf, 1965.

———. *The Discourses*. Translated by C. J. de Catanzaro. London: SPCK, 1980.

Tertullian. *Apology and De Spectaculis*. Translated by T. R. Glover. Loeb Classical Library. London: Heinemann, 1977.

———. *Early Latin Theology: Selections from Tertullian, Cyprian, Ambrose, and Jerome*. Translated and edited by S. L. Greenslade. Library of Christian Classics 5. London: SCM, 1956. http://www.tertullian.org/articles/greenslade_prae/greenslade_prae.htm.

———. *The Holy Spirit*. Edited by James P. Burns and Gerald M. Fagin. Message of the Church Fathers 3. Wilmington: M. Glazier, 1984.

Thomas à Kempis. *The Imitation of Christ*. Translated by Aloysius Croft and Harold Bolton. 1949. http://www.ccel.org/ccel/kempis/imitation.txt.

———. *The Imitation of Christ*. Translated by E. M. Blaiklock. London: Hodder and Stoughton, 1979.

———. *The Imitation of Christ in Four Books: A Translation from the Latin*. Edited and translated by Joseph N. Tylenda. New York: Vintage, 1998.

———. *My Imitation of Christ*. Translated by Joseph B. Frey. Brooklyn, NY: Confraternity of the Precious Blood, 1954.

Thomas, Aquinas, Saint. *An Aquinas Reader: Selections from the Writings of Thomas Aquinas*. Edited by Mary T. Clark. London: Hodder and Stoughton, 1972.

To Any Christian: Letters from the Saints. Selected and arranged by a Benedictine of Stanbrook. London: Burns and Oates, 1964.

Waddell, Helen, trans. *The Desert Fathers*. New York: Vintage, 1998.

Walsh, James, trans. *The Cloud of Unknowing*. New York: Paulist, 1981.

Ward, Benedicta, trans. *The Desert Fathers: Sayings of the Early Christian Monks*. London: Penguin, 2003.

———. *The Paradise of the Desert Fathers*. www.coptic.net/articles/ParadiseOfDesertFathers.txt.

Wiggers, Gustav F. *An Historical Presentation of Augustinianism and Pelagianism from the Original Sources*. Translated by Ralph Emerson. New York: Gould, Newman and Saxton, 1840.

Winkworth, Susanna, trans. *Theologia Germanica*. Edited by Dr. Pfeiffer. London: Macmillan, 1893. http://www.ccel.org/ccel/anonymous/theologia.txt.

Wolters, Clifton, trans. *The Cloud of Unknowing and Other Works*. London: Penguin, 1978.

Topical index

Action, 51, 60
Angels, 220, 316, 348
Ascetic, disciplines, 140, 249, 361
Attachment, 355, 361
Balance, Moderation, 51, 60, 80, 205, 249
Baptism, xv, 235, 253
Beauty, 6, 15, 38, 222, 236, 254, 391
Care, 180, 190, 238, 377
Celtic, 112, 124, 136, 145, 154, 183, 203, 209, 220, 239, 250, 251, 255, 274, 295, 311, 316, 322, 337, 345, 348, 352, 356, 370
Christlikeness, xiv, 42, 182, 185, 189, 199, 263, 307, 333, 354
Church, 11, 92, 118, 195, 200, 217, 247, 284, 359, 394
Comforter, consolation, 12, 44, 133, 186, 192, 224, 240, 278, 317, 370, 381
Compassion, 9, 12, 31, 61, 109, 201, 214, 245, 249, 258, 318, 362
Confession, 81, 315
Conscience, 81, 293, 304, 379
Contemplation, 6, 51, 60, 102, 122, 189, 205, 242, 246, 261, 281, 282, 362, 393
Conversion, 56, 116, 258, 276, 294
Creation, 6, 15, 144, 242, 251
Cross, 9, 18, 113, 133, 159, 182, 184, 235
Darkness, desolation, 50, 85, 103, 166, 192, 217, 251, 252, 260, 304
Desert, x, 26, 140, 149, 168, 208, 226, 290, 328

Discernment, 43, 80, 103, 126, 356
Diversity, 83, 119, 122, 219, 224, 242, 300
Encouragement, 160, 225, 312, 367
Enemies, 32, 84, 106, 129, 211, 256, 393
Equality, 177. 247, 258, 394
Eucharist, 17, 54, 61, 76, 115, 172, 299, 380
Evil, Satan, 47, 188, 194, 253, 290, 320, 360, 366, 386
Faith, 37, 42, 47, 59, 67, 68, 93, 102, 116, 126, 134, 140, 161, 179, 188, 204, 224, 253, 262, 300, 388, 391
Fasting, 140, 212, 249, 292, 334, 362
Forgiveness, 10, 32, 70, 106, 157, 210, 223, 327
Freedom, 47, 89, 117, 145, 173, 275, 355, 361, 375
Friendship, 64, 186, 227, 306
Fruitfulness, Generativity, 75, 162, 171, 359, 361
Generosity, 13, 31, 72, 76, 106, 158, 190, 334
Gentleness, 14, 157
Glory, 257, 296, 358
Goodness, 139, 194, 286, 318
Grace, 30, 67, 87, 97, 104, 126, 151, 214, 249, 279, 311, 334, 387, 390, 392
Greatness of God, 144, 222, 280, 391
Growth, 61, 271, 301, 335
Guide, 155, 209
Hiddenness, 67, 111, 130
Holiness, 16, 123, 126, 244, 310

TOPICAL INDEX

Holy Spirit, 11, 58, 108, 155, 219, 248, 270, 304, 336
Honesty, 141, 323
Hope, 166, 173, 381, 388
Hospitality, 106, 223, 237
Humility, 19, 25, 115, 120, 170, 206, 259, 288, 309, 333, 384
Immortality, see mortality
Impassibility, 9
Imperfection, 14, 187
Incarnation, 28, 82, 113, 117, 169, 251, 387
Inclusion, 210
Intimacy, 168, 234, 240
Jesus, 16, 18, 113, 167, 255, 327, 349, 366, 378
Journey, 124, 127, 179, 204, 335, 368
Joy, ecstasy, 176, 186, 216, 240, 281, 295, 339, 389
Judging, 157, 221, 245, 278, 305
Justice, 70, 137, 150, 190, 267, 305, 318, 343, 366
Light, 5, 50, 85, 128, 172, 192, 269, 350, 352
Listening, 236, 277, 283, 356, 384
Longing, 3, 9, 39, 74, 84, 181, 241, 287, 382
Loss, 138, 239, 273, 306, 360
Love, 8, 22, 63, 68, 86, 94, 109, 119, 134, 146, 148, 156, 176, 20, 210, 213, 233, 244, 259, 273, 329, 393, 395
Lover, 38, 39, 102, 163, 183, 207, 227, 240, 262, 273, 308, 357, 395
Martyrdom, xv, 216, 268
Mary, 52, 90
Meditation, 4, 6, 7, 96, 104, 199, 202, 281, 362
Mercy, 6, 12, 16, 61, 81, 109, 211, 228, 258, 291, 315, 317, 318, 334, 346, 354, 375, 381, 386, 392
Mission, 37, 57, 135, 256, 371
Mortality, Immortality, death, 91, 146, 296, 345, 373, 380
Motherhood of God, 40, 75, 97

Mystery, 204, 280, 308, 313, 333, 391
Obedience, 52, 114, 116, 126, 170, 184, 185, 285, 288
Patience, 14, 105, 208, 340, 395
Perfection, imperfection, 187, 329
Persecution, 41, 46, 269
Pilgrimage, 53, 95, 310
Political, 137, 206, 217, 229
Poor in spirit, 48, 95
Poverty, 76, 135, 140, 190, 258, 305, 325, 394
Praise, 96, 170, 346
Prayer, 32, 33, 55, 62, 87, 92, 101, 107, 110, 129, 177, 212, 234, 267, 275, 290, 319, 321, 371, 392
Prayer of the heart, 63, 290
Presence, 92, 134, 141, 161, 168, 303, 365, 370
Protection, 20, 27, 47, 101, 112, 124, 136, 183, 303, 316, 322, 348
Redemption, 28, 333
Renewal, 108, 128, 171, 187, 260, 347
Repentance, 78, 81, 128, 145, 152, 257, 281, 315, 323, 325, 326, 351, 375
Rest, 136, 154, 243, 272, 319, 342
Restoration, 90, 149, 233, 394
Revelation, xv, 79, 91, 123, 193, 215, 336, 385
Sabbath, 118, 243
Scripture, 4, 153, 172, 191, 193, 202, 336
Seeking God, 3, 22, 241, 287, 372
Self-examination, Self-knowledge, 20, 21, 64, 121, 218, 244, 245, 275, 278, 353
Service, 24, 29, 51, 60, 72, 151, 158, 160, 226, 238, 276
Shepherd, 152, 337
Sin, 64, 70, 152, 241, 293, 315, 341, 353, 355, 379
Singlemindedness, 272, 383, 393
Slander, 125, 221
Solitude, 38, 84, 88, 289, 309, 328, 362

TOPICAL INDEX

Suffering, 41, 73, 77, 133, 159, 174, 181, 182, 207, 284, 383, 395
Surrender, 56, 84, 89, 94, 95, 176, 182, 262, 314, 360, 369
Temptation, 26, 55, 188, 252
Thanksgiving, 55, 107
Transformation, 7, 128, 175, 304, 349
Trials, adversity, 111, 133, 138, 174, 179, 188, 239, 369
Trinity, 5, 23, 63, 93, 112, 344
Union, 42, 69, 163, 189, 302, 357, 368
Unity, 58, 177, 284, 344
Virtue, 7, 143, 170, 199, 210, 286, 292, 356, 376
Vocation, 142, 227, 282, 300
Vulnerability, 25, 328
Weeping, 116. 281, 334, 339, 368
Wisdom, 88, 175, 324
World, 53, 137, 234, 392
Work, 51, 55, 243, 342

Author Index

Abelard, Peter, 323, 397
Abelard, Héloïse, 323, 400
Aelred of Rievaulx, 64, 227, 243, 254, 374, 397
Ambrose, Saint, 70, 326, 394, 397
Ammonas, Saint, 386, 397
Anselm, Saint, 3, 12, 31, 44, 68, 75, 90, 129, 179, 210, 241, 318, 390, 397
Antony, Saint, 10, 121, 149, 174, 279, 313, 353
Aquinas, Thomas, 357
Arnobius, 378, 397
Athanasius of Alexandria, 28, 121, 353, 397
Augustine, Saint, 4, 21, 41, 56, 77, 88, 106, 116, 128, 187, 193, 247, 250, 300, 306, 310, 315, 334, 341, 398
Basil, Saint, 13, 107, 138, 144, 152, 188, 200, 225, 238, 248, 271, 284, 289, 328, 367, 398
Benedict, Saint, 180, 398
Bernard of Clairvaux, 89, 96, 105, 134, 171, 244, 296, 388, 398
Bonaventure, 74, 104, 167, 175, 223, 261, 275, 280, 335, 362, 365, 398
Brendan, Saint, 237
Bridget of Sweden, 83, 224, 398
Carmina Gadelica, 112, 124, 136, 154, 209, 220, 239, 251, 303, 311, 316, 322, 348, 389, 398
Cassian, John, 6, 33, 43, 150, 202, 234, 267, 282, 290, 329, 398
Catherine of Genoa, 69, 398

Catherine of Siena, 18, 119, 162, 181, 217, 293, 368, 398
Chalcedon, Council of, 82, 398
Chrysostom, Saint John, 177, 190, 204, 221, 235, 242, 278, 292, 317, 325, 342, 360, 398
Clare, Saint, 160, 272, 307, 398
Clement, 375
Clement, Saint, 86, 156, 398
The Cloud of Unknowing, 19, 67, 84, 122, 189, 205, 245, 319, 393, 398
Columbanus, Saint, 103, 185, 314, 382, 398
Constitutions of the Holy Apostles, 118, 258, 354, 399
Cuthbert, Saint, 142, 399
Cyprian, Saint, 11, 46, 351, 399
Cyril, Saint, 219, 399
De Duodecim Abusivis Saeculi, 356, 399
Deogratias, 158, 399
Desert fathers and mothers, 10, 24, 51, 149, 157, 178, 208, 236, 257, 279, 313, 358, 384, 399
Dhouda of Septimania, 48, 399
Didache, 17, 195, 399
Divine Liturgy of James, 92, 399
Eckhart, Meister, 8, 60, 73, 114, 147, 168, 169, 174, 302, 350, 361, 372, 385, 399
Ephrem, 299, 399
Epistle of Barnabus, 45, 399
Eriugena, John Scotus, 352, 399
Francis of Assisi, 7, 15, 29, 49, 63, 115, 120, 135, 160, 170, 191,

414

AUTHOR INDEX

199, 216, 229, 249, 256, 294, 320, 343, 346, 376, 399
Gertrude the Great, 38, 400
Gregory VII, 206, 400
Gregory of Nazianzus, 238, 333, 349, 387, 400
Gregory of Nyssa, 58, 80, 287, 301, 373, 400
Gregory the Great, 57, 123, 215, 371, 400
Hadewijch of Antwerp, 22, 94, 148, 182, 201, 213, 395, 400
Hilary of Poitiers, 222, 270, 286, 391, 400
Hildegard of Bingen, 5, 25, 52, 101, 117, 127, 137, 143, 163, 194, 312, 383, 400
Hilton, Walter, 16, 50, 81, 95, 110, 161, 192, 400
Hippolytus, 214, 327, 400
Hugh of Saint Victor, 30, 400
Ignatius, Saint, 246, 380
Irenaeus, Saint, 93, 184, 305, 400
Isaac of Syria, 283, 321, 400
Jacopone da Todi, 78, 85, 400
Jacques de Vitry, 212, 400
James the Holy Apostle, 92
Jerome, Saint, 26, 140, 400
John of Damascus, 153, 400
Julian of Norwich, 23, 40, 55, 71, 87, 97, 109, 130, 139, 173, 186, 207, 233, 259, 285, 339, 381, 401
Justin Martyr, 54, 76, 401
Kempe, Margery, 159, 392, 401
Lactantius, 377, 401
Letter to Diognetus, 53, 401
Lull, Ramon, 273, 401

Macarius, Saint, 260, 401
Martin of Tours, 309, 401
Mawr, Cynddelw Brydydd, 255, 401
Mechtild of Magdeburg, Saint, 63, 226, 240, 401
Meilyr, 203, 401
Methodius, Bishop, 359, 366, 401
Moucan, 145, 337, 401, 402
Mygron, Abbot, 291, 401
Nicholas of Cusa, 146, 401
O'Huiginn, Cormac Ruadh, 277, 401
Origen, 263, 324, 401
Patrick, Saint, 20, 27, 37, 47, 401
Pelagius, 249, 338, 401
Polycarp, 32, 268, 401
Porete, Marguerite, 176, 308, 401
Possidius, Bishop, 41, 401
Pseudo-Macarius, 276, 355, 402
Rich, Edmund, 79, 244, 399
Richard of St Victor, 166, 252, 402
Rolle, Richard, 39, 102, 210, 262, 281, 402
Ruusbroec, John (see van Ruybroeck)
Salvian, 253, 402
The Shepherd of Hermas, 72, 125, 228, 347, 402
Stowe Missal, 295
Symeon the New Theologian, 91, 108, 304, 336, 402
Tertullian, 59, 113, 155, 402
Theologia Germanica, 218, 369, 402
Theonas, Saint, 269
Thomas a Kempis, 14, 61, 111, 133, 172, 288, 340, 379, 402
van Ruysbroeck, Jan, 42, 126, 151, 344, 402

Scripture Index

OLD TESTAMENT

Genesis
1:1–2	79
1:27	185
27:27	171
28:10–12	348
47:39	229

Exodus
3:1–6	358
13:21	209
23:20	220, 316
33:11, 17	287
33:18–23	123
33:19	291, 318
33:22–23	287

Leviticus
16:29–31	342
19:6	125, 221
26:2	243

Deuteronomy
6:4–6	102
10:12–13	213
10:17	144
10:21	346
15:7–8	13
29:29	130
33:12	240

1 Samuel
2:1–3	91
2:22–24	228
15:26	70
15:34–35	273
20:17	15

2 Samuel
9:7	158
12:1–8	64
22:29	192

1 Kings
19:11–13	215, 385

2 Kings
6:8–10	137
6:15–19	365

1 Chronicles
21:13	334, 335

2 Chronicles
6:36–40	375

Job
1:20	360
3:20–26	77
6:14	227
7:21	89

11:7	147	90:1–2	38
35:7–8	354	90:3–6	296
42:4–6	351	90:9–10	138
		90:10	179
Psalms		91:9–12	203
3:3	112	91:14	124
4:4	218	92:1–4	107
8:1–4	193	103:13–18	259
9:1	166	105:4	287
16:9	136	117:14	234
17:6	141	119:13–16	202
17:8	374	139:11–12	50
18:1–2	27	141:2	321
18:35–36	20	145:3	222, 391
23:4	345	146:5–7	140
23:5	394	147:1–3	60
27:1	350		
27:4	15	**Proverbs**	
27:8–9	3	2:1–8	175
27:14	340	2:7–8	183
27:9	67	3:7–8	301
31:19	139	3:34	120
31:23	294	4:6	201
32:6–7	92	8:10–12	324
34:1–3	282	16:18	341
36:7–9	382	18:10	370
40:11	303	19:11	208
42:1–2	39	28:25–27	72
42:8	154	28:27	190
43:3	4	30:8	205
45:2	311		
46:1–3	125	**Ecclesiastes**	
48:9	362	5:3	234
51:1–2	145	5:4	234
51:3–6	379	7:1–14	356
51:10–12	62	11:5	313
63:1	22		
69:29	322	**Song of Solomon**	
69:30	55	1:2–4	74
70:1	290	1:15–17	236
82:6	189	2:11–12	171
84:5	310	2:16–17	357
84:5–7	95	7:10–12	94
89:5–8	6	8:6–7	176
89:8	280		
89:11	242		

SCRIPTURE INDEX

Isaiah

1:1	384
6:1–7	281
11:1–5	305
13:22	388
19:22	317
33:7	388
35:1–6	295
35:5–7	328
38:4–6	368
40:1–5	343
42:6–7	269
45:15	111
49:13	12
53:4–6	207
55:6	241
55:8	204
57:15	19
58:6, 9	267
65:24	110
66:12	388
66:13	44

Jeremiah

1:14–16	41
23:3–4	51
29:11–12	33
29:12	234
32:38–39	272

Ezekiel

1:1	347
3:1–3	191
33:13	229
34:7–11	217

Hosea

2:19–20	163

Habakkuk

2:20	246

Zephaniah

2:3	206

Zechariah

2:13	289

NEW TESTAMENT

Matthew

1:22–23	251
5:43–45	377
5:48	189, 329
6:7–15	87
6:9–13	177
6:13	369
6:33	254
7:24	285
7:24–27	143
10:16	80, 256
10:21–23	46
10:42	24, 276
13:13–16	88
15;25–27	48
16:17–19	315
17:19	267
18:10	114
18:19	267
18:21–22	10
22:37	185
22:37–40	262, 393
25:15–23	307
25:42–43	180
25:44–45	238
26:26–29	54
27:45–46	85

Mark

1:1–3	388
1:16–20	29
3:13–15	49
11:25	106
14:3–9	223

Luke

1:34–35	169
1:35–38	90
1:38	52
1:50	109

2:8–14	389
2:34–35	271
4:1–2	226
6:27–28	32
6:32–36	250
6:37–38	245
6:43–45	361
7:6–7	390
8:18	229
9:1–6	135, 256
9:23	133
10:38–42	51
11:8	267
11:20–22	366
12:15	314
15:21–24	78
16:2	256
18:13	278
22:19–20	115
22:39–44	56

John

1:1	101
1:1–5	352
1:14	113, 169
1:16	91
1:29	16
2:23–25	43
3:5	256
3:5–6	75
3:17	374
4:13–14	9
4:34	338
5:21	167
6:35	172
6:49–51	299
6:63	96
10:7–10	337
10:14–16	152
10:34	189
14:15	185
14:15–17	161
14:16–17	248
15:1–5	162
15:12	185
15:14–15	186

15:16	171
16:12–15	155, 270, 336
16:15	329
17:5	344
17:11	239
17:20–21	302
17:21, 22	58
21:9–14	237
20:22	58

Acts

1:8	58, 371
2:42–47	200
2:43–47	76
2:46–47	118
4:32	227
4:32–35	309
6:63	96
7:54–60	268
7:59–60	211
9:3–6	116
9:15–16	37
9:17–19	235
10:38–41	383
13:1–3	292
13:43	97
17:21–22	58
17:22–23	372
18:26–27	30
20:1–2	312
20:22	58
26:15–18	194
26:19–20	325

Romans

1:16–17	57
1:18–23	181
5:5	156
5:6–8	31
5:15	151
5:18–21	387
6:4	235
6:5–11	28
6:6	235
6:8	233
6:15–18	288

Romans (continued)

7:24–25	117
12:9–11	286
12:9–13	11
13:1–7	229
14:8	380
14:13	122
14:17	274
14:19	178
15:4	153

1 Corinthians

2:2–5	23
2:14–16	103
3:22	329
4:10–13	339
4:15–16	307
6:17	227
7:1–7	300
10:23–26	279
11:1	354
11:23–26	17
12:4–6	119, 224
12:4–11	219
13:1–3	395
15:42	171
15:42–44	187
15:42–49	373

2 Corinthians

1:3–7	306
1:12	293
1:20–22	304
3:17–18	210
4:7	25, 83
4:7–12	188
4:16–18	174, 257
9:6–8	249
10:3–4	320
13:5	121

Galatians

1:11–17	142
2:11–13	326
2:19–20	159
3:25–27	42
3:26–27	253
3:27	235
3:27–28	247
4:4	171
4:7	349
5:1	89
5:6	68
5:16–18	275
5:22–25	199
5:22–26	376
6:1	157
6:2	14
6:8	108
6:10	258
6:14–15	150
6:16	283

Ephesians

1:11–12	381
1:17	168
1:17–19	40
1:18–23	261
2:4–5	134
2:4–7	69
2:19–22	126
3:14–17	61
3:14–19	173
4:25–27	353
5:1–2	263
5:3–5	355
5:8–9	260
5:15–16	53
5:18–20	96
6:10–13	319
6:11–13	101
6:12–13	47
6:14	305

Philippians

1:15	108
1:29–30	182
2:14–15	45
3:10–11	216
4:6	129
4:8–9	7, 170

Colossians

1:15–20	255
1:17	18
2:2	160
2:11	235
3:13–14	386
4:12	392

1 Thessalonians

4:18	367
5:3	296
5:16–18	212
5:23	308

2 Thessalonians

2:13–16	5
2:13–17	93

1 Timothy

1:15–16	323
2:1–2	32
2:3–6	59
3:16	327
4:4–5	81
4:9–10	214
5:9–10	S16
6:6–10	195

2 Timothy

1:8–10	284
4:9–11	225

Titus

3:4–7	333
3:5	235

Hebrews

1:1–4	105
2:3	388
5:5–10	63
6:4	235
10:32	235

James

1:12–16	26
1:13–15	252
1:19	277

1 Peter

1:15–16	104, 244
2:9	128
2:13	256
2:21	73
2:24–25	184
5:10	149

2 Peter

2:21–25	378

1 John

3:18	148
2:12–14	127
4:1	43
4:7	8
4:7–12	146
4:10	185
5:6–12	82

Revelation

5:9–10	359
21:5	171
21:6–7	71

www.ingramcontent.com/pod-product-compliance
Lightning Source LLC
Chambersburg PA
CBHW021928290426
44108CB00012B/754